Utilizing the 3Ms of Process Improvement

A Step-by-Step Guide to Better Outcomes Leading to Performance Excellence

Utilizing the 3Ms of Process Improvement

A Step-by-Step Guide to Better Outcomes Leading to Performance Excellence

Richard Morrow

Foreword by Claes Rehmberg, EVP Business Excellence, SKF

CRC Press
Taylor & Francis Group
Boca Raton   London   New York

CRC Press is an imprint of the
Taylor & Francis Group, an **informa** business

A PRODUCTIVITY PRESS BOOK

CRC Press
Taylor & Francis Group
6000 Broken Sound Parkway NW, Suite 300
Boca Raton, FL 33487-2742

© 2012 by Taylor & Francis Group, LLC
CRC Press is an imprint of Taylor & Francis Group, an Informa business

No claim to original U.S. Government works

Printed in the United States of America on acid-free paper
Version Date: 20120424

International Standard Book Number: 978-1-4398-9560-3 (Paperback)

Library of Congress Cataloging-in-Publication Data

Morrow, Richard, 1956-
    Utilizing the 3Ms of process improvement : a step-by-step guide to better outcomes leading to performance excellence / Richard Morrow.
        p. cm.
    Includes bibliographical references and index.
    ISBN 978-1-4398-9560-3 (alk. paper)
    1. Organizational change. 2. Business--Data processing. 3. Leadership. I. Title.

HD58.8.M657 2012
658.4'06--dc23   2012013445

Visit the Taylor & Francis Web site at
http://www.taylorandfrancis.com

and the CRC Press Web site at
http://www.crcpress.com

Dedication

This book is dedicated to my wife, Jan, and my children,
Adam and Janelle. I could not be more proud of you all.
I love you and thank you for allowing me to follow my passions
that often took me away from being there for you in person.

Contents

Foreword

High reliability has been our focus at SKF (Svenska Kullagerfabriken) since before my career started with the company. Our culture is one of safety and integrity and we allow no compromise on quality in our products and services. Our products are found in nearly every high reliability organization's products, including submarines, aircraft carriers, and 100% of the content in the Ferrari Formula 1 cars.

SKF has been noted in reliability engineering textbooks due to its work in understanding the factors that contribute to high reliability. Those factors include product attributes such as the finish that is measured in microns on bearings used in aircraft engines. We also have discovered service attributes that include scheduled maintenance practices that affect the reliability of a vehicle wheel hub unit. As Rick Morrow points out in this book, reliability is a factor of measuring the key variables both of the product and servicing as well as variables controlled by the user. Measuring these attributes before delivering the first unit and performing accelerated testing are fundamental to our success in achieving high reliability.

Measurement is key to all of our successes. So, why are so many failures associated with a lack of measurement? How many times have we witnessed a catastrophic failure and later found that no one was paying attention to the system's warnings that something was starting to go wrong? Maybe it is because we weren't measuring in the first place or no one reacted to the measurement.

Morrow worked for SKF as vice president of Total Quality leading our Seals Business Unit's Total Quality team across the United States and Latin America. It is in this unit that his team led the first deployment of Lean Six Sigma, which we believe contributed greatly to this unit's highest quality performance in its 100-year history. He and I would later take Six Sigma across the globe in SKF's Automotive Division achieving similar results. SKF's CEO, seeing the results when he led the Automotive Division at the time, had our team deploy Six Sigma globally across the entire business.

Utilizing the 3Ms (measuring, managing to the measure, and making it easier) is absolutely vital to change that lasts. Measurement was, and still is, a requirement of each effort. The stories that Morrow shares in *Utilizing the 3Ms of Process Improvement*, I think everyone can relate to. The answer is quite simple if an organization is struggling to change and has avoided the 3Ms in its improvement efforts. What is not quite so easy sometimes is getting people to appreciate the importance of the 3Ms. Therefore, Morrow also shares in this book a step-by-step approach to change that begins with proven techniques we deploy today. He even includes templates that guide teams in driving change and utilization of the 3Ms for process improvement.

I can't think of a better book to start you on your journey in process improvement. There are many good books on the science of problem solving and I continue to read and develop our program now in its second decade of Six Sigma and in our second century of providing highly reliable products and services at SKF. Core to our longevity and success is our utilization of the 3Ms in our product and service delivery systems. I can't imagine succeeding without the concepts shared in this book.

Claes Rehmberg
Executive Vice President Business Excellence
AB SKF

Acknowledgments

Measuring the contributions to this book starts with these colleagues and friends, and is impossible to quantify. Therefore, please know there are many others who have contributed to my understanding of how to lead change and many more to come:

Alan Houser, my classmate, friend, colleague, boss, and performance excellence extraordinaire from Carroll Catholic Grade School through our Executive MBA at the University of Illinois and 30 years of applying process improvement.

Claes Rehmberg, my boss and coach at SKF, who not only taught me what high reliability really takes, but also how not to be an "ugly American" on the world stage.

Dr. Dave Munch, my friend and boss who teaches and coaches me and is always there for me when I have crazy thoughts and ideas in healthcare improvement.

Dr. Terry O'Malley, Massachusetts General Hospital, my teacher of healthcare issues and my friend.

Charles Hagood, president, Healthcare Performance Partners (HPP), who allows me to help healthcare organizations and patients every day and give back to society.

My colleagues at HPP, who are the nicest people to work with.

Sarah Cook, David Buki, Ernie Perez, Carrie Mayer. My most prized colleagues who exemplify utilizing the 3Ms for process improvement and applying the Golden Rules in Change Leadership.

Don McCann and William Kelly, who gave me my first chance and had faith in me that I could maybe solve some issues.

Tom Johnstone, CEO at SKF, who saw how Lean Six Sigma can make a High Reliability Organization even better.

George Dettloff, former president at SKF, who met Al (Houser) and me, and gave us a chance to apply Lean and Six Sigma globally for SKF.

Bill Spaniol, my dear departed friend who was a catalyst for so many actions including going for the Exec MBA and downhill skiing. I miss you dearly.

My mom, Patricia, who loves me no matter what I mess up and gave me the confidence to do what I love, whether it was piano, changing to a real musical instrument (the drums), or solving issues like how to get two glasses of water to the same place easier.

My dad, who also loved me and taught me how to do just about anything when you don't have the money to pay someone to do it.

Adam, my son, who shared his talents creating the illustrations.

Janelle, my daughter, who reminds me why life is to be enjoyed and this book is a way of giving back.

My "Band of Brothers," Mark and Mike, who are always there for me when I need them. Mark is the rock of the family who we know will always be there to protect us. Mike is the roll, who teaches me how not to get too stuck working all the time to enjoy family and Florida.

And, Kris Mednansky, senior editor for Taylor & Francis, who has had the patience to help me share with you how to improve processes.

My clients over the 30 years, who allowed me to learn from them, experiment, and then share with others how to utilize the 3Ms, their successes, and lessons learned.

About the Author

Rick Morrow is a consultant with more than 25 years of senior leadership experience in healthcare, aviation, construction, automotive, and high tech. Morrow leads the automotive industry Healthcare Performance Partners' Quality, Safety, and High Reliability unit, a MedAssets company. He has authored Lean Six Sigma performance excellence courses and taught and deployed programs internationally for Eaton Corporation, SKF, Motorola, United Airlines, The Joint Commission, and Healthcare Performance Partners.

Morrow is the author and leader of HPP's Six Sigma consulting and wrote and leads the Belmont University Lean Healthcare Certification Program for Supply Chain Professionals, which is a blend of The Toyota Production System, Six Sigma, and Change Leadership. Morrow also wrote and taught The University of Penn's Penn Medicine Leadership and Performance Improvement courses. He authored the Lean Six Sigma Program at The Joint Commission and led its Center for Transforming Healthcare, where he and his team led collaborations improving patient care and safety with major academic medical centers including Cedars-Sinai, Johns Hopkins, Mayo Clinic, Intermountain Healthcare, North Shore Long Island Jewish, and Stanford University.

Morrow earned his MBA from the University of Illinois' Executive Program and has a B.S. in business from Illinois State University. His certifications include Motorola Master Black Belt and Lean Enterprise from the University of Tennessee. He is an international speaker on Lean Six Sigma, Quality, and Safety at conferences including NPSF, ASC, and ASQ.

Morrow is also the author of the companion book, *Utilizing the 3Ms in Process Improvement in Healthcare*, and is a contributing editor on performance improvement, quality and safety publications.

He is as proud of his work coaching his son and daughter in baseball and soccer as he is of leading as the President of the Holy Family Commission of Education.

Chapter 1

Overview of Process Improvement and the 3Ms

Outcomes Are the Result of Processes

If better outcomes are desired, improve the processes. Sounds simple, so why do we sometimes struggle in achieving better outcomes? This is a "how-to book." You will discover how to improve processes and how to better achieve better outcomes. In addition, we will share how to sustain the gains, the "Achilles heel" in performance improvement for many organizations.

An outcome in any long-term business venture we want to improve is customer satisfaction. Satisfying a customer is a process, often a very complex set of processes, and one that often involves more than one person and more than one discipline. For example, if the organization is selling and supporting a service after the sale, there are at least three processes. One process is the design of the service. A second process is selling the service, and, of course, delivering the service is yet another process. Finally, there is the process of supporting the customer in the service. The best support process in the world will fail over the long run if another company offers both a better design and service and better support.

Please think of your favorite store. Write down what makes this store your favorite. Maybe it is the products it sells or the mix of products and services. Next, underneath each of the attributes that makes this store your favorite, write the names of the process or processes that contribute most to how you feel about that store.

My wife and I really enjoy going to Costco™.[1] The products are usually the quality that we are looking for and the prices are competitive. But, what really makes Costco one of our favorite stores is the uniqueness of its selection of products. I imagine I can find any product Costco sells somewhere else, but there is just something about the diversity of products along with the assurance the products meet our wish for quality and price that brings us back. Have you ever seen a listing of product categories on a company's Web site such as what Costco offers: appliances, indoor (including weather stations), home healthcare, radio-controlled helicopters, and definitely last, but maybe not least, funeral products and services? I have never used Costco for my funeral needs, but doesn't it support my point about diversity?

The process that defines Costco most uniquely, I think, must be the process of product selection and service selection. Costco's customer satisfaction *outcome* improves whenever it *improves* its process of product selection and mix. As Costco states in its marketing, customers come back for the discovery of its latest selection of products.

Process improvement can't be solely performed inside the company's "four walls." Costco, as well as the firms I have been fortunate to work for, know how to improve the processes throughout their value stream. A value stream is a stream of energy flowing among entities resulting in a service or product. When I led business designing, manufacturing, distributing, and supporting safety products for Eaton Corporation, we had to reach out to our designers to design quality in so as to prevent injuries. Eaton's core competency was its outcome in electrical and electronic products that excelled in quality and safety. I will talk more about Eaton when we discuss High Reliability Organizations (HROs). My team included the suppliers of components who were always in the value stream of a manufacturing firm to ensure their processes met our needs and also were continuously improved. And, we radically organized our manufacturing and distribution processes to build all items to order, versus trying to guess what customers wanted only to waste time and money in finished goods inventory.

Healthcare is now accelerating development of its many complex processes within its value stream. One name for a value stream in healthcare is an Accountable Care Organization. An ACO is a grouping of healthcare facilities and providers that link together to improve the quality and cost of healthcare. Some acute care hospitals are improving patient treatment and reducing readmissions by reaching out to the skilled nursing facility and even into the patient's home to improve the processes of follow-up prescriptions and diets that often fail—resulting in the patient needing readmission to the hospital. The hospital executives, physicians, and staff realize that they alone cannot assure a patient's recovery and treatment quality when other entities in the value stream have processes that fail.

Personally, enjoying our family is an outcome. Sharing time together on trips, helping our children or spouse with homework, and attending social events are processes that lead to enjoying our family. What would happen if we never improved the trips we took as the children grew? Would the same trip to the park, playing explorer with make-believe forts, bring the joyous outcomes when the children became teenagers? But, life isn't about process improvement, at least, it isn't for me. Is process improvement what you get up for in the morning?

Performance Excellence

So, why does the title of this book include Process Improvement? Why didn't I name it Performance Excellence? Isn't that why we improve processes? Better yet, why do we strive for performance excellence? Maybe we improve processes to achieve higher performance that leads to an increase in sales and margins for our shareholders? So, why didn't I include in the title Excellent Outcomes, or what some companies consider their mission, Contribute to Society? Wait a minute, I wanted this book to work for those who want to apply it in their home life as well as their work life, so how about reaching beyond the workplace and engaging our entire self with "How to Get to Heaven" if that is your ultimate goal in life? I wrote this book to help you and your organization achieve better outcomes and, in fact, excellence in performance. Process improvement is the way to get there.

3Ms for Process Improvement

- ■ **M**easure
- ■ **M**anage to the measure
- ■ **M**ake it easier to do the right thing

Measure

I can **M**easure processes that lead to the outcome. Simply measuring the outcome doesn't directly change the outcome. It doesn't improve the outcome. If I measure the process that gets me the outcome and improve the process, I can get a better outcome.

Getting to work in the morning is an example of how measuring contributes to process improvement. Measuring the time it takes me to get to work is nice to know, but if I want to get to work faster, this measure does nothing for me. However, if I measure the process in getting to work including the time it takes for alternate routes, I might be able to improve the process in getting to work, my desired outcome. If I could measure occurrences and severity of accidents relative to traffic congestion before and during my trip, I might be able to adjust my process of getting to work and achieve a higher performance—getting to work on time.

If I, and my family members, could measure the amount of gas left in the tanks when we return each other's vehicles, which, of course, we can, we could work together to improve the return process. We have caused each other wasted time in getting to work by having to refill the gas tank after someone borrows my truck. Measuring is the first M, but measuring without doing anything is not going to get to a better outcome. Simply telling each other the gas level is low does not put gas in the tank.

This entire issue is caused by my owning a truck, which is a highly valued vehicle when it comes to hauling lots of friends or stuff. You know what I think is even better than owning a truck? Having a dad who owns a truck. My kids borrow my truck frequently and I find myself driving my son's or daughter's little Mustangs to the airport instead of my nice comfortable four-wheel drive truck. What we decided to do is to **M**easure the gas level in each vehicle before returning and holding the keys hostage.

Manage to the Measure

With measuring being emphasized, we now needed to *Manage* to the measure to improve the process. Holding the keys to each other's car managed to change the process to ensure that we return the vehicles with at least enough gas to get to work. However, it wasn't always easy to replenish the gasoline late at night. Gas stations in our area are not open late, so it is difficult to bring the vehicles back after a long day on the road. We needed an easier way to bring the vehicles back with gas in them. Well, for every will there's a way, and for every son and daughter, too.

Make it Easier

Adam also borrows my lawnmower and its gas can. One morning, I had an early flight and found my truck's tank too low on gas to make it to the airport. In a hurry, and not wanting to look for a gas station on the way, I reached for the gas can in my garage and fueled my truck. Voila! We now have improved the process to make it easier to return a vehicle with some gas in it. Keeping that container in my garage *Makes* it easier for all of us to return vehicles with that spare gallon or two in the container for those really late nights or horrible weather we get back home. There you have it, utilizing the 3Ms for Process Improvement. Measure the amount of gas, manage to get it filled, and make it easier to replenish.

Any time I can *Measure, Manage,* and *Make* it easier to do the right thing, I progress toward performance excellence. It's that simple, yet so many organizations fail to do one or more of the Ms. I bet that is often the cause of the failures you see in achieving your desired outcomes.

Science of Process Improvement

Process improvement best occurs using a scientific methodology. What I can't do in this one book is show you all the tools in the process improvement tool chest. However, utilizing the 3Ms and using a few tools that are taught in this book will improve most of the issues organizations face today. Dr. Ishikawa, professor of engineering at the University of Tokyo and leader of the Japanese Union of Scientists and Engineers, promoted team problem solving and developed much of the training given to problem solvers today. He also is considered the "Father" of Quality Circles (teams trained in continuous improvement), and inventor of the Cause and Effect Diagram, aka the Ishikawa Diagram or "Fishbone" chart used in root cause analysis.[2] He also was a promoter of mistake proofing methods. Dr. Ishikawa believed that just 7 to 10 tools would solve 95% of the quality issues and should be taught to all employees. The Quality Foundational Process Improvement tools include:

- Chartering: Defining the problem
- Stakeholder resistance analysis
- Brainstorming
- Data collection techniques (check sheets, concentration diagrams, etc.)
- Cause-and-effect analysis and "Five Whys"
- Pareto analysis
- Histograms and scatter diagrams
- Control charts
- Stratification

I also include in this list tools for productivity issues not caused by quality issues. These include tools to reduce the wasted time from disorganized areas, excessive motion looking for supplies, and excessive resources including inventory. Toyota[3] and others have developed these and the Productivity Process Improvement tools include:

- Eight wastes
- 5S (sort, store, shine, standardize, sustain)
- Standard work
- Value stream mapping
- Just-in-time inventory methods of pull replenishment including kanban
- Continuous flow

As you can see from his list of preferred tools and the list of productivity process improvement tools, Dr. Ishikawa and leaders in quality and performance like Toyota are firm believers and teachers in measuring, managing to the measure, and making it easier for people to do the right thing.

You probably have already used most of these tools, but I find many people aren't confident about how to get started or which tool to use and when. To thank you for reading my book and utilizing the 3Ms, I include an example of each tool in the appendix with my Roadmap for Performance Excellence™. Please see Appendix 1. This roadmap guides the process improvement team in asking the right questions at the right time and suggests the tool that best answers the question. All of the foundational tools can be found on the Roadmap and also in Appendix 2 where I show them graphically or in figures for easier understanding. I teach more advanced performance improvement methods for more complex issues and speedier process improvement, but I always rely on these fundamental tools first.

Change Leadership

To improve is to change. To be perfect is to change often.

Winston Churchill

Learning and applying Change Leadership is as important as utilizing and depending on the 3Ms at the same time. I will cover Change Leadership in its own chapter because it is that important to process improvement. Leading change is a skill everyone can learn and one that cannot be over-emphasized. All the science in the world and all the tools in the tool chest are worthless if one leading a team cannot lead them through change. I will share stories of great Change Leaders and share their methods in leading others in change and process improvement. I will also share sad stories of failed changes because of a lack of Change Leadership. I think we learn best by learning the good and the bad.

We Need All Three Ms to Sustain the Improvements

Here is an example of what happens when just one M is weak or missing. We have all been measured by others and probably have failed to achieve the improvement or outcome desired. In this story, my team was to improve the yield of a motor control device used in virtually every factory and commercial building to control machines and air handling equipment for heating and air conditioning. The failure was the product's inability of correctly calibrating itself to restart a machine. A "soft start" feature in our product reduced the wear and tear on the machine our device was restarting and, thus, extended its reliability.

We measured the success of the calibrating product and found failures in calibration. This is the first M. We were also managing to the measure (the second M) by organizing a team to find the root cause of the calibration failures and meeting daily to review the prior day's measurement of yield. The team worked for months trying to find the root cause of this rather complex device. The manufacturing and test processes were themselves complex with two major manufacturing sites spread from Wisconsin to Puerto Rico. Each site's manufacturing and test equipment were aptly described as a bunch of wires, conveyors, computers, sensors, and people.

Despite measuring and managing every day, we could not get the outcome of reliable calibration solved. It just wasn't easy to calibrate. We needed the third M—Make it easier.

Case Study in Process Improvement

A team was formed to discover why the calibration failed. The team was trained in how to improve a process using a scientific methodology. A scientific methodology is a standard method to define the issue clearly, calculate the current state of performance, analyze for contributing factors or root causes to the issue, develop countermeasures to improve the issue, and, finally, to control the process to sustain the gains. I will share with you the scientific method with a unique "roadmap" included in the Appendix 1 that helps you navigate even the most complex of issues.

My team also knew science alone would not improve a process. Even in the simplest of issues, there can be many people affected in a process improvement. We engaged the people in the processes in Wisconsin, Puerto Rico, and the suppliers asking them to apply their process improvement skills. We enabled them by allowing time to work on the issue. Not engaging them and trying to solve it alone might work, but how much can one person do?

Utilizing the 3Ms for Process Improvement

The team members introduced themselves, reviewed the issue, and went to the process. To make this long story shorter and illustrate the prior point about the need to include the entire value stream, the team discovered an error in the microprocessor purchased to read voltage and convert it to amps. This conversion is vital to calibrating the product to know how "soft" to restart the machine. The error was rather silly. The equation of a line is $y = (mx) + b$. The firm "burning" the equation in the microprocessor made an error in where the parentheses were placed. The equation initially in the device read $y = m(x + b)$. After fixing the error, it was easier to calibrate the product. The third M was in place.

Measure was happening and adding value by highlighting the issue. Managing to the measure, the second M, also was occurring as evidenced by the director and staff watching the measure and creating a dialogue among staff on how to get the measure moving in the right direction. Because the measure was not moving simply from awareness, the team knew process improvement was needed. The director managed to the measure more fervently by engaging and enabling a team to work on the issue.

The teamwork *Made* it easier to calibrate the device. The *Measure* of yield improved as well as staff satisfaction. And, the team continues to *Manage* to the measure to continuously improve.

Change is difficult for most of us, especially when we are not the instigators of the change. I often don't know at the beginning of process improvement efforts what changes are necessary to get to performance excellence. I sure don't profess to know how to get the desired ultimate outcomes, especially in complex organizations like healthcare. What I do know is that process improvement leads to higher performance, which, in turn, leads to better outcomes.

3Ms, Scientific Methodology, Change Leadership

Utilizing the 3Ms of Process Improvement is about how to utilize the 3Ms to improve processes to achieve performance excellence. It is as much about the science of process improvement as it is about how to lead process improvement utilizing the 3Ms. Without both the scientific methodology of process improvement and how to lead others in change, we will fail. We also know it starts with an effective Change Leader. It takes a Change Leader to instill the need for the science of process improvement. I will share with you how to utilize the 3Ms in process improvement and lead change that sustains the gains. The 3Ms work every time and I have never seen sustained improvement without the 3Ms. It is truly this simple.

I believe it helps to practice, so throughout the book, there are exercises to practice. I hope you try them all because practicing will build your confidence. I sincerely hope you enjoy our time together utilizing the 3Ms for process improvement with stories of some of the greatest Change Leaders of all time.

Key Points

- A better outcome is with the end in mind. Performance excellence achieves better outcomes. Process improvement leads to performance excellence.
- The 3Ms are:
  - **M**easure what is important.
  - **M**anage to the measure.
  - **M**ake it easier to do the right thing. Make it happen, Make it work, Make it better, Make it worthwhile.
- A scientific methodology and Change Leadership combine to enable teams to improve processes.
- It doesn't take advanced tools to improve most process issues. Seven to ten tools will solve 95% of most quality issues.
- Change Leadership is vital to process improvement and is as important as utilizing the 3Ms.

Endnotes

1. http://www.costco.com/Browse/MainShop.aspx?cat=24091&eCat=BC|24091&lang=en-US&whse=BC
2. Don Dewar, *The Quality Circle Handbook*. (Chico, CA: Quality Circle Institute, 1980), F2–4, F9–14.
3. Yasuhiro Monden, *Toyota Production System, An Integrated Approach to Just-In-Time*, 2nd ed. (Norcross, GA: Industrial Engineering and Management Press, 1993), 237.

Chapter 2

Change Leadership

Change Leadership: As necessary as the science in the greatest process improvements.

What Is Change Leadership? Change Management? How Do They Differ?

Leadership is the key word that differentiates the two terms: *Change Leadership and Change Management.* You have probably heard of both of them and thought the terms to be synonymous. They are not. Change requires someone to lead. If we wanted only to manage, we would not have change. Have you experienced a change gone wrong in your organization?

The Need for Leadership in Change: A Case Study in Healthcare

The Improvement Champion and I were called in to help a hospital's chief executive officer (CEO), chief nursing officer (CNO), and chief financial officer (CFO) find why a change to help nurses spend more time with patients and less time in charting had failed. Who would argue that such a change made sense? The change was to buy computers on wheels so nurses could roll the cart into the patient's room and do the required charting while spending time with the patient. In the past, the nurses would leave the patient's room, walk to the nurse station, and enter the data on computers at the desk. What we found was a complete failure to achieve any additional time with patients.

It's no wonder. When we first walked onto the floors, we found the computers on wheels outside the patient rooms, not inside the rooms. We observed nurses still doing their charting at the nurses station or at one of the computers on wheels parked near the nurses stations. In addition, 50% of these expensive tablet computers that cost far more than a desktop computer found at the nurses station, were inoperative, having been unplugged and their batteries drained. They were now taking up vital space in the corridors or stashed away in a storage area.

What went wrong with this change? It's not that the computers did not work as well as the desktop computers. In fact, they had features such as biometric scanning that made signing on as easy as swiping a thumb over the sensor. But, not one nurse was using this feature and many nurses complained about the many keystrokes needed just to sign in. They had touch screen capability and a strap to allow one hand to hold the tablet while the other hand was free to enter patient data. So, why did we see large, desktop-sized keyboards added to these handheld computers and hear that nurses found the touch screen frustrating? Worse, why were the "COWs" (computers on wheels) never, ever, taken into the patient's room to achieve the primary objective of nurses charting in real time and spending more time with patients?

The computers worked, technically. What did not work was someone leading the changes. The nurses told us they had little input into the changes. No one could remember anyone from the supplier coming to observe how a nurse from these units performs the tasks. No one spoke to them and asked them for their ideas and/or suggestions. Most nurses had not been trained in the unique features of the tablet computer. None even knew what the biometric sensor was on the front of the tablet. Even more surprising, more than one nurse did not realize the computer had a strap on the back so it could be taken from the mount and held in one hand.

After the computers arrived, not one nurse could remember the tablet maker or distributor coming to demonstrate the computer or to address their complaints. Managers were as frustrated as the nurses about the new computers and the lack of support by the instigators of the change.

We reported our findings and recommendations to the hospital executives and to the corporate CFO and chief information officer (CIO). The CFO was told originally that the changes would improve patient and nurse satisfaction. We shared how 100% of the investment was wasted. The CFO promptly canceled the program. He then looked to the hospital's CNO and promised he would support whatever she and her staff decided they needed for charting that increased time with patients, improved charting for better patient care and information, and made the nurses' work life better.

Too Many Examples of Not Leading Change Well

We see similar changes that have failed in every industry. In the 1980s and 1990s, we witnessed countless organizations launching Quality Circles in America. I led the Quality Circle program for several years at one of Eaton Corporation's largest sites and overall it was successful. However, resistance to change was a constant struggle. We saw managers as frustrated as the staff at leading the changes.

We also saw changes that have made significant impact, such as the change from a functionally aligned organization where similar manufacturing processes and equipment were physically arranged in departments to a customer-centric product alignment. This customer-focused, physical alignment change is where the equipment was moved out of departments and grouped together to create a continuous flow line. This change worked well and we found continuous improvement (change) was much easier in this arrangement with people who may never had met those using their products now working side-by-side as a team, and respecting each other's opinions. What we find different between the changes that fail and the changes that succeed is not so much the management, it is how change is led. Why did this enormous change—where people were physically relocated, some middle managers lost independent authority to make decisions, and workers had to work with people they had previously not met—succeed and some other simpler change initiatives fail?

Management and Leadership: Scientific Management

Frederick Taylor (1856–1915), the father of "Scientific Management," is considered the first consultant to management. Scientific management is the science of management whereby tasks and behaviors are measured against outcomes. He pioneered the differences in management and leadership by working with an organization's leadership, management, and the workers. He worked both in industry and healthcare, with workers caring for the patient or workers shoveling coal.

Leaders, Taylor believed, were responsible for developing managers who developed workers. Measurement is key to know how well work was being done. Taylor found that measuring a task allowed management to know what was needed and how much work could be done by each person. This measurement allowed managers to predict the number of workers needed and to respond. Scientific Management starts with leadership's vision of a more productive workplace with better outcomes.

Perfect Example of Scientific Management

In 1912, Taylor testified before congress that the perfect example of Scientific Management was found at the Mayo Clinic.[1] Perhaps, he judged it based on the Mayo Clinic being the world's first privately integrated group practice and that it stressed a teamwork approach. Patients discovered the advantages of doctors pooling knowledge by being cured.

The late Peter Drucker, arguably one of the foremost experts on management and leadership, suggested there have been seven assumptions close enough to reality until the early 1980s to be operational. He goes on to write,[2] "They are now so far removed from actual reality that they are becoming obstacles to the Theory and even more serious obstacles to the Practice of management." One of these assumptions is that "there is, or must be, ONE right way to manage people." He postulates that "one does not 'manage' people. The task is to lead people. And, the goal is to make productive the specific strengths and knowledge of each individual."

Drucker honored Taylor's work in developing management theory and practice. However, he suggested these assumptions are no longer valid, or maybe we misunderstood Taylor. For even Taylor recognized that the importance to management is outcome. Patients at the Mayo Clinic recognized value was how the doctors performed, not how they managed their workers. Drucker writes, "Maybe we will have to redefine the task (of management) altogether. It may not be managing the work of people. The starting point both in theory and in practice may have to be 'managing for performance.'" Measuring performance seems like the thing to do. Managing to the measure to get performance is the logical next step. How do we get started? Do we manage ourselves into starting or will it take a leader?

Definition of Manager and Leader

The Small Business Administration[3] differentiates managers and leaders. Managers are defined as those who adopt impersonal, almost passive attitudes toward goals. Managers choose goals based on necessity instead of desire and, therefore, are deeply tied to their organization's culture, and they tend to be reactive because they focus on current information. Management is planning, organizing, staffing, directing, and controlling.

Leaders, however, tend to be active because they envision and promote their ideas instead of reacting to current situations. Leaders shape ideas instead of responding to them, have a personal orientation toward goals, and provide a vision that alters the way people think about what is desirable, possible, and necessary.

Leaders are to change what inventors are to innovation. We don't get innovation without inventors, and we don't get change without leaders who create a vision and motivate others in changing.

What Happens When There Is no Leader?

Ballroom dancing requires a leader. The leader takes an active role in creating a vision of the routine in movements and timing. Both dancers will manage the routine to achieve the vision, but the leader initiates change from one location to another, in one direction to another, from one move to another. The aggressiveness and pace of the dance comes from the leader. The maintenance of rhythm and sequence may come from either partner as they manage the routine. The leader's intensity during the routine will change based on the management of the routine and performance quality. The leader may intervene during the routine to adjust the dance if the vision is to win a competition or to create a sensual experience between two lovers waltzing romantically as one across the dance floor.

What happens if the leader's vision is not the same as his or her partner's vision? Are you envisioning what I am? Not a pretty picture. We have all seen video of the falls in the popular ballroom dancing shows or pairs in figure skating competitions when one partner is not in synch with the other. When the leader and partner are working together, it can be a beautiful scene and story. Leading change is beautiful, but like ballroom dancing, it takes practice. Getting good at Change Leadership can result in quite a few bumps and bruises. It's worth it when one looks back on successful changes that seemed so impossible before they occurred.

Think back to changes you have been a part of that succeeded beyond expectations. Who was the leader? What was different about the leadership of those successes versus changes that failed? Maybe you were the leader. How did you feel at the beginning of the change, midway through, and at the end? Has the change sustained? If change has not sustained, why not? We will explore successes and failures in leading change and help you with techniques that work to achieve and sustain changes in healthcare.

Change Leadership becomes more successful and easier once one achieves success and momentum. This comes with practice. Great Change Leaders continuously analyze their successes and failures and improve their skills.

Leadership Principles

In this chapter, you will learn that process improvement should start with a vision, engage others, and include methods to sustain the improvements. Later chapters will detail how to create vision statements and how to engage others with methods to sustain changes. You will learn step-by-step with templates, whenever possible, and I have included examples from health-care as well. You will learn how to communicate the vision, and to whom it is necessary to communicate. Most importantly, I will share the pitfalls to avoid. You will learn more on leading change. Unless the one leading the change has the skills we are covering in this chapter, managers won't know what change to plan for, how to organize, staff, direct, and, last of all, control. Leading change differentiates this book from others that talk about managing change.

Abraham Lincoln on Leading Change

Abraham Lincoln is one of the greatest leaders of all time. A Change Leader could learn many lessons from Honest Abe. Honesty is perhaps the first and greatest lesson of a Change Leader if you want to achieve more than one change with the same organization.

You can fool some of the people all of the time, and all of the people some of the time, but you cannot fool all of the people all of the time. Abraham Lincoln

Just about anyone can get one change through, especially if the person has organizational authority. However, revolutions and death have come to some who force change dishonestly and against the interest of the people. A Change Leader's skills go well beyond being honest, but a Change Leader could do well starting out with being honest about changes coming, and observing Abe's principles of leadership that he consistently used to govern managerial conduct and change.[4]

Lincoln's principles of leadership:

- Advocate a VISION and continually reaffirm it.
- CIRCULATE among followers consistently.
- Build strong ALLIANCES.
- Search for INTELLIGENT assistants.
- Encourage INNOVATION.
- PERSUADE rather than coerce.
- Influence people through STORIES.
- Be RESULTS oriented.

You will learn how to practice each of Lincoln's principles with exercises along the way. Let's start with the end in mind. A Change Leader gets results. And Change Leaders often achieve results beyond expectations. How do they accomplish so much? What can we learn from others' failures? To learn Change Leadership, I share lessons learned from those who failed to achieve results as well as those who have succeeded. We start with one who led one of the most significant changes for humanity.

Leading Change to a Slave-Free America

Lincoln was a Change Leader who envisioned a slave-free America and engaged the North and the South in one of America's most significant changes. He was also a Change Manager during the war because he planned, organized, staffed, directed, and controlled the North's war effort.

Lincoln's leadership to abolish slavery started with advocating a vision of abolishing slavery. His means to that end, however, was to stop its growth, believing it would eventually die out. His intention was not to act immediately to abolish it, believing this change to be too great a change for the nation. At the time, a civil war was not beyond comprehension. One certainly does not want to manage a nation into war against itself. Manage a war effort, yes, once the change started, but leading includes having a vision of change and not reacting to a change. A Change Leader knows well how much change can be managed at any one time and place.

We know Lincoln and America were successful in the change to a slave-free land. We also know change is very difficult at times, and Change Leaders may pay the ultimate price. We all benefit today from Lincoln's Change Leadership, and we will use Lincoln's story to become better Change Leaders leading to better process improvement.

Industry's Change Leaders

All industries have had their share of Change Leaders. In automotive, Henry Ford was a Change Leader and highly successful to the point he has been credited with creating the middle class though his practice of paying front-line workers well above what they had been previously making.[5] Dr. Brent James, a physician at Intermountain Healthcare in Salt Lake City, Utah, is identified as one who could reform healthcare. Ford, Dr. James,[6] and others who have led significant change often focus on reducing variation. We all know the quote from Ford: "Any customer can have a car painted any color that he wants so long as it is black."

Variation, in this example, was not to inhibit a customer's wish of color being met. Ford reduced variation to minimize cost to allow more people to benefit from having a car. What good is a car for the masses if so few can afford it? Another reason for black was its reduced drying time, and the reduction in variation that one drying time had over multiple drying times based on color. Change Leaders rely on measuring to know if changes make an impact. Ford and Dr. James use statistical charts highlighting variations and differences between methods. I will teach you how to use these charts in later chapters.

Intermountain had worked on heart failure and discovered that a beta blocker could make a difference in the outcome. This beta blocker treatment was not discovered by Dr. James, but by measuring its use and the outcome, Intermountain was able to validate improvements. Physicians are schooled in evidence-based medicine and appreciate having such measures of processes and outcomes. Dr. James manages to those measures in Intermountain and expects the same of others in this environment of evidence-based care. Sharing the measures in real time and acting upon them are key to success. Dr. James focuses on the charts instead of arguing. He lets the charts prove the theory. This is his leadership philosophy.

In my work inside Intermountain and with staff and physicians, it is clear that Dr. James believes in measuring and managing to the measure. He, like all good leaders, teaches his methods of using data and charts, and he does this in a well-orchestrated training program. He also offers this training to others outside of Intermountain.[6]

Walking the Talk

We are going to learn techniques that Change Leaders, like Ford, use. Process improvement leaders, like Change Leaders, use measurement instead of merely debate or arguments about philosophy. In Phillips' book, *Lincoln on Leadership*,[4] we read how Lincoln would personally walk to the War Department's telegraph office to know as soon as possible the "score" of the battles being fought. What message did his desire to measure progress constantly and quickly send to the generals in the field who knew the president's practice? They knew their measure, and they knew Abe would manage to that measure. Lincoln managed to change general-in-chief four times in the course of the Civil War until finally finding the general who could achieve the measure—winning the war. We see measurement as a differentiator, but it takes more than measuring. Process improvement leaders measure and then they manage to the measure. Lincoln didn't simply measure progress. He wrote letters to the generals sharing thoughts, coaching them, and asking for their ideas. We also see that making change easier is what Change Leaders do better than those who fail. The 3Ms must all be in place and, when they are, they can change a nation. They are helping improve processes in healthcare today.

Definition of Common Terms across Methodologies

"Go to the *Gemba*" seems to be what Lincoln was suggesting. "Go to the *Gemba*" is a Japanese and English term that means "go to where the work is and the people are." The reverse is to not go, yet still make decisions and promote change without ever being in the process. *Genchi Genbutsu* is yet another term for this same concept. *Takt* time is used by Toyota and it means the rate at which the process should flow. *Takt* is a German word that means "beat."

Alas, we would all be "Leaner" if we simply minimized the number of recipes, tools, and terms in process improvement. Some terms are simply the same words, but in different languages. Throughout this book, I hope, in whatever language it is translated, to avoid words that are not self-evident. Do not get me wrong, I explore and attempt to learn the language of the country where I am working. However, my purpose is to be able to learn and share in the leanest, most effective fashion. Using another language to share a Change Leadership term seems like a waste of time. Worse, this use of an unknown term often hinders change because we may be perceived as demeaning and arrogant. Arrogance is not an attribute with which we believe process improvement people should be labeled.

Key Points

- Change requires someone to lead. If we want only to manage, we would not have change.
- Changes that succeed are not so much the work of management as they are the leader's work. Changes that sustain are very much the manager.
- Measuring a task allows management to know what is needed and how much work can be done. This is Scientific Management.
- Management is planning, organizing, staffing, directing, and controlling. Managers react to change.
- Leaders shape ideas instead of responding to them. We don't get change without leaders who create a vision and motivate others in changing.
- Abe Lincoln's Principles of Leadership:
  - Advocate a VISION and continually reaffirm it.
  - CIRCULATE among followers consistently.
  - Build strong ALLIANCES.
  - Search for INTELLIGENT assistants.
  - Encourage INNOVATION.
  - PERSUADE rather than coerce.
  - Influence people through STORIES.
  - Be RESULTS oriented.

- A Change Leader knows well how much change can be managed at any one time and place.
- Sharing the measures in real time and acting upon them are key to success.
- Use the 3Ms to know the best treatment and reduce the debating and arguing.

Endnotes

1. http://www.mayoclinic.org/history/
2. Peter F. Drucker, *Management Challenges for the 21st Century*. Copyright © 1999 by Peter F. Drucker. Reprinted by permission of HarperCollins Publishers. San Francisco: Jossey Bass Publishers, 1999).
3. Small Business Administration, *Leading vs. Managing: They're Two Different Animals*. Online at: http://sba.gov/leadvmanage
4. From *Lincoln on Leadership* by Donald T. Phillips. Copyright © 1992 by Donald T. Phillips. By permission of Grand Central Publishing. All rights reserved.
5. Henry Ford and Samuel Crowther, *My Life and Work*. (New York: Doubleday, Page & Company, 1922), 72.
6. Intermountain's Institute for Health Care Delivery Research. Online at: http://intermountainhealthcare.org/qualityandresearch/institute/courses/Pages/home.aspx

Chapter 3

Resistance to Change and Process Improvement

Everybody has accepted by now that change is unavoidable. But, that still implies that change is like death and taxes—it should be postponed as long as possible and no change would be vastly preferable. But, in a period of upheaval, such as the one we are living in, change is the norm.

Peter Drucker

Forces against Change: Resistance, Time, Natural Laws

One of the most valued skills in our work in leading change is how to reduce resistance. Resistance is the greatest force acting against change. In this book, we will teach you how to reduce resistance. There are other forces that a Change Leader needs to recognize and address as well. Time, whether it is too much time or a lack of time, also can be a force against change. Procrastination may occur when people are given too much time for a change.

Of course, too little time for people to change does not allow process improvement either. Trying a change that defies the laws of nature is a waste of time. A Change Leader cannot change time itself or the laws of nature. A Change Leader has to address other variables, and we will show how to indirectly reduce the effect of these two forces on change. A Change Leader can, however, directly reduce resistance, with the force of resistance often the most common force.

A Quick Win against Resistance

If you have any expectation about how to reduce resistance, as most do, perhaps we can get a quick win in our very first chapters. Let's start with a question. Do people resist change? I have asked this question of hundreds of people in support centers, plants, customer sites, conferences, hospitals, surgical centers, waiting rooms, and even to concert goers when asking them what they thought about the band performing. I get the same answer. Yes, of course, people resist change.

Some organizations actually pride themselves on not making changes. One business venture I helped lead definitely capitalized on not making changes and we were successful. My brother and I played in a rock band for years. We enjoyed being one of the most popular "copy" bands in the area. A copy band is one that performs music of other artists instead of music it writes. People in our audiences reacted most favorably when we played the song exactly as the original artists recorded it. Reduced variation at its extreme, I guess we could say. Granted, this reduced variation might drive a lover of jazz improvisation right out the door; however, we found many audiences resisted bands that improvised too much. Even though we won a contest for our original material, our fans came to hear the songs of other artists. Another lesson about change and resistance can be learned from our band's experience. The frequency of being exposed to a change (our original songs) makes the change a nonchange over time. Resistance to our original material faded after we "slipped" the songs in and fans began to applaud. This is my first quick-win suggestion for you. Introduce change in small batches in between pleasing experiences.

Speaking of audiences, one afternoon after delivering a speech on leading an organization in performance improvement, another speaker asked me if people resist change. After initially being perplexed that such a wise person would ask such a question, I answered with a "yes." I will never forget his next question. "Or do people resist being changed?" Peter Senge,[1] a prominent business consultant and author, has been credited with this interplay.

"People resist being changed" is a phenomenon that has stuck with me since that question by Senge. I have learned to use it to my advantage every time I lead change. I had to try it out, of course, to prove it to myself. I tried helping people be a part of the change instead of directly trying to change them or their process. Instead of promoting what I thought the change should be, I engaged the team and guided them in discovering the issues that convinced me we need a change. Lo and behold, once they understood what was causing the issue, they chose and implemented the same changes. Try it. Let me know how it works for you. Just trying what we share in this book should make you better at leading change because practice builds confidence to become better at process improvement.

Want another quick win that saves lives? Check how many people don't wash their hands after using the restroom. Look for sinks and soap dispensers that are broken or empty. Find a person working in the area and ask how one knows the dispenser is getting low or broken. Next, find out who is supposed to refill it. Lastly, find where the stock is located. As I was writing this book at night, I thought I was finished with this chapter until the next day. In my client's workplace, we found four out of six dispensers in the surgical center hallway were empty. We looked at the dispenser and there was a little window in the cover of the dispenser, but none of us could figure out if the window was an indication the alcohol was running low. When we asked the people in the process who refills the dispensers, they said, "Housekeeping." We asked if they could refill it, and one said they could, but they didn't know where the refills are kept. When we asked the housekeeping manager why this was happening, she said that there was a problem ordering. Each day, 247 people die in U.S. hospitals from healthcare-acquired infections that often are passed on by healthcare professionals' hands. Make it easier, folks, and wonderful things happen to your measure.

Role of the Change Leader

The Change Leader is the first role we will discuss among the roles in process improvement. What separates those who initiate the change from those who are targets of the change? Is the answer simply the organizational hierarchy? In organizations with top-down decision making, this may be the case. Can the amount of change needed be done in this manner? Peter Drucker states, "Unless it is seen as the task of the organization to lead change, the organization—whether business, university, hospital, and so on—will not survive. In a period of rapid structural change, the only ones who survive are the Change Leaders."[2]

A Policy of Change and Continuous Improvement

Drucker believes there are four requirements for Change Leadership beginning with "making policy to make the future." Simply stated, the organization must make change a policy. Measuring an annual rate of change is living it. Abandonment is a policy used by Change Leaders as a means to prune old products and services. The second requirement of the organization is to drive continuous improvement because continuous improvement starts the chain of events that leads to fundamental change. This chain goes like this: Continuous improvement leads to product innovation that leads to service innovation that leads to new processes, then new businesses, and, finally, to fundamental change. Steve Jobs and Steven Wozniak (Apple®) improved the computer, which started a chain of events that created new businesses and, fundamentally, changed the way we buy music, read books, and work. This is transformation and it all starts with continuous improvement.

Piloting Changes

Drucker's third requirement is to pilot on a small scale. "Neither studies nor computer modeling are a substitute for the test of reality," according to Drucker. He recommends the right way to introduce change is through piloting of new or improved systems. This is why the more successful improvement programs have piloting built in. Later, we will introduce to you a Roadmap to Performance Excellence. Change is never introduced perfectly despite some valuable methods to get it right the first time. Continuous improvement works best when we start small and test our changes. It can really reduce the anxiety and make change easier too, as we will see is a fundamental skill of Change Leaders. Piloting is a requirement and comes before full implementation.

What Can Happen If Change Is Not Piloted First

In October, 2011, the U.K.'s National Health System (NHS) announced scrapping the biggest civilian IT (information technology) project ever initiated. After wasting 10 years and over £12 billion, the NHS has decided that smaller local solutions are better able to provide the electronic aids that healthcare needs. Maybe piloting the concepts locally on a much smaller scale would have exposed the issues that eventually convinced one of the largest health systems in the world that fundamental change comes from continuous improvement.

Focusing on opportunities is more important than focusing on problems. The Change Leader should measure the opportunities and resource them from a budget immune to economic cycles. Time spent is time lost. The "opportunity cost" of having knowledge workers working on the past versus building for the future can kill a company.

Balancing Change and Continuity

This opportunity cost leads us to Drucker's fourth requirement, the need to balance change and continuity. The organization needs to engage its partners. Partners include its knowledge workers and all workers as well as its suppliers, customers, and community. Dr. W. Edwards Deming's (American statistician, author, and consultant) name for balancing change and continuity is "constancy of purpose." Change is difficult for many, especially in an organization where change is not yet the norm. Stability in the mission, strategy, and rewards provides a balance to changes. Strong relationships will be seen in this book as fundamental to making change the norm. Information sharing is vital between partners, and reinforcements to sharing and learning and who gets new challenges all provide constancy of purpose. What will crush change and result in losing the knowledge workers is an organization that does not promote those who deliver continuous improvement. After all, the knowledge worker is the worker of the twenty-first century, according to Drucker. To lose him or her is to lose a Change Leader who will lead many others to performance excellence.

The Emancipation Proclamation

Abraham Lincoln practiced all four of Drucker's requirements. Lincoln's policy included writing the Emancipation Proclamation, which prohibited the expansion of slavery to states: "That on the first day of January, in the year of our Lord, one thousand eight hundred and sixty-three, all persons held as slaves within any State or designated part of a State, the people whereof shall then be in rebellion against the United States, shall be then, thenceforward, and forever free."[3]

The president attempted in this historic document to look for and anticipate change and resistance to freeing slaves by writing" "… will recognize and maintain the freedom of such persons, and will do no act or acts to repress such persons, or any of them, in any efforts they may make for their actual freedom."

Now, the third policy, the right way to introduce change within and outside the organization, was argued by the South. However, the Emancipation Proclamation was not Lincoln's first attempt to introduce a change to freeing the slaves. In fact, The Emancipation Proclamation came a year and a half after the first shots of the Civil War were fired by cadets from the South at Fort Sumter on April 12, 1861. Lincoln had tried engaging the South in dialogue well before the start of the Civil War, to no avail.[3]

And evidence that Lincoln also practiced what Drucker would describe as a Change Leader's fourth and last policy—to balance change and continuity—is found in Lincoln's words that the freed slaves should continue to labor faithfully for reasonable wages after receiving their freedom versus impose an imbalance of change among U.S. citizens.

"And I hereby enjoin upon the people so declared to be free to abstain from all violence, unless in necessary self-defense; and I recommend to them that, in all cases when allowed, they labor faithfully for reasonable wages."

Lincoln continues with: "And I further declare and make known, that such persons of suitable condition, will be received into the armed service of the United States to garrison forts, positions, stations, and other places, and to man vessels of all sorts in said service."

Lincoln ends with a statement of balance and continuity: "And upon this act, sincerely believed to be an act of justice, warranted by the Constitution, upon military necessity, I invoke the considerate judgment of mankind, and the gracious favor of Almighty God."

Count the recent changes in your organization, and how many were initiated by the people doing the work versus the manager. How does leading change work in a top-down organization when changes are initiated by the frontline? I promised we would learn from those who excelled.

Another good way to learn is from those who failed.

What Happens When One or More of the Ms Is Missing?

The answer to this question can be answered with a story from healthcare. A story about a Hungarian physician, Dr. Ignaz Semmelweis, who practiced medicine in the middle of the nineteenth century. He is best known for a discovery that saved the lives of many mothers during his work at the

Vienna General Hospital's Obstetrical Clinics (Austria) and countless lives since the time of his discovery. However, his story is also one of failure in process improvement due to a failure in Change Leadership. His story is also a lesson in how missing one of the three Ms can devastate a change that could have saved many more lives. This is our first lesson on how change can fail.

He had a vision of a safer hospital for mothers. He used a scientific method to test his hypothesis of how to save lives. He also engaged his colleagues and superiors, and instructed them in a safer practice. Before we hear his story of change, let's have an overview of the force against change so we can appreciate Dr. Semmelweis's story even more.

Dr. Semmelweis and Washing Hands: The Right Change, but ...

The time is the 1840s. Dr. Semmelweis discovered the benefits of physicians washing their hands to prevent mothers from dying after childbirth of puerperal fever. He practiced at the Vienna Obstetrical Clinics in Austria. These clinics could be any clinic or hospital in any country. Mothers were dying after giving birth assisted by physicians in hospitals. One may ask: "Aren't these unfortunate practices and deaths the reason most births today are not in the homes, but in hospitals?" The cause of mothers dying was correlated with where and with whom mothers gave birth. However, these horribly unfortunate and devastating fatalities may not have been occurring where you would think. Mothers who were perfectly healthy and had chosen to give birth in hospitals with a physician attending were dying at a significantly higher rate than the mothers who gave birth with assistance of a midwife.

Dr. Semmelweis found a correlation with physicians who assisted in births after they had conducted surgery or autopsies, and the deaths of those mothers giving birth. Beyond any doubt, a mother giving birth in a hospital in these circumstances had a higher rate of infection and death than one who gave birth outside of the hospital or even within the same hospital by a midwife. An Oscar-winning short film, *That Mothers Might Live*,[4] shares Dr. Semmelweis's story.

His technical skills in performance improvement resulted in one of the most significant discoveries in healthcare, if not in the history of humankind. He reduced the mortality rate from a mean of 10.5 to 2.5% (Figure 3.1). Researchers believe even the first percentage numbers are conservative because mothers who left the clinic and then died may not have been counted in this data.

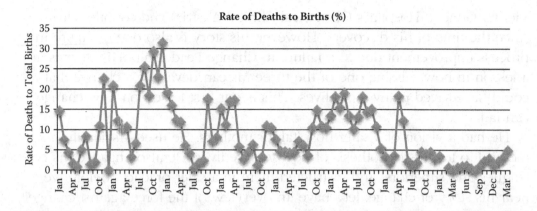

Figure 3.1 Rate of deaths to births.

Why Is Change Needed In Healthcare?

There are 247 people who die each day from healthcare-acquired infections in the United States according to the World Health Organization (WHO).[5] In the Vienna Clinic in Austria where Semmelweis practiced, if his changes would have been implemented in 1841 when the mortality data started, 1,532 mothers might have survived.

Beyond the number of mothers who would have died, how many other patients, doctors, and hospital staff would have died if it were not for Dr. Semmelweis? Weren't we told by our parents to wash our hands? How many of us today would not be reading this story if it were not for Dr. Semmelweis? How many people are not here today because mothers died before having a chance to have another baby?

Semmelweis's Improvement Dies with Him

This brings us to the point of sharing Dr. Semmelweis's story. He died an early death in a mental institution, depressed and destitute because of his lack of Change Leadership skills. Washing hands, a simple, proven solution, was itself not enough to create sustained change. Change Leadership is as important as the science in healthcare's discoveries.

What went wrong in his process improvement? His own colleagues resisted the change to the washing of hands. His superior resisted even the thought that he, Dr. Semmelweis, and the very surgeons who have achieved the highest respect of any profession, could be the cause of death. Who could think that these same surgeons who had saved so many from so many illnesses were actually causing death? Despite the evidence so clearly showing a correlation with their actions and mothers dying, they resisted scientific evidence. Did they resist because of poor Change Leadership skills, despite knowing that washing their hands was effective?

The resistance to Dr. Semmelweis was clear. In the film, an early scene showed a man carrying instruments in the hospital. He drops several on the floor and picks them back up as he continues his journey. This same man was shown later in the film resisting Dr. Semmelweis as he demands this behavior be changed. Dr. Semmelweis's colleagues openly resisted, as well. A passive regressive colleague is shown mimicking washing, instead of actually cleansing. Dr. Semmelweis catches him and berates him in front of his colleagues. Even Dr. Semmelweis's superior resisted the change.

Forcing Doesn't Always Work

Dr. Semmelweis tried to police his peers and staff with stern warnings, but resistance only grew stronger. There is no evidence that Dr. Semmelweis maintained a chart showing the correlation of washing hands and the reduction in mothers dying. We don't know if he ever posted the chart for all to see after his initial tests. So strong, in fact, was the resistance, he was dismissed from the clinics. Having failed at leading the change within his hospital and actually being dispelled, he reached out to the community, wrote letters to other doctors and institutions, and still failed to lead the change. The simple change of washing one's hands was resisted.

The point of the story is not that we resist washing. The point is that his colleagues resisted the *doctor* more than his *ideas*. The best changes can be lost due to poor Change Leadership.

The Force of Resistance

Change Leadership can be learned using the principles of electricity, especially in understanding the force of resistance against change. Don't worry if electricity, or reading a book about it, scares you. We'll mix in some little known facts and entertain you a bit. And, no, we don't recommend shock therapy or cattle prods if that is what you think we have in mind in getting people to change.

Benjamin Franklin, Electricity, and Change Leadership

Benjamin Franklin was a great Change Leader, wouldn't you say? Who was more important to America's change to independence? Ah, yes, he knew a bit about electricity, too. I hope you enjoy his story as we learn how the principles of electricity help us believe in, and understand, Change Leadership and its power.

Electricity flowing to power devices to make our lives better is analogous to change flowing to make our lives better and those of our stakeholders. What prevents electricity from flowing is resistance. If this isn't enough to convince you, let me explain. We will stay close to healthcare as we learn Change Leadership through Franklin's leadership stories and his discoveries about electricity.

We have all experienced an electrical shock, whether the minimally risky static shock delivered when shaking hands or while kissing our loved ones, to the more painful household electric shock. Electrical resistance is a barrier to the free flow of electricity. Components in your computer, television, and hair dryer manage the flow of electricity by using components named, not surprisingly, resistors. Resistors! We'll learn more about these stakeholders. For now, do you know some of these folks who might be scheming to prevent the change you are looking for in your organization?

Principles of Electricity Explain Resistance to Change

How electricity works for us and against us also explains how Change Leadership works. Let me start with a lesson learned early in my career in electrical safety products: "What you can't see can kill you, so don't touch it." We learned better ways to handle the energy than ignoring it and proceeding. Being aware, such as in an analysis of who the stakeholders are, is a way of "seeing" the potential danger before "touching" the process and stakeholders with changes. Channeling that energy is what we do in Change Leadership, too. To prevent lightning from damaging your house or worse, starting a fire, we install lightning rods to channel the energy to the ground where resistance works for our safety, earthworms, excluded (Figure 3.2).

Change Leadership and electricity also have in common a method to actually benefit from the energy. What if we could channel that energy and resistance to do good?

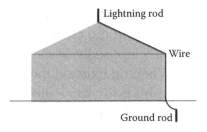

Figure 3.2   Lightning rod and resistance.

What You Can't See Can Hurt You

Ben Franklin's experiment showed that what you can't see can hurt you. His actual experiment involved flying a kite into clouds to prove that lightning is electricity (Figure 3.3). All we knew in 1752 was that lightning looked like an arc of electricity. Arcs at the time could only be produced an inch long, nothing like a miles-long lightning bolt. Franklin wanted to test the hypothesis that lightning is electricity.

Franklin and his son theorized that if they could get the kite in the clouds, the invisible electricity could be captured by channeling it down the kite string

Figure 3.3   Benjamin Franklin and his kite.

to a jar with a key in it. Lightning did not actually strike the kite, we understand, but enough negative charges in the clouds traveled down the kite string to the key in the special jar that supposedly stored electricity. Franklin proved that lightning was electricity. When he touched the key, he received a shock because the positive charges in his body were strongly attracted to the negative charges in the metal key. Franklin now knew how to channel the energy from lightning to a safer level of resistance. Again, "what you can't see can kill you, so don't touch it." If you can't see resistance, don't touch it. What Change Leaders do is eliminate the resistance, or reduce it safely to achieve the changes desired. Learn to see it even if it is invisible to the naked eye and channel it. Electric meters were invented to *see* electricity. Stakeholder analysis is to see resistance—the energy that can work against your team's efforts to improve healthcare.

Using Resistance to Help Lead Change

The next lesson in dealing with high energy is to use resistance in our favor. To manage electricity, we actually use a component aptly named a resistor. One is pictured below in Figure 3.4.

If there is too much energy for what is needed, or what a device can handle, a designer inserts a resistor to restrict the flow of electric current. An example is to place a resistor in a circuit to lower the flow to an alarm that warns that a machine is starting to fail. If we want to increase the flow, we reduce the resistance. The same is true in leading change. Reduce the resistance to get the changes flowing.

Electricity and Forcing Change Can Be Dangerous

The next lesson is really helpful. Electricity is dangerous. You are probably reading this book because you fear change. Or, perhaps you fear leading the next change. Even if you have all the confidence in the world, you are reading this book because you know change can be dangerous to you

Figure 3.4   An electronic resistor component.

Figure 3.5 What a resistor might look like in your organization.

and your company if not done well, and you want to improve your Change Leadership skills. Leading major changes can be career limiting if you aren't careful "what you touch."

Getting Change to Flow

Back to Franklin's experiment. We also know others have died from shock trying the same experiment he did on that stormy day. Change is like electricity. We want change to flow. Therefore, the best way to increase changes is to reduce resistance. Shock occurs when our body's resistance is low enough that the current through the body allows the high voltage to flow. The voltage required for electrocution depends on the current through the body, which depends on the resistance our body puts up to the voltage wanting to flow to a state of equilibrium. There is actually a law about this called Ohm's law. For those who learn better through math, it is $I = V/R$ where I is the current passing through your body, V is the voltage, and R is resistance. When R goes down, I goes up. This is what we want in Change Leadership. So, our goal is to flow change by reducing R.

Resistance to Change Can Vary within the Same Person

There is more to be learned from electricity in leading change. As in leading change, the same person at different times of the day can be more resistant to change. So, too, is his/her body's resistance to electricity as the moisture in the skin varies through the day. Hmmm, another quick win? What if we announced the next change at a swimming pool party because wet skin is less resistant? And, better yet, wet the insides of everyone, too, with some enticing drinks? (My attorney wanted to scratch this little humor, but I left it in anyway with a statement that you should not attempt this yourself. This should only be tried by a professional on a closed course.)

As in Franklin's key, and Benjamin himself, the greater the differential, the greater the shock. Therefore, engage stakeholders early and often to reduce the differential of knowledge and potential for shock between what you know and they know. "If we both know what each other knows, then we will feel like each other feels, and we will do as we each would do."

Resistance between Two Bodies

Change has the same properties. We have a differential between two bodies, the Change Leader and a Stakeholder. The phrase: "There is electricity between these two people," is appropriate. And, remember, that like electricity, there is energy in each party and a desire to reach equilibrium. The two bodies with different potential energy coming in close contact results in the shock and a new state of equilibrium. Remember the negative charges in the metal key and Franklin's positively charged body. After the shock, both the key and he were again in a state of equilibrium. Wow, who would have thought kissing your loved one on a dry winter day on carpet is part of the science in Change Leadership? In addition, we see that two bodies do not have to be in direct contact. Think of when that person identified on the Stakeholder Analysis walks into your team's meeting with his arms folded.

Electricity also teaches us that the higher the differential between two bodies, the greater the shock when they come near each other. If there is not much differential between two bodies, the shock will be minimal or nonexistent.

Resistance at Home

Think of when you and your loved one are picking a color for the kitchen. If you and your spouse both want to change the kitchen to blue, no shock or resistance here, and off you go to the paint store. My wife, Jan, is good at Change Leadership. As proof, let me share with you how she leads change that makes for a great marriage inside and outside our home. Jan loves green. Blue is by far the color for me. There is something about blue that makes it the right color for just about any wall. Come to think of it, blue is the right color for anything. Anyway, we have been married for over 30 years, so whenever we are picking colors for a room, the differential is just how green it will be. Here is how Jan's mastery of reducing resistance from me inside our home works. Although our house is usually a palette of green, we usually have a blue car in our garage. Compromise is a wonderful thing and is a great tool in reducing resistance. By the way, did I tell you we still have the '65 Mustang with blue and white seats we drove in when we were teenagers? And, she sold her green Cougar before we married. Jan and I have a nice marriage with compromises inside and outside our home. This is a lesson for Change Leaders.

Key Points

- Change Leadership is as important as the change itself. The greatest scientific discoveries may fail if leaders do not lead others to benefitting from the science.
- Change Leaders envision a change, engage stakeholders, and start the change. Change management plans, organizes, staffs, directs, and controls the change process.
- Every industry has many examples of change, including frontline workers, managers, and executives who are either reducing variation or increasing variation for changes to improve customer value. What is common is that changes are led, not just managed.

Practicing Change Leadership

- In the foreword, we asked you to list your expectations of this book. Take time now to review your expectations and update any expectation that has begun to be met.
- Read more about your favorite leader to see if what we share in this chapter is true as well with your favorite leader of change.
- We are ready for an experiment for you in your organization. We will apply the rules of electricity in a small, and we think fun, exercise. Pick an object that you think is better located elsewhere, maybe the mail trays for your office, a picture hanging in your room, department or lobby, or supplies in the store's room or on a common desk. Practice your Change Leadership where the item is better located. Reflect on what you did and who resisted the idea. How could you have led change better?

Endnotes

1. Peter Senge, *The Fifth Discipline: The Art & Practice of The Learning Organization*. (New York: Doubleday/Currency, 1990).
2. Peter F. Drucker, *Management Challenges for the 21st Century*. (San Francisco: Jossey Bass Publishers, 1999).
3. Donald T. Phillips, *Lincoln on Leadership, Executive Strategies for Tough Times*. Copyright © 1992 by Donald T. Phillips. By permission of Grand Central Publishing. All rights reserved.
4. *That Mothers Might Live*. (Warner Bros. Home Entertainment, Broadway Melody of 1938, Special Features).
5. *World Alliance For Patient Safety*. Director Fred Zinnemann. (World Healthcare Organization Guidelines on Hand Hygiene in Healthcare, Geneva, Switzerland, April 2006).

Chapter 4

Process Improvement Methodologies

We don't need any more recipes. We need cooks to change groceries into meals. That is adding value.

Richard Morrow

Overview of the Most Popular Methodologies

PDSA (plan, do, study, act), PDCA (plan, do, check, act), Lean, Six Sigma, and other scientific performance improvement methodologies adorn the walls in many different industries. Recipe madness, it is. I wish I had a nickel for each time I heard debates about one methodology being better than the other, which one should we start with first, and how complex one is compared to the other. Most problem-solving or process-improvement methodologies are described below using the steps and sequence in the methodology.

An example is Dr. Walter Shewhart's PDSA and it is useful to remember the four steps. Dr. W. Edwards Deming modified Dr. Shewhart's PDSA to plan, do, check, act (PDCA). Dr. Shewhart and Dr. Deming were on friendly terms and, in the effort to continuously improve, Dr. Deming added his own recipe.

In Six Sigma, Bill Smith and Mikel Harry originally described the Six Sigma methodology as MAIC: measure, analyze, improve, and control. They and others using Six Sigma found that issues needed better definition, so "define" was added. Thus, DMAIC.

The Toyota Production System (TPS) is Toyota's methodology for improving a production system. TPS is now used widely in virtually all industries. I have seen my teams use TPS for improving electrical safety products and call center support, reducing wait times in the airline industry, eliminating inventory, and improving surgical safety. Lean is another methodology and it is not an acronym. Lean includes TPS and is a very popular performance improvement methodology in many industries. Lean is a term coined by an MIT group who studied the auto industry. In the book, *The Machine That Changed the World* (Macmillan Publishing, 1990),[1] James Womack and Daniel Jones shared the term's origins. Lean describes the Toyota processes compared to Ford, GM, and Chrysler processes. The amount of time and resources to do similar tasks at Toyota were much less than at Ford, GMC, and Chrysler.

We could list many more methodologies and acronyms, but this book is about making process improvement simpler for you and your organization. Therefore, I will walk the talk here and purposely be "Lean" by sharing the vital few and most popular "recipes."

You need at least one recipe and don't forget a "heaping tablespoon" of Change Leadership. The key point I want to leave you with in this chapter is that these methodologies are all you need, and you need them all with Change Leadership. I could point to elements of Six Sigma, Lean, PDSA and Change Leadership in each of these methodologies. Reducing waste is often associated with Lean, and statistical process control by many is considered Six Sigma by some.

Which recipe delivers the culture and Change Leadership skills? Some consultants have hijacked culture change and leadership development claiming that only their Lean or their Six Sigma delivers skills beyond the tools of a methodology. Untrue. Certainly some Lean "purists" have hijacked culture change to be delivered only through Lean. And, I have heard some Six Sigma purists claim that Lean-trained people don't use data or other quality tools. Many Six Sigma consultants have helped organizations change their cultures in much the same way as those consultants who describe themselves as primarily Lean.[2,3] This is a shame and a waste of time to even debate.

Work with Toyota and for Motorola

I have worked with Toyota, taught its former employees Lean and Six Sigma, and toured its sites. I am one of the few who also has worked for Motorola.

The two most popular methodologies were developed by these two leading organizations. At Motorola, I coached and trained process improvement teams while in its Corporate Initiatives Group. I also led performance excellence in Motorola's automotive business unit. However, Motorola did not sell to Toyota, so my experience with Toyota comes from time with SKF (Svenska Kullagerfabriken) as its vice president of Total Quality and Lean Six Sigma.

Motorola and Toyota Use Lean and Six Sigma Tools

I know firsthand that Toyota and Motorola use the same tools that some want to categorize as Lean or Six Sigma. Jeffrey Liker states in his book, *The Toyota Way*,[4] that the tools that some associate with Six Sigma are used in Toyota. Although Liker makes a statement that quality specialists and team members use only four key tools, I can assure you that Toyota teaches its team members many of the same tools that are taught in Six Sigma courses, such as fishbone charts, control charts, and data collection methods. Toyota also values and uses histograms, statistical process control charts, data analysis, and failure mode and effects analysis, and they often demand the same from its suppliers as Liker states later. The key is to teach what adds value. It is also true that there are tools taught in both Six Sigma and Lean courses that may never be needed.

I may never forget a former Toyota employee's "aha" moment at a United Airlines process improvement course my staff was teaching. She had joined UAL after many years on the shop floor at a Toyota vehicle assembly plant. She stood up during a module on statistical process control, histograms, and how to test if there are statistical differences between two methods, exclaiming, "Oh, now I understand why quality was so good at Toyota." Not every Toyota employee is taught all the tools that make Toyota quality a benchmark as in most companies of such size. That doesn't mean the tools aren't used.

PDSA and PDCA Compared to Six Sigma

Experimentation is the essence of PDSA and PDCA. Drs. Shewhart and Deming were scientists and experienced at experimentation, and they believed in cycling through plan, do, study, act until success is achieved. The PDCA cycle refers to the practice of continuous improvement through repeated successive experimentation. PDCA describes experimental design we were all taught back in primary school. Terry Howell, chief quality officer at Hennepin County (Minnesota) Medical Center and co-creator of a modified PDCA, and others have helped those applying PDSA by clarifying that a few steps should occur before planning an experiment.

Drs. Shewhart and Deming knew to answer these questions before PDSA, but others have missed these steps. FOCUS is an acronym for focus, organize, clarify, understand, and select. IHI, the Institute for Healthcare Improvement organization,[5] also added similar questions before PDCA. IHI's Improvement Model authors recognized that not all of us are so skilled in setting up an experiment. These questions, not surprisingly, make PDSA and PDCA as complete as DMAIC. Those questions include:

- What are we trying to accomplish?
- How will we know a change is an improvement?
- What changes can we make that will result in an improvement?

Question 1 closely mirrors the define phase of Six Sigma where the team brings consensus to the issue, customer-centric metrics, goals, scope, and impact.

Question 2 refers to measuring the current state to know when change has occurred. Too many times, people show a line chart with a few points going in the favorable direction without a representative baseline period. This baseline period should be measured to validate change has really occurred. We will discuss another tool often associated with Six Sigma, Statistical Process Control (SPC), in Chapter 13 about Measure. For now, consider that all of these methodologies reinforce measuring the current state early on to know if change has really occurred.

Question 3 is the weaker connection to Six Sigma's Analyze Phase. Let's start with what Analyze Phase entails and then relate it to the third question.

All Good Methods Analyze for Root Causes before Solutions

Analyzing for contributing factors and root causes is what the Six Sigma team discovers in this phase. PDSA, PDCA, Lean, and Six Sigma all focus on analyzing to find root causes and contributing factors before implementing countermeasures. In PDCA, Drs. Shewhart and Deming promote analyzing before the "plan" step. Otherwise, they would have wasted doing, checking, and acting on, every single possible variable. One must remember that both of these experts in process improvement were well-versed in experimentation that starts with defining the issue, stating a hypothesis, and then planning an experiment. If one knows the root causes, improvements are often self-evident.

Case Study of Late Shipments

Keeping a "Big Box" retailer happy is not the easiest thing to do. They are demanding, short tempered at times, and can always find someone else from which to buy. This particular retailer was a "Do-it-Yourself" international chain and one of the biggest and most successful. We went to extraordinary measures to ensure we had processes that could deliver complete orders to each of their sites on time. Occasionally, we would miss a shipment. A team was organized, trained, and given time to improve the shipment performance. Some team members and a manager or two believed the solution was simply to increase inventory. Such a "solution-in-mind" approach to problem solving instead of using PDSA, Lean, and Six Sigma is a warning sign to be more mindful.

The support from my fellow executive members was tremendous, having been one of the first organizations in the corporation to train and empower teams in process improvement. This newly formed team might have requested and gotten more inventory if it were not for the team leader and members knowing they should first analyze for the causes.

Don't get me wrong here about the leadership. They would have asked about the root causes, having been trained as champions and aware of the Define, Measure, and Analyze phases. They might have assumed the team validated that a shortage of inventory for the retail customer had resulted in the bad outcome of missed shipments.

Visible measures of the current state are required in the Measure phase. Depending on the consequences, if wrong on the root causes, Six Sigma team leaders trained in measuring capability can achieve this validation statistically. I and my team may have supported the request for more inventory with confidence that the team validated root causes. We would have looked for the statistical analysis of demand and service.

The team came into the project with a clear definition of the work to be done, measured the current state, and then used the tools in the Analyze phase to find the contributing factors to the issue. The team used a simple value stream map and time series chart showing demand patterns of the retailer and the export customers who also bought the same product, but in

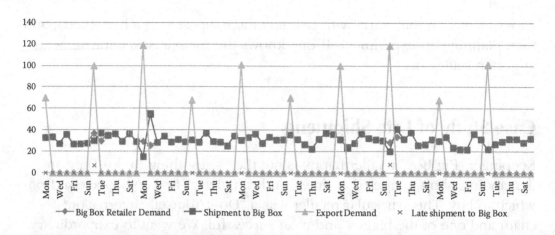

Figure 4.1 Demands and shipments.

a different package (Figure 4.1). Notice there are four lines in this chart. The lines represent the demand daily by the Big Box retailer, the demand for our export customers that were shipped weekly, the shipment quantity to the retailer by day, and a point showing any shortage to meet the Big Box retailers' demand for that day.

Was increasing finished goods inventory the solution? Note the demand patterns of the Big Box retailer compared to the export customer shipment pattern. When did the shortages occur? Each shortage occurred when a shipment was made to the export customers. We could have increased inventory for the Big Box retailer and solved the problem, perhaps. But inventory is waste. The team took a different approach. They used their Lean Six Sigma skills and created this baseline to analyze why exactly we missed some shipments.

The team went out to the floor and the distribution center on Monday. What they found was not expected. They found more inventory. The inventory was being staged for the following week's export shipment. In other words, there was plenty of inventory, but the export shipment team had continually missed shipments the year before. They found that the inventory was always prioritized for the Big Box retailer and they often did not have enough. So, they started reserving products for the export customers as production produced them. Once these products were allocated to the export shipment, they were not visible on the inventory screen to anyone else in the plant. The team went on to find that in every case of a missed shipment to the Big Box, there were enough products reserved for a later shipment to the export customers.

The production line people could always recover the extra production needed the next day, as is shown in the chart. They also were not very happy to find they had an "emergency" on Tuesday to make up for the Big Box retailer. They also were not very happy to find out that their production was reserved for export customers and "gathering dust" waiting on the once-per-week shipment six days away.

By diving deeper to find the root causes before jumping to the solution to add inventory, the team now knew to consider using the inventory staging for the export customers if they ran short for the daily Big Box shipment. The team also found that manufacturing seldom had to make an emergency order because they had up to six days advance notice to ensure the export shipment had enough products.

Cross Reference of PDSA, Six Sigma, Lean, Change Leadership

I have created a table that may help cross reference PDSA, PDCA, Six Sigma, and Lean process improvement methodologies. I also include a band describing the Change Leadership methodology (Figure 4.2), Process Improvement Principles. The Roadmap for Performance Excellence™ also

Process Improvement Principles				Act → Plan ⇩ Study (Check) ⇦ Do	
PDSA Cycle with leading questions*	What are we trying to accomplish?	How will we know a change is an improvement?	What changes can we make that will result in an improvement?	What are the possible solutions and how do we implement the best solution?	How do we maintain the gains we have achieved and standardize?
Six Sigma	**D**efine the work to be done	**M**easure the current state	**A**nalyze for root causes	**I**mprove and Design	**C**ontrol to sustain the gains
Lean Principles	Specify what customers value	Identify all steps and inputs in the value stream	Eliminate waste and variation at the root cause	Stabilize, reduce variation and defects to create flow, letting customers pull	Standardize, level flow, sustain and continuously improve
Change Leadership	Prepare for Change -Train, Envision, Engage, Enable and Empower	Explore Together	Explain	Experiment, Explore, Build Consensus	Train, Enable, Empower, Hold Accountable, Celebrate

Figure 4.2   Process Improvement Principles.

has this information with more details on the tools. We share this Roadmap in Appendix 1.

Human Factors and Ergonomics in Process Improvement

Human Factors is a term describing how humans perceive a situation and react. Human Factors work often is cited with the airline industry, which has been studied often due to catastrophic accidents.

Ergonomics is closely related to Human Factors. Ergonomics is sometimes relegated to the physical and mental stress associated with work. Let's relate Change Leadership and Human Factors and Ergonomics with a story.

Case Study: Human Factors Added to Lean Six Sigma

A nurse who is a Black Belt trained in Six Sigma joined a collaboration I led with other hospitals to improve hand hygiene. She asked early in our first collaborations if we intended to use Human Factors in our work to improve hand hygiene. I quickly answered "yes" to her question and thought how odd to ask what seemed obvious. We know performance improvement in human-controlled activities versus automated processes always has to factor in the human element and our variation we add to a process. To others in the group trained by certain Six Sigma consultants, the question seemed reasonable and needed. We discovered that each other's definition of Six Sigma, Lean, or whatever recipe we all knew, varied as to the degree of human factors in Change Leadership. All of us agreed Human Factors are critical in leading change. I had no idea some consultants did not teach Human Factors and certified Black Belts without this knowledge.

Hand Hygiene Change Leadership Issue

The 3Ms have not only worked in reducing the resistance to handwashing, the 3Ms are vital to leading change when humans are key in the process. Here is why. Dr. Deming said, "If I had to reduce my message for management to just a few words, I'd say it all had to do with reducing variation."

The best technical solution may fail due to variation in how people have different interpretations of the same issue. Understanding the change by all parties leads to more effective change.

If people know what each other knows, they may feel like each other feels, and they may do as each other does.

Dr. Semmelweis understood the issue of unclean hands. but could not teach others the issue to understand the impact. Self-preservation is innate and still not enough of a motivation to understand handwashing's value. There is something different about pediatric units. We often see hand hygiene practiced better by those entering these units than adult units. Maybe those entering have done a stakeholder analysis of those impacted?

Could it be that the chart that Dr. Semmelweis had showing clear correlation was not shared with all? Could it be it was a one-time presentation and hidden away by those who feared that this chart in the hands of others would result in humiliation of the surgeons by the hospital staff? There is no evidence that this measure was shared in the hospital.

We need to understand measures used in research and measures used in processes. They are similar, but have important differences in purpose and use. We will cover this in Chapter 14, Managing to the Measure.

Dr. Semmelweis's discovery is also considered a catalyst for Dr. Louis Pasteur discovering the process of pasteurization, which itself has saved millions of lives worldwide. His discovery is linked with the microscope to discover what we could not see killing mothers.

Failure to Engage Others with the Measure

Performance improvement needs Change Leadership. The 3Ms (measure, manage to the measure, and make it easier) are the binding force that is necessary to achieve significant and sustained change. How will we know if improvement occurred without a measure? We don't know with whom Dr. Semmelweis and his superior and colleagues actually shared the measure. There is nothing in the film showing that he shared the measure with anyone. The film suggests he tried sharing the measure, but many failed to even open his correspondence. Sharing a measure is often not enough to change behaviors and improve a process. We must manage to the measures for the measures to have their impact with those who resist the measure. Regardless if managing to the measure failed in Dr. Semmelweis' work, we see winners managing to the measures every day.

Baseball and Managing to the Measure

Baseball is often regarded as one of the most measured sports. I had a young college intern join my staff one summer. His goal was to become a statistician because he loved the statistics in baseball. He loved the stats so much that he had entered thousands of statistics for fun and became very skilled in statistics for one so young. He had studied the pitch count to see if there is a correlation between the pitch count and the performance of the pitcher. Coaches and players count the number of pitches thrown and this stat is considered a key measure to manage changing to another pitcher.

The manager of the team will manage pitching changes when the pitch count is high and other factors suggest a pitcher may start varying. Note that here is that variation concern again. Some managers will make a change on pitch count alone. Loss of control may be felt a hazard with a pitcher nearing his or her pitch count threshold. Pitch count is especially important with young boys and girls to avoid potential injury.

As we see in baseball, measuring pitch count is one thing; however, managing to the measure is what is critical. Did Dr. Semmelweis and his superior manage to the measure? They had the measure, so what went wrong? Was it a one-time study or did Dr. Semmelweis frequently measure and display to the surgeons? Was it all data in the past that he then "sprung" on his boss and colleagues who may not have understood what the measure was telling Dr. Semmelweis? We don't know. What we all have experienced are people resisting our changes saying things like, "Well, that is just one sample." "How do we know if tomorrow shows different results?" "You haven't proved anything."

Measures for Research Purposes

Data and measures for research result in statistics that describe a period in time. It is a "batch" versus flow of data. Measurement in research is often done to test if there are differences between two or more groups. There is usually a probabilistic determination in research that requires knowing the sample size to estimate the confidence in the decision. Research is nothing about real time analysis and early knowledge if a process is changing.

Measures for Process Improvement Purposes

Process improvement is about knowing if the process is in control and helping us make decisions about the process as it runs. Think of research data as a batch, and process control data as a flow of data. Process control data continue to be gathered, thus process control sample size tends to be infinite.

Cedars–Sinai Using Measure and Manage to the Measure

Sharing that data with people in the process is also necessary in process control. In addition, sharing as the process runs is also necessary. A 20% increase improvement in one unit at Cedars–Sinai Hospital was achieved with the help of measuring and managing to the measure. Make change easier with measuring and managing to the measure, and we can achieve amazing changes. A 95% hand hygiene compliance is just one outcome, making healthcare organizations safer, resulting in fewer healthcare-acquired infections or conditions (HAI or HAC) and more lives saved.

Key Points

- Scientific methodologies include PDSA, PDCA, Six Sigma, Lean, and others.
- Acronyms often shorten the steps describing the methodologies and help us remember the steps.
- Change Leadership is critical in addition to the methodologies.
- A step-by-step process improvement approach provides higher quality improvements in less time.

Endnotes

1. James Womack, Daniel Jones, *The Machine that Changed the World.* HarperPerennial, 1991.
2. Ronald D. Snee and Roger W. Hoerl, *Leading Six Sigma.* (Upper Saddle River, NJ: Prentice Hall, 2003), 184–186.
3. Michael L. George, *Lean Six Sigma.* (New York: McGraw-Hill, 2002), xii, 127.
4. Jeffrey Liker, *The Toyota Way: 14 Management Principles from The World's Greatest Manufacturer.* (New York: McGraw-Hill, 2004), 135, 252–253.
5. IHI Improvement Model. Online at: http://www.ihi.org/knowledge/Pages/HowtoImprove/ScienceofImprovementTestingChanges.aspx
6. With permission of Cedars-Sinai.

Chapter 5

Roadmap for Process Improvement

Introduction

The 3Ms (measure, manage to the measure, make it easier) are for everyone. Process improvement should be taught to everyone. Keeping it all straight, such as the steps in PDSA (plan, do, study, act), can be difficult, though. People who are part-time process improvement practitioners find it more difficult to remember the steps in process improvement because they don't get the repetition that a person who works full time in performance improvement gets. The third M is to make change easier. The best way I have found to make process improvement easier is to develop a step-by-step plan. The Roadmap to Performance Excellence™ is a step-by-step plan. It is called a roadmap because it is much like a highway map. Its purpose is to make it easier to navigate to your destination—a successful improvement and celebration with the team. We will use the Roadmap for the balance of the book to keep you on the right path for process improvement. I also hope it prevents you from getting lost (see Figure 5.1 for the Roadmap). You also can see the Roadmap on my Web site: www/rpmexec.com.

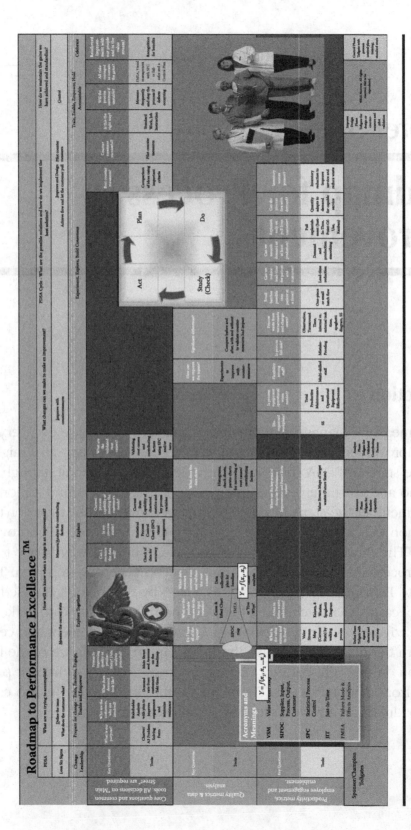

Figure 5.1 Roadmap to Performance Excellence™.

Start the Journey on Main Street

We start in the upper left corner and we will follow the Change Leadership path in this book (Figure 5.2). Notice that I have included the Lean Six Sigma path above the Change Leadership path. I also include the PDSA path with its leading questions. These are high-level paths that guide many teams well enough in process improvement. These are the steps to process improvement we discussed earlier and one can see how the methodologies are similar and follow the same flow. For the purpose of this book, the upper paths provide enough granularity to know how to utilize the 3Ms for process improvement. I teach and use the more detailed areas below for advanced skills. For those who need to know how the lower Roadmap paths work, I will share a brief "how-to." This brief lesson will satisfy most of you who want to know how to use the Roadmap in its entirety.

Below the Change Leadership path is the more detailed part of the Roadmap that guides the team by posing questions to consider in process

PDSA		What are we trying to accomplish?			
Lean Six Sigma		Define the issue What does the customer value?			
Change Leadership		Prepare for change - Train, Envision, Engage, Enable, and Empower			
Core questions and common tools. All decisions on "Main Street" are required.	Key Questions:	What is our purpose?	Who are the customers, who are involved?	What does demand look like?	Primarily improving quality or productivity? Data analysis potential
	Tools:	Charter/ A3 Problem-Solving Form	Stakeholder Analysis with plan to improve engagement and minimize resistance	Demand rate from customers. Takt time.	Main Street and Avenues on the Roadmap

Figure 5.2 Paths and streets.

improvement. The Roadmap has three "streets" including "Main Street," which holds the questions that are core to any process improvement and design effort. Depending on the measure and the issue, there are two other streets. The middle street holds the questions and tools for reliability, quality, and safety issues. The lower path adds value by guiding the team in possible questions that are important to answer to improve productivity and reduce waste and time. (See Figure 5.3 for the Quality and Productivity streets.)

Getting Started on Our Journey

We start with the Change Leadership path above Main Street. Every project should start with the step "Prepare for change." Note, we purposely do not write "Preparing for *the* change." Process improvement leaders don't presume they know the change well enough at the beginning of the plan. Change Leaders know a change is needed, and stay flexible to stakeholders helping create the specific change required. The 3Ms work in every organization that uses it. (See Figure 5.4 for the steps in Change Leadership.)

At the top of the Roadmap, look for the Change Leadership Plan. By the way, the Roadmap is also an integrated training system to learn process improvement, and it is a management tool to support teams. This Roadmap is everything you need to navigate to performance excellence. We will take each element in order. If you have heard that process improvement is not linear and, thus, more complicated than we think it is, keep an open mind. Like the best scientists, work to disprove your theory versus working to reinforce it. I think you will find it quite linear.

Possible Shortcut

If you consider yourself a novice or want to take the full route so you don't "get lost" on the Roadmap, you might want to stay with me here. If you consider yourself fairly well trained in process improvement and Change Leadership with a well trained executive team joining you in leading the change, or if you are acting independently for now and have confidence in

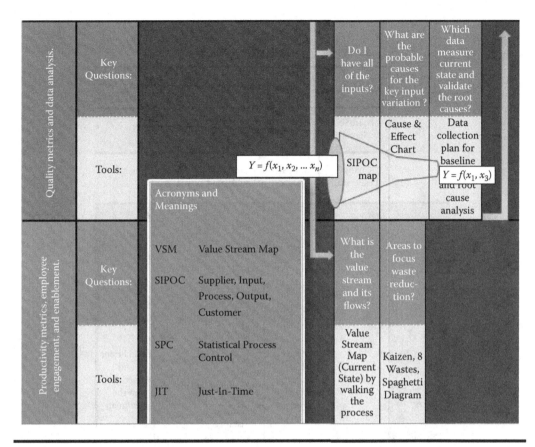

Figure 5.3   Quality and Productivity streets.

Roadmap to Performance Excellence™

PDSA	What are we trying to accomplish?	How will we know when a change is an improvement?	PDSA Cycle - What are the possible solutions and how do we implement the best solution?	How do we maintain the gains we have achieved and standardize?
Lean Six Sigma	Define the issue What does the customer value?	Measure the current state	Measure /Analyze for	Improve and Design Achieve flow and let the customer pull	Control
Change Leadership	Prepare for change - Train, Envision, Engage, Enable, and Empower	Explore Together Explain	Experiment, Explore, Build Consensus	Train, Enable, Empower, Hold Accountable Celebrate

Figure 5.4   Change Leadership steps.

Roadmap to Perform

	PDSA	What are we trying to accomplish?			
	Lean Six Sigma	Define the issue What does the customer value?			
	Change Leadership	Prepare for change - Train, Envision, Engage, Enable, and Empower			
Core questions and common tools. All decisions on "Main Street" are required.	Key Questions:	What is our purpose?	Who are the customers, who are involved?	What does demand look like?	Primarily improving quality or productivity? Data analysis potential
	Tools:	Charter/ A3 Problem-Solving Form	Stakeholder Analysis with plan to improve engagement and minimize resistance	Demand rate from customers. Takt time.	Main Street and Avenues on the Roadmap

Figure 5.5   Prepare for change.

your skills, then consider taking the shortcut to the Engage section. We will share the shortcuts as we progress. We know your time is valuable. (See Figure 5.5, Prepare for change.)

Prepare for Change

- Train the Change Leadership team.
- Envision[1] the desired future state.
- Engage the stakeholders now, not later.
- Enable the stakeholders and the Change Leadership team to contribute using the Roadmap to change, including co-leading and even debating assumptions.
- Empower the workforce; truly empower.

Train

The training in this path refers to training the process improvement team in process improvement. We will see "train" as a principle again later on the Roadmap referring to training in the new changes. This training refers to training the people in the process in the changes and new ways. Just like Change Leadership benefits from a vision of the future, leading change benefits from knowing the vision of Change Leadership's elements. It is much more effective to have your process improvement (PI) team trained in Change Leadership before you set out on the Roadmap.

Envision

Change Leaders and process improvement leaders create and share a vision of the future. Note, we do not say a brighter future, for not all change promises that. In our tremendously ever-changing world, we have had, and will have, changes that set us back. Vision should be a powerful graphic that can move nations to a new state. What comes to mind right now for you? Kennedy's speech in 1961 to Congress and the world that: "I believe that this nation should commit itself to achieving the goal, before this decade is out, of landing a man on the moon, and returning him safely to Earth."[2]

Vision is what many CEOs love to talk about. Maybe your CEO's recent letter posted in the break room reads something like, "Our hospital will be in the top percentile in patient satisfaction by the end of the year." How about your vision as a worker? How does a vision of a better future strike you? What about envisioning your dream of traveling through Europe?

Articulating a Vision

You, the leader, see a current state that does not meet your expectations. Sorry for the lack of bravado here. One might be expecting a grandiose statement to launch this lesson in articulating a vision. My reason to stay somewhat scientific is to share with you that creating a vision can be as much science as art and bravado. In fact, starting your vision statement with unbiased eyes will help you lead others to the change. Most likely, the majority of the targets of the change, those whom your vision will surely affect, may not initially share your view and emotion for the need to change. Taking a more scientific approach now will allow your words later to be created for the ears of the targets and the emotions to build to a crescendo at that time. The best vision shared before the targets are ready to accept your "vision" will be wasted.

Develop your vision statement to speak to your stakeholders where they are now in understanding, not where you are. In fact, a vision statement should be in the present versus future tense as we see in the elements below.

Elements in a Vision Statement

- Positive: Safety versus risk, health instead of sickness, satisfied instead of complaining.
- Present tense: Our clients are ... employees experience ... stakeholders receive ... .
- Succinct: Our customers experience safe and affordable travel.
- Challenging: Our citizens live in the most secure and highest standard of living country in the world.
- Relevant to stakeholders: Our products and service deliver the reliability expected.

What is the probability of achieving the vision? First of all, the vision may be years away from realization. Progress, therefore, is important. In The Progress Principle,[3] the authors state that people in your organization need to see progress to have any chance of staying engaged and committed. There is nothing like collecting some data to estimate the probability of your success. Note that my questions to you come in order. It is much easier to collect data on a change with a well-crafted vision statement. Try your vision statement with stakeholders.

Include stakeholders who will be important to engage and stakeholders who are targets of the change. Try it with those who will most resist, although "spilling the beans" can backfire at this stage in your Change Leadership, so choose these representative voices carefully. Confidentiality is nice to ask for, but keeping secrets is often not an attribute of others, especially if your change is considered highly desired or you expect heavy resistance. Many will desire to share your vision and what may be coming. This premature communication to others makes managing the change process all the more difficult.

Try Out Your Vision Statement

Once you selected your sample to try your vision, what did you find? Did they feed back to you an understanding of your vision? Alternatively, did your vision statement confuse them? If confusing, what words created the confusion? A good trick to check their understanding is to ask them to paraphrase. You might find using their words may improve your vision statement. This is another benefit of trying out your vision statement early in the improvement process.

How did they react to your vision? Did those you expected to welcome the change glow and vow to commit with you in reaching the vision? Were they even more positive than you hoped? Alternatively, did it fail to ignite any emotion or commitment? This will be a hard vision to achieve and makes for a very difficult change process.

Did those you expect to resist, resist less? More? The same technique of asking them to paraphrase often identifies confusion, which fortunately may be the major contributor to resistance. Remember, if others know what I know, they may feel the way I feel, and will do as I do.

If their resistance comes not from misunderstanding of your vision, but from other reasons, the two most likely reasons are fear or political resistance. Change Leaders have techniques to address both types of resistance. Don't worry at this point. Use this early data to know the reasons for resistance and we will address tactics to minimize resistance.

How Does One Communicate the Vision?

Assuming that the small sample that you tried the vision statement on has not completely communicated the change, now we discuss tips on how to share. Rule no. 1: Share the vision in person versus remotely. Unless we are the world's best vision statement writers, most of us don't get it perfect the first time. Our ability to read audiences tells us how our vision is being understood and we adjust accordingly. We get feedback and fine tune our communications improving understanding and, perhaps, actually adjusting our vision with new knowledge from our stakeholders.

Campaigns are vital to communications. The management portion of change now bears fruit. As we confirm our vision's value, we begin to develop others in their ability of sharing the vision. Planning, organizing, staffing, directing, and controlling these "disciples" allow us to exponentially communicate the vision and engage stakeholders. Yes, that is what is meant by sharing a vision and engaging.

Abraham Lincoln's Vision

Abraham Lincoln's principles included having a vision. Lincoln would consistently govern by his vision statement. Vision statements were to be taken seriously and not just a media relations tactic. His principle was to advocate a vision and continually reaffirm it.[4]

Advocate a Vision and Continually Reaffirm It

Let's share a true story of a great Change Leader and how he envisioned a better future, his actual vision statement, and how he communicated the vision and engaged his organization and other stakeholders.

Preserving the Union was Lincoln's vision and mission. Abolishing slavery was also Lincoln's vision, but preserving the Union was most important. Although abolishing slavery was not his entire platform as he ran for the presidency of the United States, it was what differentiated his campaign from his opponent's in 1860. Lincoln's vision was more precisely to first abolish slavery's expansion. He thought that trying to get the nation to change to a slave-free America in one step would meet with too much resistance. His vision is found in The Emancipation Proclamation. This historic speech and document were shared later in his presidency after a series of events and time. See Apendix 3.

A few weeks before signing the Proclamation, he wrote a letter in response to an editorial by Horace Greeley of the *New York Tribune*, who had urged complete abolition. Lincoln writes, "My paramount object in this struggle is to save the Union, and is not either to save or to destroy slavery. If I could save the Union without freeing any slave I would do it, and if I could save it by freeing all the slaves I would do it; and if I could save it by freeing some and leaving others alone, I would also do that. What I do about slavery, and the colored race, I do because I believe it helps to save the Union; and what I forbear, I forbear because I do not believe it would help to save the Union. I shall do less whenever I shall believe what I am doing hurts the cause, and I shall do more whenever I shall believe doing more will help the cause. I shall try to correct errors when shown to be errors; and I shall adopt new views so fast as they shall appear to be true views."

For Whom the Bell Tolls

What are the pitfalls to sharing a vision and people "marching" to the vision? Ernest Hemingway's book, *For Whom the Bell Tolls*, shares a vision of a military leader taking a bridge in battle.[5] It remains unclear if all the effort to destroy the bridge made an impact on the final outcome of the Spanish Civil War. Many lives were lost and many resources were expended. How do we ensure the vision is worthwhile? How do we know this vision is for a positive change? I suggest we all spend time creating our vision because many changes affect many people. And, make sure that the vision is understood.

What will help you achieve your and your company's vision? What differentiates achieving the vision from those other visions that never were achieved? Were the milestones along the way well laid out and achieved? Did you support achieving your vision with some measure if you reached it? Maybe you had goals with dates to achieve? Did you actually measure progress along the way? Did you have early warning that you needed assistance when the measures showed risk of achieving the milestones?

For the first time, perhaps, you now have a scientific approach to leading change by starting with the vision statement. The next step is to engage others.

Engage

Envisioning a better future while not engaging the entire organization—its customers, suppliers, community—is destined to fail.

Engaging stakeholders in the vision is part of the envision step. Kennedy's vision of getting a man on the moon before the decade ended is one of the more famous visions. The nation achieved it, too. Change Leaders also get plenty of help, if they are wise. Do not be so tough on yourself. Kennedy had NASA and thousands of others. Process improvement and creating a vision statement are not meant to be tried alone the first time. Coaches should be provided. This is a part of enable, which is the next step.

Enable

Providing resources to the team to proceed in process improvement is the next step. Have you ever been given an assignment without the tools or resources to carry it out? Once the team has been engaged, it is critical to give them time to work on the improvement process, to explore, to train others in new ways, and to control the process for long-term gain. It is cruel not to enable team members. Why would anyone train people in process improvement, but not give them any time to actually work together to improve a process?

Quality Circles

In 1980, Quality Circles[6] were gaining popularity in America after a very successful start in Japan. The one thing most companies got right was to give an hour or so a week to train and apply the learning. I can't count the number of times I hear from organizations both at the leadership level and at the frontline level that their programs are struggling. They train, they have projects to work on, and they get nowhere. Well, enabling them to work is a good start. I know that the pressures are tremendous and margins are low to nonexistent. I share a story of one of my first managers and what he did in the same, if not more difficult, situation.

Enabling during the Recession of the Early 1980s

I was a first line supervisor in one of the largest plants in the company. I was also the least senior management person at this site of over 600 people. The recession hurt our business deeply and people were being laid off in droves. The plant manager came up one day and said he had an idea. He started with what I expected him to say, "Rick, we are shutting down your department for lack of work." Oh no, I thought. Just out of school and now out of work. However, his vision of the future was different from mine. He envisioned a much leaner and higher quality facility when the economy recovered. His idea was to train me and a few other supervisors in process improvement. They, too, had no one to supervise. Although I was hired to improve processes, I was never trained specifically in process improvement.

The next week started with learning industrial engineering that enabled us to spend our time working on the biggest issues. The plant manager's strategy paid off. When the economy returned, the teamwork and solutions and improvements paid off handsomely. None of this would have occurred without being enabled.

Quality Circle training also taught employees how to work together in teams. It is not natural for many to engage others in process improvement. I have too often seen people with great pride in their training also feel that it is their responsibility to improve processes alone. After all, they are the ones trained by the university. In getting these people trained in team process improvement, we found we also needed to train them how to enable others to find truth and allow debate. We need to enable team members to participate, knowing that assumptions and decisions are part of the process.

Assumptions and Decisions

Debating assumptions is what good teams do, not debating decisions. This is a good time to train your team in:

- Assumptions
- Truth
- Consensus
- Decisions

Assumptions facilitate getting us to the truth. Another term for assumptions could be *hypotheses not tested*. Assuming is what we do when we do not know. Assuming is a short-term condition that must be respected for what it does for us in Change Leadership and what it does not do. Assuming that there is danger looming when walking down a dark street in an unknown area may be the reason you are here today reading this book. So often, we have to assume because we can't be sure of everything and devote the time to validate. In process improvement, we make assumptions and then explore those assumptions to find truth or different assumptions. Truth is what we have validated to occur. For Descartes followers who want to debate the truth that we even really exist, you need to be reading another book. Change Leadership is not for you, yet.

Consensus is what we achieve after making assumptions and before decisions. We work to turn assumptions into truth and then all commit to the findings. Consensus is critical in Change Leadership because it is the glue that holds the change process together and ultimately sustains the change. It may be easier to define consensus by what it is not. It is not everyone in agreement. One may still have different assumptions from the team and question if the assumption or decision is the best, but for the sake of progress, everyone commits to the decision and actions. Think of this situation as team members agreeing to move forward together in the same direction, never in different directions. A good technique in gaining consensus when there are team members in disagreement with an assumption is to promise to continue listening. Use the exploration with the countering assumptions in mind. Setting up formal reviews periodically shows respect for everyone's opinions and assumptions.

A decision is the choice of direction when multiple choices exist. Direction is based on assumptions proved either to be truth or still to be determined with consensus reached. Decisions are progress. The Progress Principle described earlier supports that change is facilitated by teams achieving progress frequently. The breakthroughs are nice to have, but small progress keeps the change progress alive.

Empower

Empowerment entrusts decision making with others and includes sharing of responsibilities with those being empowered. Peter Garber, in his book, *Managing by Remote Control*,[7] shares that empowerment enables everyone to make greater contributions to the organization and to reach his or her highest potential. Empowerment also includes the one who empowers others setting boundaries. These boundaries make it safer for both parties and clarifies the empowerment.

Those boundaries can expand as you and the team mature. If you are not a good communicator and confuse your team, you may very well be concerned about some of the team's decisions as they near what you perceive to be the limits of their skills and your uncommunicated boundary. It takes skill and trust to set boundaries, but set them and communicate them clearly. Soon, relaxing boundaries will be a sign of your maturity and your team's success. Everyone wins, but start with boundaries.

We have completed the first step in the Change Leadership path. Next, we will drop down to "Main Street" for the mandatory questions to answer in process design or process improvement.

Key Points

- The Roadmap makes process improvement easier by giving us a step-by-step route.
- The paths in the upper area of the Roadmap may be all that are needed to guide the team. More details are in the lower section of the map.
- Prepare for change is the first step on our route to process improvement.
- This step includes train, envision, engage, enable, and empower.

Endnotes

1. Adapted from sources including Dream Achievers Academy, www.dream-achieversacademy.com/five-elements/
2. history.nasa.gov/sp–350/ch–2–1.html
3. Teresa M. Amabile and Steven J. Kramer, *The Progress Principle: Using Small Wins to Ignite Joy, Engagement, and Creativity at Work*. (Cambridge, MA: Harvard Business Press Books, August 2011).
4. Donald T. Phillips, *Lincoln on Leadership: Executive Strategies for Tough Times*. Copyright (c) 1992 by Donald T. Phillips. By permission of Grand Central Publishing. All rights reserved. (New York: Hachette Book Group. 2009).
5. Ernest Hemingway, *For Whom the Bell Tolls*, Scribner, 1950.
6. Don Dewar, *The Quality Circle Handbook*. (Chico, CA: Quality Circle Institute, 1980).
7. Peter Garber, *Managing by Remote Control: How to More Effectively Manage People and Resources When You Can't Always Be There*. (Boca Raton, FL: CRC Press LLC, 1999).

Chapter 6

Chartering the Process Improvement Work

The Charter

The first question is: What is our purpose? In PDSA (plan, do, study, act), the question is the same: What are we trying to accomplish? The tool that we will now learn answers the question best and avoids the danger of missing any key element. Chartering work is actually the most important skill in process improvement and design. Chartering is the act of defining the work to be done. We will walk you through the chartering process using a charter template provided to you in Appendix 3 at the back of the book. Again, I want to make process improvement as easy for you as possible and provide several templates that I have used in launching Performance Excellence initiatives for global companies.

Feel free to think of an issue now that you would like to lead a change to improve. This will make chartering easier to understand. I also include an exercise after the instruction with a completed charter.

There have been many authorities who have asserted that the basis of science lies in counting or measuring, i.e., in the use of mathematics. Neither counting nor measuring can however be the most fundamental processes in our study of the material universe—before you can do either to any purpose, you must first select what you propose to count or measure, which presupposes a classification.

Roy Albert Crowson[1]
British biologist (1914–1999)

What to measure is often very difficult to determine. I spent a winter in the middle of Wisconsin because what I thought was being measured is not what my client thought was being measured. This also taught me a lesson on managing to the measure and specifically managing to the measure in real time. If I had shared what I was measuring more frequently with the sponsor, I would have been able to move on to a much more interesting assignment, such as in Puerto Rico and turning a failing site around with a beachfront cottage at my disposal. No, because I did not have consensus on what to measure, I had to stick around in snow and cold at a plant in Wisconsin. Process improvement teams, I hope you learn from my mistakes. As I learned in Wisconsin, what to measure is a decision of multiple stakeholders who aren't necessarily in agreement. Resistance to change was more than our company could handle due to confusion as to what should be measured. Hindsight being 20–20, I should not have gone to Wisconsin until I had the measurement in writing and signed off by the sponsors. It is clear our team did not have the measurement right for who turned out to be the key stakeholder.

Rest assured, if you followed the steps in this book, this story that follows would have had a happier ending. Here is a story of what can happen when people don't follow the process improvement steps—and in order.

No Charter? Big Problem

A long time ago, I received a call from our headquarters asking if I could do an assessment in the surgical operating rooms at a major medical center for my fellow project executives. Right away, warning bells should have gone off in my head. Three leaders? Usually, we have one person in charge.

Two project executives called my colleague and me. The purpose of the call was to share the purpose of our work at the client. The third project executive was not available at our first meetings and not until the meeting right before our visit. As it turns out, I didn't know everything that happened before my involvement. The measurements shared by our colleagues were common to assessments and this was a relatively simple project. We were to observe procedures and record the reasons and times when surgical staff had to leave the operating room (OR), paying special attention to events when the case was delayed. We agreed that the deliverables would be:

■ The count of occurrences when the staff had to leave the OR once the procedure was started
■ The time away
■ The reason for needing to leave
■ The time the case was delayed

The scope was to include only the time during the actual case. The time *between* cases was not in the scope. We can do this type of assessment plus observe other activities, which the project execs thought would be useful, but we were to stick to the intraoperative time only. This concerned me because, typically, the clients need to understand what happens between cases that might give a clue as to why someone would have to leave the room. There are failures that can occur between cases that will increase the occurrences of staff needing to leave the OR. I asked our team to confirm that this study was to include only the time between the patient arriving in the OR and the patient leaving the OR. We will come back to this in following paragraphs.

If the turnaround and setup of the OR for the next case is not done well, retrieving forgotten supplies can create a revolving door to the OR during a case. Besides wasting time and delaying the case, possibly, there is evidence that improper entries and exits may contribute to surgical site infections. Therefore, I suggested we stay between cases to observe any variation and deficiency in the turnaround. My colleagues agreed, but stated the client wanted us to only observe intraoperatively.

We thought we had a good definition of the issue and the measurements and scope. We knew there was some risk because we never spoke directly with the client. We had nothing from the client confirming the measurements, and we had multiple project execs on this assessment. My strategy is always to meet with the sponsors upon arrival, especially when we have no signed charter with metrics.

The two sponsors were the director of OR and a surgeon. These sponsors were not available by phone prior to the visit, but we were told, and did receive, an email from the director that he would arrange for us to be greeted by his scheduling manager.

We also did not get a stakeholder analysis (SHA). (I will teach you this important tool after chartering. But, you already know that because it is the next step on the Roadmap). So, I drafted an SHA based on what I heard. Our strategy was to introduce ourselves after arriving and before starting. We find it is best to confirm the purpose of the study and the measurements we would deliver at the end of the study at this point.

We arrived at the site and were graciously met by the director's assistant, who was also the scheduling manager. I offered to meet with the sponsors, but the assistant said they were tied up. She would leave them a note. The scheduling manager confirmed we were to watch the intraoperative processes and off we went to get in scrubs and observe. She had us scheduled so that there was little chance to observe turnarounds. I volunteered to step out when the sponsors had a minute to chat about the week ahead and make sure we met their expectations.

Despite asking for a meeting as soon as we arrived, before the trip, and daily offerings to meet with the sponsors when I arrived, I could not get an audience with the sponsors until four days later. The sponsor I did get a minute or two with was the surgeon. I caught his case thanks to the director's assistant knowing I wanted to ensure we were on the right track.

Sharing Findings before Departing

I shared with the surgeon our preliminary findings and he confirmed that is what they wanted. He also asked me to validate the reasons reported for delayed case starts. This was a new request because this supported us also observing turnarounds of ORs. As in so many failures, there are data coming at people in the process showing something isn't quite right. After receiving the surgeon's request, I immediately left the OR to find the other sponsors to offer to do this in addition to the original metrics. This is something we do often, and there is usually data to help me help the client, so I asked the director via email to share the data on delays. I got no response after two requests. I was a bit concerned now that we may be viewed as ignoring this new request from the sponsoring surgeon. So, I let my colleagues know I could do this, but the director had not responded indicating that he received my request for data.

On Friday morning, five days later, I met with the scheduling manager and another surgical safety manager to discuss the week. I still had not had the chance to meet with the other sponsor, so I took this opportunity to confirm with his "right-hand person" what we had done and when our report would come back. I showed them the preliminary report with the measures that we had. They remarked that this was exactly what they wanted and seemed very pleased. The director's assistant seemed especially delighted in the findings because they confirmed what she thought was happening. We know there is usually someone in the client's organization who has an understanding of many of the issues and answers, but the person struggles to find a way of getting others to listen and act.

Clear Definition of the Issue and What Was to Be Measured Are Key

This story has several benefits to learning process improvement. First, the obvious one is that clear definition of the issue and measurements should be confirmed. Secondly, process improvement leaders who excel are ones who seek out those who already have a good understanding and may just not have been able to share. In a top-down culture for decision making, these people are surrounding the Change Leader if she can draw them out. That is, if they haven't already left the organization due to frustration. The scheduling manager was one of those stars. Sadly, she remarked twice during the week when I showed up that she thought I was there to fire her. My colleague and I shared notes Thursday night on how we were going to compile the observations. My colleague had previously shared a well laid out form with the measurements clearly detailed. We agreed to enter our observations into this report.

The week ended with observing the last case on Friday. I returned to the scheduling manager's office to bid adieu, and was told that she had left for the day. I headed off to the airport feeling good about what my colleague and I had observed and recorded.

My colleague and I received a call from the project executive that the client wanted a preliminary report. Upon review and some editing of the report, the project exec said she had what she needed. After she met with the client to share the preliminary report, the client wanted some tweaks made before the final report came out. We thought this was promising confirmation of our work meeting their needs. We made the tweaks, which included adding some turnaround information (as we expected), and prepared to share the final report. The final report had a title slide, the purpose and objectives, and, on the third slide, the answer to all measures. The balance of the report contained facts and analysis supporting the findings and offering suggestions.

The Final Report and Surprise

The final report was done with the project executives at the client site and my colleague and I teleconferenced in. The plan was for us to succinctly cover the first three slides, share some of the turnaround information requested after the preliminary call, and then open it up to questions. I expected the director and perhaps the surgeon to be leading the call. Surprisingly, a director we had not known to be a sponsor described herself as the client and asked us to begin.

A process improvement leader's bad day was starting to unfold. She did not let us finish the first slide before she said we were focused on the wrong issue. She said some of our findings were taken out of context, despite the fact we had not even covered yet on this call.

I share this story because it has so many lessons in it, and I want you to avoid this at all cost. Peter Block, in his book, *Flawless Consulting*,[2] states there are four steps to achieving a strong consulting agreement. We never got to the third step, which is what the client needs to do. All the client had to do was spend two minutes looking at the measurements we were collecting. Hindsight is 20/20. Being clear about roles and responsibilities was another responsibility.

A process improvement leader ensures in the chartering process, and preparing people for change, that we know who the sponsor is. One last lesson is that we touched a nerve with the client who fielded the final report. Our report mentioned an observation that the nurses were complaining about how much time they were spending reading bar codes to manage inventories and to charge customers. For implants, they had to enter the same information in up to four different places. We found out that she was the sponsor of the system that required the nurses to enter this data. Should we have known this and adjusted our report? I guess if we knew both this information and that she, alone, was the deciding client sponsor, then maybe. Ah, the joys of leading change.

In summary, get confirmation that your measures are customer-centric. It's that simple. Here is a better way to ensure success. We want to make this so easy for you that we include a charter (Figure 6.1). Also, all of the templates in my book may be downloaded at www.rpmexec.com.

Charter Title:		Business Case:				Role	Responsibility
1. Issue Statement Elements a. Customer Name:						Executive Sponsor:	Senior Level manager who selects work. Has authority to solve cross-functional issues.
b. Characteristic to Improve:						*Signature*	
c. Process Name(s):						Champion:	Leader who owns the process and manages staff. Prime responsibility with Project Leader for success.
2. Product/Unit: *Name of what is produced in the process*						*Signature*	
						Clinical Leader	Decision-maker for clinical issues
						Signature	
3. Defect: *How we sense a failure in the product or service*						Process Owner(s):	Responsible for the design, continuous improvement and sustaining the process.
4. Metric(s) to Improve		Current Baseline	Goal (S.M.A.R.T.)	Date to Achieve		*Signature(s)*	
						Project Leader:	Leads the team and execution of the methodology. Shares prime responsibility with Champion for success.
						Signature	
5. Financial Impact Metrics:		Type of Impact	Traceable	Non-Traceable		Mentor/Coach	Coaches and mentors sponsor, champion and project leader in their roles
		$ Annualized Amount				*Signature*	
6. Scope: Process Begins and Ends when....		7. Scope: What must be included or excluded is...				Team Members	Key contributor to work. Participates with Project Leader in methodology and responsible for success.
						Core Member	
						Core Member	
						Core Member	
						Core Member	
						Core Member	
						Core Member	
High Level Project Plan: Rick Morrow						Core Member	
Phase	Planned Start Date	Planned End Date	Actual Start Date	Actual End Date			
Define/Charter signed							
Measure/Baseline obtained							
Analyze/Root Cause validated						Subject Matter Expert	
Improve/Improvement piloted						Subject Matter Expert	
Control/Sustainability plan						Subject Matter Expert	
						Author name:	

Figure 6.1   The Charter template.

The Issue Statement

This work is clearly defined by stating the issue, the customer, the process to be changed, the product or service the process delivers, and what a defect is in the product. If the work is to design something new, the defect is the gap in what the design is to fill. Once the defect is known, determining metrics is much easier.

The Measures or Metrics

Always start with a customer-centric metric and ensure the metric is relevant to the defect. For instance, if the issue is to reduce the missed shipments to a customer, then a metric should measure the occurrence of such. As we detailed in the story of the OR delays, the charter would have prevented any confusion.

Outcome and Process Measures

The measures or metrics might include both an outcome metric, such as the count of missed shipments and a metric of the inputs. One input we usually include in these studies is the service level, or percentage of time an item is available. There is a correlation between stock outs and having missed shipments. Remember that in leading change to different outcomes, we benefit from measuring inputs. In achieving higher reliability, measuring and managing the inputs are most important before their variation results in an unfavorable outcome.

Goals

The amount of change desired is detailed by filling in the goal statement. It may help in setting the goal if we know from where we are starting. A baseline performance level in each metric "grounds" us in reality. In health-care, we often don't have a measurement system, or one that we trust, so often baselines are determined later in the work. The goal is the amount of change we are hoping to achieve. The goal should be SMART:

- **S**pecific to the issue, product, and defect
- **M**easurable
- **A**ttainable: A Change Leader is cruel when expecting a team to defy the laws of nature
- **R**elevant to the customer
- **T**ime bound: We need a time for when the goal should be reached

Progressive Goals and Successive Successful Approximations

Progressive goals are often used and should be detailed in chartering. A process improvement leader knows setting SMART progressive goals to get to the ultimate goal is wise. Change is hard enough for many, and achieving successive successful approximations to the goal[3] is rewarding and provides renewal. Successive approximations are a conditioning of people to progress in behaviors to achieve the desired final outcome. Progress toward the goal is rewarded with additional progress. However, it also is important to stop rewarding earlier progressions toward the goal.

Measures and Goals to Build a Safer Culture

In process improvement, we might reward a staff member bringing up a concern about safety to his supervisor with our ultimate goal for the staff member to feel safe enough to address the situation himself. When a person is confident in speaking to a supervisor, we coach the person to act on his own with the same quality of judgment. Once the staff member begins to act on his own and not rely on the supervisor to act, we cease rewarding him to come to his supervisor instead of acting on his own. It is important in Change Leadership to not reinforce moving in the wrong direction. This can set change back and gives the wrong impression that the Change Leader may be changing the vision, if, in fact, the Change Leader is not. Again, honesty is the best policy always. If, with new information, the Change Leader decides to change the goal, then she should share it quickly with reasons. The leader should show how it might affect the team and Stakeholders.

The Progress Principle is a perfect term for leading change in complex long duration work. The term coined by Teresa Amabile and Steven Kramer in a *Harvard Business Review* article[4] describes a finding that: "Of all the things that can boost inner work life, the most important is making progress in meaningful work." A Change Leader's motto, maybe?

Hold Off on Financial Metrics Until …

Important to note is that we don't mention financial metrics before we mention outcome and input metrics or process metrics. Often, the process improvement team and sponsor are interested in financial impact. However, financial impact is *always* a function of changing a nonfinancial metric. Unless you actually make money, which only governments do, making money is a bit of a misnomer. We "make money" by changing revenue and/or costs. Thus, we list metrics that change revenue and cost and then list financial metrics calculated from changing process or input metrics.

Reducing inventory is an example of how a process measure improved will result in an improved financial measure. We may want to reduce the amount of money we have in inventory. There is nothing inherently wrong with that because all inventories are waste. We help organizations reduce inventory just about every week. Inventory is a result of a process that is not flexible enough to provide a supply just when the customer needs it. Some industries have developed their suppliers, or suppliers have assisted their customers in reducing and eliminating inventories. Consigned inventory, which is actually inventory owned by the supplier until used by the organization is still waste and should be reduced, too. It is naïve to think suppliers don't try to capture the money they have tied up in consigned inventory on your site. Lean practices drive both supplier and customer to reduce inventory. Reducing the amount of money we have in inventory frees up money to spend on providing valued services. To reduce inventory dollars, euros, pounds, or any country's currency, we have to reduce a nonfinancial metric. This could be reducing the quantity, the price, or both. We work to change one of these variables, and then "dollarize" the impact. If the item costs $1 and we reduce 1,000 items, then we reduced inventory $1,000. We didn't directly reduce $1,000. We had to change one or more of the other variables.

Scope the Work

After detailing the metrics, we need to scope the work. Will this be a change that spans the entire value stream or just one unit in one building? We split the question of scope into two areas:

- Defining the start and stop of the process to be changed
- Defining what is in scope and out of scope helps bind the work and is consistent with the Progress Principle

A process improvement scoping strategy is often to achieve the change in one area, say a pilot or test area, and then replicate the work to achieve the change across the entire organization.

Charter "Signatories"

The next feature in chartering is listing the sponsors, champion, process owners, leader, coach, team members, subject matter experts (SMEs), and others, such as a process expert or technical leader. Oh, how this tool would have saved the day in so many projects.

Sponsor

The sponsor's role in change is as the ultimate decision maker. His or her name goes at the top due to the importance of this role. We list other stakeholders on the charter including the process owner and, perhaps, the clinical leader. All of these roles could be filled by one person or others. The charter is actually the first tool followed by the Stakeholder Analysis. We lead with the Stakeholder Analysis only when we are not clear who the sponsor is. Once the sponsor is found and the work clearly defined using the information detailed in the charter, we are now ready to better do the Stakeholder Analysis. Until we know the details including the process, the product, the defect, and the scope, we cannot be confident we have the correct stakeholders.

Chartering Is Iterative

The chartering process is iterative.[5] We may think our first time through the charter that we have a clear definition of the issue and consensus. We then speak with the customer about the metric and the customer does not agree that metric describes the change needed. Once we get the metric to be customer-centric and has his/her approval, we go back to the defect and other issue elements and correct them. Don't be frustrated, especially if you are drafting a charter without the customer with you, and you don't get it right the first time. The document drives the dialogue between team, customer, and sponsor to ensure in the end we have a very clear understanding of the change and amount of change needed and, most importantly, consensus. (See the completed charter in Figure 6.2.)

A tip I have for you is to have the charter template "in your back pocket" at all times—maybe on your smartphone as an app, in your purse, or memorize the essential elements. I don't know how many times someone has started rattling off a great idea that I want to capture the issue clearly. Writing down what someone is describing, especially when that someone is the CEO, shows respect for his/her idea and can speed the process improvement. And, being clear right from the start may get you to that warm beach in the winter.

Sign the Charter

The signatories should literally sign off showing their personal commitment. It may give them pause to read the charter carefully and ensure the team

Charter Title:	Increase Patient Capability to Follow Discharge Instructions			Role	Responsibility
1. Issue Statement Elements a. Customer Name:	Patients	Business Case: Patient surveys show a lower level of satisfaction than our competitors. Our reimbursement will be affected if we don't meet threshold levels.		Executive Sponsor:	Senior level manager who selects work. Has authority to solve cross-functional issues.
b. Characteristic to Improve:	Information shared by nurse to patient or advocate.			Signature	**Wendy Sitty**
c. Process Name(s):	Discharge			Champion:	Leader who owns the process and manages staff. Prime responsibility with Project Leader for success.
2. Product/Unit: *Name of what is produced in the process*	Information and instructions on safe care and possible changes to be aware of.			Signature	**Freddie Silver**
				Clinical Leader	Decision-maker for clinical issues
				Signature	**Dr. Welby**
3. Defect: *How we sense a failure in the product or service*	Patient or advocate confused about instructions.			Process Owner(s):	Responsible for the design, continuous improvement and sustaining the process.
4. Metric(s) to Improve	Current Baseline	Goal (S.M.A.R.T.)	Date to Achieve	Signature(s)	**Elway Pode**
Initial readback accuracy by patient of instructions given by nurse	22%	80%	90 days from project start	Project Leader:	Leads the team and execution of the methodology. Shares prime responsibility with champion for success.
				Signature	**Adam**
5. Financial Impact Metrics:	Type of Impact	Traceable	Non-Traceable	Mentor/Coach	Coaches and mentors sponsor, champion and project leader in their roles.
Readmissions due to instruction confusion.	$ Annualized Amount	$36,000 per Readmission		Signature	**Janelle**
6. Scope: Process Begins and Ends when....	7. Scope: What must be included or excluded is...			Team Members	Key contributor to work. Participates with Project Leader in methodology and responsible for success.
				Core Member	Jan
				Core Member	Layla
				Core Member	Mark
				Core Member	Mike
				Core Member	Brenda
				Core Member	
High Level Project Plan: Rick Morrow				Core Member	
Phase	Planned Start Date	Planned End Date	Actual Start Date	Actual End Date	
Define/Charter signed					
Measure/Baseline obtained					
Analyze/Root Cause validated				Subject Matter Expert	Jeff
Improve/Improvement piloted				Subject Matter Expert	Pat
Control/Sustainability plan				Subject Matter Expert	Donna
				Author name:	

Figure 6.2 A completed charter.

has the issue, metrics, goals, and other fields correct. A signed charter also enables the team by giving proof of the importance of the effort. The charter template is in Appendix 3 and is ready to use in your process improvement. An electronic version is also available at www.rpmexec.com.

Key Points

- Chartering is the most important tool because it clearly defines the improvement needed.
- Chartering is often iterative. As you input fields, another field later in the charter may help you discover more clarity is needed in an earlier response.

- The signatories should literally sign off showing their personal commitment.
- A signed charter enables the team and tells all that this process improvement is important.

Practicing Skills: Chartering

Your organization is a good one, but your customers report defective products after only a short time in use. Warranty claims are "through the roof." A recent analysis by your claims team finds that 22% of the products fail early. The impact financially of the average failure is estimated to be about $350 in product, shipping, analysis, and goodwill. Wendy, the chief operating officer, is supportive of a team to improve the product quality. Freddie Silver, the manufacturing manager, has volunteered to join Wendy in supporting this team. He is a real champion of change. The chief engineer, Marcus, will be happy to answer any questions on the product's functions and design. Dr. Welby can act as the technical leader. Elway Ode is the day shift manager when most of the production occurs. Confidentially, he just doesn't seem to want to change. We are glad that Freddie will support the team and help remove barriers that Elway may put up. Adam, our black belt trained in Lean, Six Sigma, and Change Leadership, has agreed to lead the change on this one and he will be supported by Janelle, our master black belt. The team includes the key stakeholders, such as our PR representative. We also will have a few subject matter experts who know all about the distribution channel and regulatory requirements.

Take the role of Adam and draft a charter based on the information above. Show your Sponsor for approval by all listed as signatories on the charter. A charter example is on my Web site: www.rpmexec.com. Good luck.

Endnotes

1. www.todayinsci.com. Classification and Biology (1970), 2.Science quotes on: | Classification (46) | Mathematics (262).
2. Peter Block, *Flawless Consulting. A Guide to Getting Your Expertise Used*. (New York: Pfeiffer, 1981).

3. BF Skinner, et al, Differential reinforcement (shaping) response is gradually changed across successive trials towards a desired target behavior by rewarding exact segments of behavior. Online at: http://en.wikipedia.org/wiki/Shaping_(psychology)
4. Teresa M. Amabile and Steven J. Kramer, "The Power of Small Wins," *Harvard Business Review* (May 2011).
5. Peter Pande, Robert P. Neuman, and Roland R. Cavanagh, *The Six Sigma Way: How GE, Motorola, and Other Top Companies Are Honing Their Performance.* (New York: McGraw-Hill, 2000), 197–204.

Chapter 7

Stakeholder Analysis

Purpose of Stakeholder Analysis

I find it easier to learn process improvement in a very linear and methodical way. This allows us to practice each skill based on the prior skill and outcome and you can see the step-by-step approach. We are teaching you the fundamentals just like a good coach teaches piano or a sport. In learning piano, we first learned where to place our fingers on the keyboard and then practiced scales. In basketball, we learned how to dribble much earlier than how to hit a three pointer. In process improvement and Change Leadership, one of the most critical fundamentals is stakeholder analysis (SHA). The purpose of doing the SHA is to reduce resistance to future changes. The SHA accomplishes this by first identifying stakeholders, who might not buy into the change, and a strategy to reduce the resistance.

Are you the advocate of this change coming up and want to lead the change to a brighter future, with minimal resistance, and faith that the change will sustain? Do you fear that change is coming to you? Have you just witnessed yet another upset customer storming out of your store knowing you just helped your competitor? Are you picking up this book totally frustrated at having great solutions that no one seems to want to hear?

Case Study in Stakeholder Analysis

Stakeholders include the targets of the change. They are the ones for whom the change is intended. Here is a story of nurses in a dramatic change in the perioperative services of the largest private hospital in the United Kingdom, The Wellington. The Wellington's CEO, Keith Hague, had a vision of a higher quality healthcare organization with more satisfied patients. He launched The Wellington on a transformational journey in 2010. A transformation includes a focus on leadership skills, cultural change, and process improvement skills for all. In less than eight months, they achieved significant improvements in nearly every major service line within the hospital by engaging his executive team and through every organizational level. The patient-facing staff, including nurses, therapists, admissions staff, porters who transport patients, pharmacy staff, dietitians, housekeepers, and staff in the surgical instrument sterilization department, have been the most engaged. Also included in the process improvement is the "front of house" staff that is often the first point of contact as patients and family enter the hospital.

Key to this improvement was naming a dedicated Champion, Chris James. Catherine Hanrahan, CFO, chose Chris based on his high potential. Giving up one of her best for the role of process improvement was a big decision by Catherine, but she sees the value to the organization, its patients, and Chris. Chris is now participating on Hague's executive team based on his accomplishments. In addition, the CFO of Healthcare Corporation of America (HCA) UK, Jim Petkas, now has Chris expanding his role to spread the engagement throughout all six HCA hospitals at their request.

One way to measure a transformation that is intended to change the culture is to measure the number of people engaged in the work. From a percentage of total staff, 100% of major departments and 30% of all Wellington staff have been engaged. Even better, many of the staff have participated in more than one major project, or week-long projects. At Princess Grace Hospital in London, a part of the HCA Group, Sheila Enright, CNO, and Stephen Maxwell, CFO, Measure, Manage to the measure, and Make it work with Healthcare Performance Partners' (HPP) Steve Taninecz as their coach. At least one major project has been accomplished monthly that has been chosen based on priorities to improve outcomes. To get this much done in just the first five months, Steve and Princess Grace's first Champion, measure and manage the inputs including:

■ People development: 107 individuals have received process improvement training.
■ Engaging the people who do the work and managers; 63 have participated in the projects applying their new skills.

■ Taking a value stream approach reaching out to multiple areas that all must work together to improve patient care and operations. Nursing, surgical services, and outpatient services have been most active and, thus, their patients and physicians are reaping the most benefit.

The Wellington Hospital and Princess Grace Hospital also have reached out to their other sister hospitals and engaged staff for projects. The momentum in process improvement is building for this HCA Health System in an amazingly tough environment—private hospitals in a free healthcare environment.

Stakeholders' intellect is a terrible thing to waste in leading change. Chris tells the story of brainstorming for solutions to speed the patient journey in surgery. The Wellington has theatres (ORs) on several different floors and patient rooms on still other floors. The time to access an elevator and transport the patient to theatres and back can take quite a long time. The porters are people who transport the patients with a nurse joining the patient and porter for safety. Three people including the patient often wait for the lift and then wait as the lift often stops at each floor. The patients are often embarrassed as the lift stops, door opens, and people enter. Brainstorming occurred on countermeasures to improve this situation. The first idea was to speed the lift. That wasn't very achievable. But, it created an idea to provide lift keys to block off stopping. Speed achieved.

In their book, *Reengineering Health Care,*[1] Jim Champy and Harry Greenspun claim that any dramatic reform in healthcare must be by clinicians. Not engaging stakeholders who are targets is destined for failure, I guess. The key point is engaging the people in the process is much more respectful of the very "targets" of the change and we find results in speedier change. We have found including others outside of the process is beneficial, too. The saying: a "fresh set of eyes," and the tool of asking "why five times" unlocks creativity and may result in solutions never thought possible before. Therefore, engaging those in the process is necessary. Engaging key stakeholders is necessary. Engaging interested parties is recommended.

Mission and Values of the Organization

Sharing the vision and engaging the troops are aided by stating the mission of the organization at this point in their change. Values should be developed with Change Leadership principles clearly stating the leader-ship's desire for positive change engaging all stakeholders. Competing and dysfunctional value statements make no sense in organizations that desire continuous improvement. A good test to ensure consistency of message, constancy of purpose, as Dr. W. Edwards Deming (American statistician, author, and consultant) stated, is to ask the organization how the values support positive change. Be prepared to not get the understanding right the first time. Above all, do not avoid asking the question. Perception is reality. As we discuss the critical importance of measurement in leading change, let us share a key point now. Measure the change in perception as you start your change.

Stakeholders

Before we share what engagement in process improvement is and why it is important, let's understand the term stakeholder. A stakeholder is any one or more of the following:

Customer
Supplier
Process owner
Decision maker in the change
Interested party
Target of the change

I include a SHA template in Appendix 5 and an electronic version at www.rpmexec.com (see Figure 7.1).

I arranged the form to guide us in the correct sequence for stakeholder analysis. The SHA will improve the flow of the change by reducing the resis-tance. In stakeholder analysis, the form actually teaches us the fundamentals of SHA as we progress left to right.

Overview of the SHA

We start with the organization's name and enter it on the far left. The orga-nization's name is a high-level description of a group of stakeholders. Next, we scroll down farther to a person's name, or a subgroup of the organization.

Stakeholder Analysis									Contributor names:			
Project				Stakeholder role								
Date												
Organization/ Location/Area	Name (or group name)	Role or Title	Customer of the process	Process owner	Decision maker/ Approver	Target of the change	Interested party	Supplier to the process	Current level of buy-in to change. Rate 0 - 10 with 0 being no buy-in - heavy resistance	Needed level of buy-in to change. Rate 0 - 10 with 0 no buy-in needed	Gap	Strategy to close the gap
Scheduling department	Bobbie	Scheduler				x			6	10	(4)	
Scheduling department	Petra	Manager, Scheduling		x	x				5	5	-	
Scheduling department	Michael	Scheduler				x			9	10	(1)	
Scheduling department	Gemma	Scheduler				x			4	8	(4)	
Operations	Carrie	Director of Operations			x				10	10	-	
Clinic	Adam	VP, Clinic	x	x	x	x			7	10	(3)	
Clinic	Sophie	Nurse Manager	x						8	9	(1)	
Patient			x						9	9	-	
Physician offices		Physicians					x		4	10	(6)	

Figure 7.1   Stakeholder analysis template.

This level could be the name of a person. The SHA is done confidentially with your team, and respect is tantamount. We list the role(s) the stakeholder has. A stakeholder may have multiple roles. An example is a person who owns the process and is the decision-maker.

We then rate the stakeholder's expected level of buy-in to future changes on a scale from 0 to 10 with 0 being no buy-in; in other words, the stakeholder is expected to put up heavy resistance. The needed level of buy-in for a decision maker, or a target of the change, can be helpful in differentiating stakeholders who are important to buy-in to changes from those where their buy-in is not as important. An example is if an interested party has low buy-in. The team feels the needed level of buy-in is rather insignificant relative to the decision maker in this change.

We don't share the SHA outside of the team, usually due to its confidentiality and need to be truthful with how much buy-in stakeholders may have.

Measuring the Gap: The Level of Resistance

Measuring the gap between the current level of buy-in and needed level is a relative measure of the stakeholders who may resist the most. These stakeholders need to be led in the change, and the strategy is now listed to reduce their resistance. We will give strategies for each stakeholder. For now, let's see a stakeholder analysis created. We invite you to do one for an upcoming change you are considering. Better yet, use the SHA with your team. We think you will find the SHA one of the most important and valuable tools in process improvement.

Highlight the one stakeholder whom you expect to get the largest resistance from with the upcoming changes. Now, think about the differential between what you are thinking needs to be changed and how this person might feel. It is a good idea at this time to consider engaging the person and finding out exactly how he/she feels about the issue. Perhaps, he/she feels the same way and now that you both know what each other knows, you find you feel the same way, and you will both do something about it to improve. Yes, sometimes the differential is minimal, if not zero. The SHA pays off with strategies to reduce the resistance and gets change flowing. One strategy is to interview the potential resistors to seek out how they feel and ensure they understand the chartered work.

Three SHA Scenarios to Know Your Strategy Upfront

More times than not you will find change is not easy for some stakeholders. Don't make this condition difficult for you. Understand upfront in your process improvement effort that your discussion with stakeholders will take one of three courses:

- You and the stakeholders might already share an understanding of the issue and find they want change. Therefore, there is little to no resistance to change in this situation.
- The stakeholder is not yet convinced there is an issue, or as much of an issue as you believe. Resistance or apathy early and throughout the process improvement effort affects your ability to enact change.
- All have agreement about the issue, but they disagree on the solution or method of finding a solution. Resistance to the change or the process of determining the change results.

My intention is to give you methods to process improvement and leading change for all three scenarios. I am confident you will be successful in process improvement and leading change if you apply what I share in the order I share it. The most important measure of any teacher is if the student learned. Please measure me on this ability as you read and practice the skills.

Designing the "Circuit" to Achieve Flow and Manage Resistance

By now, you should be gaining competence and confidence in distilling your vision, identifying stakeholders, and analyzing their potential buy-in to change, identifying where the resistance may come from, and starting your strategies to reduce the resistance to create better flow of changes coming. In other words, you should be designing a "circuit" to manage the resistance for the flow of change you desire. You don't have to eliminate all resistance, but you have to manage it to a level that allows change to flow at the rate you wish.

If you want more practice with a measure of how well you do SHA, try the following scenario:

Pick a change that someone who works with you will certainly resist. Both of you think out loud as you list stakeholders, their roles, and as you rate their buy-in. Reaching agreement is a good measure of your ability to do SHA well. If you tend to disagree on who the stakeholders are, work to include more rather than less. It is better to list those who might have a stake than to miss stakeholders. You are doing well if you get consensus on who are the decision makers, customers, and process owners; missing those who might be interested is a minor issue. In judging current level of buy-in and needed level, the key measure is if the same stakeholders are identified as the ones with the largest gaps. These are the ones in which strategies are needed to reduce resistance. The absolute numbers are not important in the buy-in columns because we all judge differently. Any areas that team members differ considerably in judging should use the lesson: "If we both know what each other knows, then …"

Difficult to Be Perfect

Cockpit Resource Management (CRM) was developed to change the culture among the flight crew. The airline industry accelerated the move to CRM after the improvement rate in fatal crashes stalled. CRM essentially engages everyone in the cockpit and includes hard and fast rules for escalating and engaging under emergency situations. Some captains tended to think they were perfect or at least more perfect than everyone else in the cockpit. These captains thought the pilot in the right seat and navigator had little to contribute and certainly did not respect their concerns at times.

If you think your manufacturing, service business, university, or family has some tough resistors, think about the airlines and healthcare. Significant progress in leading change has occurred in both industries despite some feeling they are perfect.

A physician friend of mine described his first day of med school. The instructing physician opened with how smart the person must be who has been accepted into his prestigious medical school. Although not infallible, the students will learn medicine, and perform the best that can be expected, and who is an equal to question this? Sounds a bit like the "Will of God" response again, right? Who would embrace change if he or she has been taught from day 1 that one will be as good as can be, and better than others?

The source of change is not always the person who leads the change. We will not always be the one leading the change, so we need to learn both how to lead and follow. We will learn how to lead and follow by starting with Change Leadership fundamentals—walking the talk, shall we say. Anything else would be hypocritical and a waste of your time.

Them Is Us Eventually

We need to know the stakeholders and their roles in process improvement. We will eventually be in every stakeholder role over our lifetime, sometimes simultaneously, so there is no end to the benefits of knowing how to do a stakeholder analysis. While we understand that leaders play a role as sponsors of change and the people doing the process improvement work are the change agents, we also have to consider those who will be asked to change as a result of the improvements.

Empathy is a powerful emotion in leading change. Empathy is gained by understanding each role's potential experience in the drama as sponsors, change agents, and the people impacted. The people impacted may experience confusion, pain, and, hopefully, if we do our jobs well, joy. Are we the ones leading the change, managing the change, or being asked to change in this change? The majority of stakeholders are often the "targets of change."

Jeanenne LaMarsh, President of LaMarsh and Associates, taught me about the targets of change. This is the group that will be asked to change. They often have no decision-making authority, may have a lot of issues with the change, and may put up heavy resistance when they are ignored, as they have been in other change management approaches. The Managed Change Model™ from LaMarsh's firm is one of the better approaches in Change Management.[2] We will learn to consider the targets of change and how to engage them in helping us improve the process.

Let's Learn Stakeholder Analysis by Doing

Using the SHA Template

A new service line is starting in your consulting firm. Like too many start-ups, milestones are starting to slip past their due date. Thank goodness things slowed down a bit from the hectic pace because the team failed to do what every high reliability organization does before starting a major initiative. The program manager has taken this delay to conduct a failure mode and effects analysis on the scheduling process, ultimately determining the amount of bookings taken—and, thus, margin. She joined the team late after the prior program manager quit due to the stress. She doesn't feel that there is enough capacity in certain skills in the consultants, and she wants to prevent failure when the service begins.

Who is involved with the launch? Who has a stake in its performance? What if we validate there aren't enough consultants who are skilled? Who might have to change knowing availability includes more processes than just training existing consultants? Let's use the form to answer these questions.

Starting at a macro level, let's list the first organization that comes to mind. The service design organization is a natural start, but it doesn't matter. Sometimes the customer may come to mind and we could start there. See Figure 7.2 to know who the stakeholders are.

We populated the role of the stakeholders as we entered their names. Let's detail each role. The customer is the one who receives the service of the process. In our example, it seems clear the medical imaging operator that we are providing this service to is the customer. What about our technician who has to service the equipment at the client's site and answer questions on the services we provide? Does the technician value the process changes to get back on track? Is he or she also a customer of our new service consulting? We think so. In many cases, we have internal and external customers, the operator being the external-to-the-organization customer. We don't differentiate external or internal in stakeholder analysis (Figure 7.3).

Stakeholder Analysis											
Project			Stakeholder role						Contributor names:		
Date											
Organization/ Location/Area	Name (or group name)	Role or Title	Customer of the process	Process owner	Decision-maker/ Approver	Target of the change	Interested party	Supplier to the process	Current level of buy-in to change. Rate 0 - 10 with 0 being no buy-in - heavy resistance	Needed level of buy-in to change. Rate 0 - 10 with 0 no buy-in needed	Gap	Strategy to close the gap
Scheduling department	Bobbie	Scheduler										
Scheduling department	Petra	Manager, Scheduling										
Scheduling department	Michael	Scheduler										
Scheduling department	Gemma	Scheduler										
Operations	Carrie	Director of Operations										
Clinic	Adam	VP, Clinic										
Clinic	Sophie	Nurse Manager										
Patient												
Physician offices		Physicians										

Figure 7.2 Clinic SHA stakeholders.

Stakeholder Analysis											
Project			Stakeholder role						Contributor names:		
Date											
Organization/ Location/Area	Name (or group name)	Role or Title	Customer of the process	Process owner	Decision-maker/ Approver	Target of the change	Interested party	Supplier to the process	Current level of buy-in to change. Rate 0 - 10 with 0 being no buy-in - heavy resistance	Needed level of buy-in to change. Rate 0 - 10 with 0 no buy-in needed	Gap	Strategy to close the gap
Scheduling department	Bobbie	Scheduler					x				-	
Scheduling department	Petra	Manager, Scheduling		x	x						-	
Scheduling department	Michael	Scheduler					x				-	
Scheduling department	Gemma	Scheduler					x				-	
Operations	Carrie	Director of Operations				x					-	
Clinic	Adam	VP, Clinic	x	x	x		x				-	
Clinic	Sophie	Nurse Manager	x								-	
Patient			x								-	
Physician offices		Physicians					x				-	

Figure 7.3 SHA with roles.

Now that we have brainstormed and listed all of the stakeholders, let's use the template to guide us in finding where we need to focus to improve our chances of achieving the changes. Notice I avoid using the typical negative-sounding resistance term. Change Leadership is not just about reducing resistance. It is as much about increasing the engagement of those who want change. It is far better to have an army with you, than trying to reduce resistance alone. Creating more open support for change is what we will share. We also will consider the "underground resistance" movement as a strategy when the culture is just not quite ready for everyone to be open. As you can see, we will have strategies for you when it is time.

Time to Assess Each Stakeholder's Buy-In

Now is the time to assess each stakeholder or stakeholder group as in this example where equipment operators and our technicians do not need to be identified by individual. They are a homogeneous group with common concerns and we believe all will react similarly to any changes we make.

Your team will assess each stakeholder's current willingness for the changes expected. We don't know at the start of a project what the changes will be exactly. What the team is rating in the initial stakeholder analysis is the willingness to change. After we find the contributing factors and issues with changes, we will develop the actual changes. We will use this stakeholder analysis again at this phase in our Change Leadership to rate their willingness to accept the specific changes devised (Figure 7.4).

- Current level of buy-in to the change
- Needed level of buy-in
- Gaps identified
- Change strategy created

There are a few common strategies for those that have a large gap. Resistance will be felt if one does not have a strategy and execute on the strategy to reduce resistance. The number 1 strategy is to inform the stakeholders about the process improvement. Gather input as to their feelings and invite them to share how it got that way and if they have solutions. We don't want to jump to solutions, and letting them share ideas may increase the buy-in. Why? Because many people are frustrated because no one valued their intellect.

Stakeholder Analysis											
Project								Contributor names:			
Date					Stakeholder role						
Organization/ Location/Area	Name (or group name)	Role or Title	Customer of the process	Process owner	Decision-maker/ Approver	Target of the change	Interested party	Supplier to the process	Current level of buy-in to change. Rate 0 - 10 with 0 being no buy-in - heavy resistance	Needed level of buy-in to change. Rate 0 - 10 with 0 no buy-in needed	Gap	Strategy to close the gap
Scheduling department	Bobbie	Scheduler				x			6	10	(4)	
Scheduling department	Petra	Manager, Scheduling		x	x				5	5	-	
Scheduling department	Michael	Scheduler				x			9	10	(1)	
Scheduling department	Gemma	Scheduler				x			4	8	(4)	
Operations	Carrie	Director of Operations			x				10	10	-	
Clinic	Adam	VP, Clinic	x	x	x	x			7	10	(3)	
Clinic	Sophie	Nurse Manager	x						8	9	(1)	
Patient			x						9	9	-	
Physician offices		Physicians					x		4	10	(6)	

Figure 7.4   Stakeholder Analysis with buy-in.

Other strategies include putting the resistor on the team. Engaging him or her helps each party understand each other better and allows you to manage "bad press" that might have been more gossip than fact. Resistors are often on the outside and unaware perhaps of why the process improvement is really needed. In his book, *Flawless Consulting*, Peter Block shares another strategy. Ensure shareholders know what is expected of them to make the change work.[3] Delaying the inevitable will increase resistance. Engage potential resistors early.

Key Points

- Stakeholder Analysis is a must.
- Strategies are key to leading change when people resist.
- The SHA may expose that the charter is not quite finished. The team may need to add charter signatories to manage resistance. The team may also benefit by adding the process owner to the team.

Endnotes

1. Jim Champy and Harry Greenspun, *Reengineering Health Care*. (London: FT Press, 2010).
2. Used with permission of Jeanenne LaMarsh, president of LaMarsh Associates.
3. Peter Block, *Flawless Consulting: A Guide to Getting Your Expertise Used*. (New York: Pfeiffer, 1981), 139–159.

Chapter 8

Finding the Root Causes, Improving, and Controlling

Experiment, Explore, Build Consensus	Train, Enable, Empower, Hold Accountable	Celebrate

Circulate among followers consistently.

Abraham Lincoln[1]

Explore Together

This chapter is about finding the root causes. If we know the root causes, we are better able to target solutions and improve the process.

Doctor Livingstone

Circulate among followers really means to circulate among the people in the process. Lincoln's intent was not to only circulate among those with his same interests, but with those who have dissenting opinions. As we circulate, we should consider being among others physically as well as mentally and emotionally. Explained in the opposite, do not expect to explore a process in a remote room. That would be like Dr. David Livingstone, a Scottish explorer, saying he explored faraway lands in his flat in Britain.[2] Dr. Livingstone also understood the mentality of the natives of Africa but also those with differing goals and expectations and where they were emotionally. Although the physical location may not change, process improvement leaders understand that the mental and emotional states vary constantly and can be a challenge in leading change. One must appreciate the right time for the right changes to be successful.

Dr. Livingstone also had an effective method to change minds that allowed him to succeed. Let us explore Dr. Livingstone's ways and benefit from his success in Change Leadership.

He had qualities and approaches which gave him an advantage as an explorer. Others attempting to explore Africa were often not trusted because they appeared to be potential slave traders and over-zealous missionaries forcing change on the natives. Livingstone usually travelled lightly and he had an ability to reassure chiefs that he was not a threat. Other expeditions had dozens of soldiers armed with rifles and scores of hired porters carrying supplies, and were seen as military incursions or were mistaken for slave-raiding parties. Livingstone, on the other hand, travelled on most of his journeys with a few servants and porters, bartering for supplies along the way, with a couple of guns for protection.[2]

Explore Together with Empathy and Patience

Dr. Livingstone preached a Christian message, but did not force it on unwilling ears. He understood the ways of local chiefs and successfully negotiated passage through their territory. He was often hospitably received and aided, even by powers in the tribal community.

Dr. Livingstone explored and engaged with the natives. He understood their needs and their wants and was successful in getting what he wanted: safe passage to find the source of the Nile, as well as his second motive to change the spiritual beliefs of the natives. One should know that Dr. Livingstone initially considered missionary work. His success in exploration moved him to more exploration, but he succeeded in leading change among the natives, too. The abolition of slavery is perhaps the greatest change that Dr. Livingstone contributed. Well before the United States abolished slavery, Britain led its reversal of such an atrocity.

Building the Team

In Explore Together, we emphasize the word together. Process improvement leaders know how to build a team with the right people. This does not mean just those who share our beliefs and values. A Change Leader circulates among those who often hold different opinions than she or he. A Change Leader recognizes that there are reasons others do not share the same opinion and, perhaps, it is because they know something the Change Leader does not know. A good team is a team that has the same vision, perhaps, but diversity in the reasons for the current state.

Case Study

Poor Service for a Major Customer and Its Customers

After 15 years and still going well is a process improvement between two major corporations that are both competitors and value stream partners. The Change Leadership to make the changes 15 years ago could only have happened between organizations that valued employees enough to empower them to reinvent the way they did business. The way they did business not only changed between themselves, but also how the distributor and end-customer did business.

This was an arrangement where my factory configured fairly complex product with unique specifications to the customer. The customer shipped to its finished goods distribution center. The distribution center would receive orders from local and regional distributors to replenish their stock or they would buy-to-order for an end-customer. We brand labeled the product, but, as mentioned earlier, it wasn't merely taking similar product under our brand name and slapping their label on it. The products were significantly different.

The issue was that both companies struggled to be able to ship the right items on time. Both of us had finished goods to try to meet their service levels of each of our customers. It just wasn't working. To make the business issue even more critical, the margins on these products were razor thin. It was a complex line of product with hundreds of SKUs (stock keeping units) and somewhat regulated because the local utility specified some of the design. I had to make a different product for Colorado than I did for Alabama. The customer sold into the same areas we did, so this doubled virtually every product SKU. And, some people think healthcare is the only industry that needs standardization.

We were a vertically integrated site meaning that we manufactured many of the components that we assembled into finished devices. We also ran the corporation's largest distribution center at the time within the walls of my factory. This afforded us the ability to ship complete sets of product to customers. This distribution role also added to the complexity. We had responsibility for everything from order receipt to shipment. This worked to our favor, though, as we shall see.

The processes included customer order entry where my team of customer support personnel was on call to help specify products. The master scheduling process was operating simultaneously. My master scheduler did his best to take the marketing forecast by family (not by specific product) done by headquarters in another state, develop a forecast by subfamily that we needed to load into our MRP system (a system that was designed to help know what to build and what to buy from suppliers), and determine finished goods inventory levels to meet the demand. The manufacturing process included many processes. We took steel coils and sheets, copper and aluminum bars, and hundreds of other raw materials and purchased components and processed each of them in a variety of processes. I could go on, but I think you get the picture that this was not simply buying a box and slapping a label on it.

Fortunately, the site manager in 1981 had the foresight to start training everyone in process improvement. This was the organization that was one of the first to train frontline employees and let them have an hour a week to work in improvements. This organization also knew virtually all of the tools taught in Lean and Six Sigma because we had to know them. We had to know how to find waste and organize workplaces and use pull replenishment systems. We also knew how to prevent failures by ensuring Failure Mode and Effects Analyses were performed before any production started. We knew how to use Statistical Process Control to know how our processes were performing now, not a week later.

We believed in and utilized the 3Ms. We shared the most important measures daily, if not more frequently in what today many call visual management. We displayed the measures on every screen at initial sign on by the users so they didn't have to do a single extra click to get the measures. We managed to the measures every day, too. If a measure was varying out of control, we were expected to take action. We also made it easy to know when to act and when we didn't have to act. This made us more comfortable when we didn't take action knowing the difference between common variation and special unexpected variation. And these measures were accessible by virtually anyone who wanted access. We knew yesterday's sales, the inventory on hand at the moment, the number of late shipments the day before, and what today's and tomorrow's order volumes were shaping up to be. This visibility to the measures was also a catalyst to focusing on the

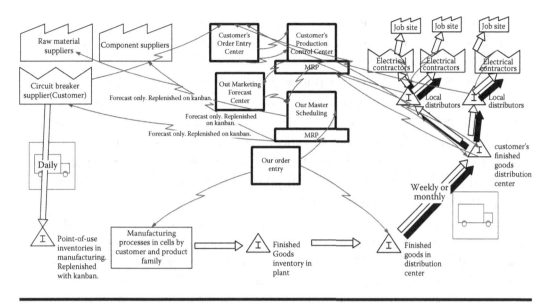

Figure 8.1 Current state Value Stream Map of brand-label customer and local distributors.

service issues with this major customer. This customer was so important to my factory, we displayed our ship-on-time daily.

We had trained, enabled, and engaged our employees who were instrumental in accomplishing what we did. Our customer was also well versed in these techniques. Their CEO was one of the biggest proponents of Six Sigma and leading change. The CEO of our company continues as CEO today leading the organization and achieving remarkable returns.

We knew not to jump to solutions to solve the on-time service issues. We created a team that spanned both companies and applied Lean Six Sigma and Change Leadership. Our marketing director, the client's lead sourcing agent, and I co-led the team. We signed our charter, did our Stakeholder Analysis, and continued down the roadmap.

Our next step was to walk through the processes creating a Value Stream Map (VSM) to record the processes (Figure 8.1).

A VSM purpose is to help teams identify value from nonvalue and it is also a graphical way to show issues. A VSM shows the value-added steps and the nonvalue occurring, such as the inventory that was found throughout the value stream. We circulated among the people in the processes early and added some of the key players to the team. One key player was our customer's customer service manager that gave us forecasts of the finished goods they wanted. We wanted him on the team especially because we felt he had the most to lose with the changes we thought might be needed.

He was a great advocate for us for years and treated us well even when we really messed up. He also knew more about the issues and potential causes than anyone else at his company.

We used Statistical Process Control (SPC) charts to analyze the stability of demand by item. It was surprising when we compared the SPC chart of what we saw the customer ordered from us against what the customer saw its customers ordered from its organization. Our SPC chart showed significantly higher variation than the demand from the thousands of end-customers placed on our customer. Each person going into the project had a different view of the issue and cause. What we discovered in the process is that we all were wrong to some degree. And, each discipline, marketing, manufacturing, sales, sourcing, customer service, distribution, scheduling, and end-customer also discovered their first impressions were not always accurate.

We validated the root causes. It was emotional at times, especially when we had to explain why the customer often created the issue. We also had to share with our customer *and* competitor, remember, that we had failures. We definitely didn't know what each other knew when we started. We did by the end of the analyze phase.

The root causes turned out to be:

- Finished goods inventory had the wrong items in stock and not enough of what was ordered.
- The forecasts were always wrong.
- Raw material and component suppliers had the same issues of not being able to supply us the right materials at the right time.
- End-customers did not know very long in advance what they needed.
- It took days to ship products from our site to the customer's warehouse, and then from their warehouse to the distributor. This lead time was longer than the lead time the end-customer had.
- No one knew what each other had in stock.

Both companies had valiantly worked around the issues by apologizing to each of our customers when shipments were missed. Other work-arounds included pushing even more inventory into the distribution centers. Our customer service teams tried to forecast better only to be wrong again every month.

Work-Arounds in the "Factory of Hidden Defects"

These work-arounds had been going on for years. Dr. W. Edwards Deming (noted American statistician and author) called this behavior the "factory of hidden defects." His point about work-arounds is that people will continue working around the root cause of a problem for a greater good. If the work-around continues for a time, people will become too accustomed to the work-around and begin to not even notice or complain about the problem, in this case, making emergency demands of manufacturing and shipping to satisfy customers. The work-around becomes the way people work. Changing people's behavior becomes more difficult when the work-around is no longer seen as a reaction to a quality abnormality. Therefore, another lesson learned is to start change early before work-arounds become the way people work. Fortunately, both companies had tired of the work-arounds.

Exploring Using the "Five Whys"

Although we know we have the root causes, we often need to drill down deeper to better design improvements. We used the tool of asking why five times to better understand some of the root causes. We know we reached the deepest cause when we didn't know the answer to the next "why." They learned this technique in their training. See Figure 8.2 for the section of the Roadmap to the Five Whys.

Here is how this root cause tool helped drill down on one of the root causes. The team starts by asking the first question. Note that this is not blaming or asking who did what. That type of questioning will hurt your Change Leadership effort next time. It is Root Cause Analysis, not Root Who Analysis.

Here is a re-creation of the exercise. We were asking the questions of the customer's inventory planning manager.

Why couldn't you ship the right quantity to your customer?
He didn't have every SKU in his center and the customer can't install the equipment unless all items on the order are shipped.
Why didn't you have every item?
The forecast was wrong last month and he knew he was running low and tried to expedite with us.
Why was the forecast wrong?
The end-customer found the utility wouldn't accept the original order and he had to change the SKUs he had ordered earlier.
Why didn't you have enough of the other item in stock?
The local distributor that the distributor shipped to had more than expected demand earlier and sold out.

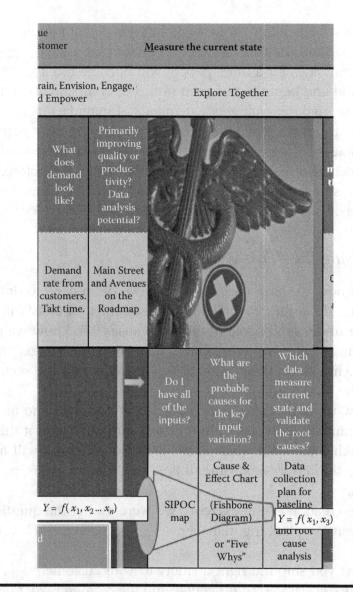

Figure 8.2   Roadmap for the "Five Whys."

Why did the local distributor not carry more inventory?

They don't make any money on the sale and these items take up a lot of space that they want to use for inventory on which they make money.

Why don't they order more frequently and with more lead time so they don't need to stock as much?

It took a lot of effort to order because our customer always wanted to check their stock and they never knew what they had on hand. So, the distributors would grow tired of waiting on the phone so long. Many of them felt the sales of these products weren't worth the effort, but knew they had to sell them to keep their customers. But, they tended to only order once a week instead of as soon as he knew he had demand because of the hassle.

Now we knew where we had to work more.

Asking why five times is a wonderfully simple and, most importantly, effective exploration tool in process improvement. My mom said I learned asking why early in life. I think all three-year-olds do.

Explain

Explain means to take the root causes and connect them to the problem. A process improvement team can lose focus on the charter and its measures if they don't connect the activities back to the charter every once in a while.

Explaining also is aided by filling in a storyboard of the effort. An A3-size piece of paper is a common way to create storyboards and, thus, engage others in your project. This A3 is a great way to explain the project and status. Next on the Roadmap is to start improving the process.

We moved to the Improve phase knowing very clearly the root causes. We created a Future State Map exploring together our experiments performed to see what could be eliminated, simplified, and improved. We all knew we had to get the right product to the end-customer at the right time (Figure 8.3).

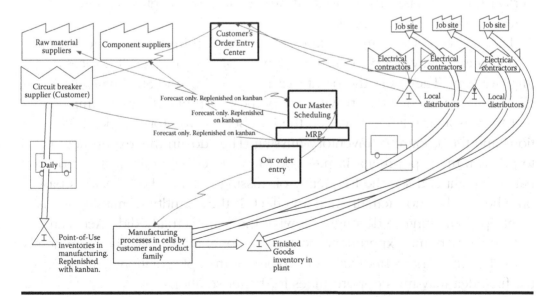

Figure 8.3   Future state Value Stream Map actually implemented of brand-label customer and local distributors.

Experiment

> The suggestions of the operators should definitely be included in this stage … the results must be understandable, capable of being communicated, the analysis should not require too much time or expertise, and the analysis should reliably detect the signals.
>
> **Donald Wheeler**[3]

Experimentation is fundamental to change. Process improvement experimentation must also be practical. In agricultural experimentation, it might take a year before results are known. In process improvement, we are looking to know now, or tomorrow. How often has a change that you wanted occurred exactly right the first time? You experimented, although perhaps initially you thought the change would go easily the first time. Thus, we find experimentation is mandatory because we did not get the change we wanted the first time. So, let us learn experimentation so we are better prepared for the inevitable as we lead change.

Dr. Deming was one of the world's leading experimenters. He and Dr. Walter A. Shewhart (American physicist and statistician) are credited with developing two of the first methodologies for process improvement as we learned in Chapter 4. Now is the time that PDSA (plan, do, study, act) and PDCA (plan, do, check, act) add value. PDSA and Dr. Deming's PDCA are perfect for this phase. To be good at process improvement, you need to be at least good at experimentation.

The first step is to plan the experiment. We plan in this phase to validate a root cause. Many people confuse "plan" to be the first step in process improvement. They miss the point that Drs. Deming and Shewhart, like all good experimenters, start with a hypothesis. An hypothesis example is that there is a correlation between the number of inventory stocking locations and the amount of inventory missing. The "do" in this experiment is to perform the experiment. It might be to increase the number of components at night and see the frequency of missing orders. The "check" is based on whether the "do" actually had an effect. If the quantity of missing feeds went up, something to do might be what the team actually did. "Act" is the last step. Often, the experiment creates additional questions. The team needs to explore the various findings and explore for multiple solutions. Jumping to the first idea may miss opportunities for better solutions.

The experiment I share here continues the root cause of the customer not knowing in time what its distributor customer wanted. The Five Whys analysis highlighted that the local distributor found that the process took too long to order and to batch orders, but hoped our customer could expedite every order like it had been doing. This was the work-around that we both were doing for years. Some of our folks thought they were heroes fighting these fires day in and day out.

We went back to the Value Stream Map and the SPC charts and discovered that the end-customer demand was a lot smoother looking at end-customer demand in aggregate. That is, when we looked at any one customer, it was highly variable. But looking at all the customers in a larger area, the demand was much smoother. The team made a Future State Map that suggested we and our customer experiment in order to transmit the local distributor's order directly to our customer who, in turn, would electronically transmit the order directly to us so we could see immediately the end-customer's order.

We tried this in a pilot, the "do" in PDCA, and it worked the first time. We found this in the "check" phase. We received the end-customer order within a minute of him ordering. It was interesting that some of the first orders proved to be the other root cause. Our customer did not have the right inventory in its finished goods warehouse. Lastly, we moved to the "act" phase by starting the process to make this direct entry transmission the norm.

This move made our customer's order entry staff aware that their tasks were no longer needed. What followed was one of the most powerful Change Leadership moves made in my career. Our customer informed each of its employees affected (Stakeholders) that his or her employment would not be affected if we could make this solution work.

In the past, these employees would manually enter the orders daily, which went to its distribution center. We would not get their customers' orders, only a forecast order for the next month as a guess to replenish what they forecasted to sell. Our solution would now eliminate all of the manual entry and the forecast order. We would start receiving our customer's end-customer orders directly and in near real time.

Explore: Builds on Experimentation

Explore goes deeper into what one is finding in experimentation.

> The primary objective (of experimentation) is exploration.
>
> **Donald Wheeler**[3]

Explore after experimentation means to explore alternative solutions. The team in this case study actually did. Brainstorming is another tool on the Roadmap and is very valuable in this phase due to its ability to create solutions that one person thinking alone may have missed. The rules of brainstorming, such as don't debate, are easy. I find, however, very few teams do it well. They miss the opportunity to explore other thoughts and suggestions. For the sake of the team, I suggest always brainstorming in Explore or risk the sponsor or someone else getting frustrated at a lack of creativity and effectiveness.

The team brainstormed next on how they could take the waste out of the piles of inventory at the customer, the customer's distributor, and improve the ability to get the right item at the right location. This is where Change Leadership can pay off. No one wants a team to fall apart at this stage because each individual has his or her favorite solution. Once they have enough solutions ideas, the team will move to gaining consensus on the best solutions.

The team pulled out the VSM again and made another change in the Future State Map. Now that the orders were coming directly to us, we were getting essentially two to four weeks advanced notice of the end-customer's true demand. We found that the end-customer usually had at least two weeks lead time to get products to the job site. We had leaned out our manufacturing process for our sellable items under our brand to be able to ship any item in small quantities any day.

Thus, we thought we could experiment shipping to the local distributor directly from our plant. Note, I said directly from our plant not from our finished goods inventory. With two weeks lead time, we could build-to-order knowing the aggregated demand provided rather smooth overall demand. We could always build some buffer stock of the highest volume items knowing they would always sell and smooth the production demand and all of our demand to our suppliers.

We experimented taking the end-customer order and manufacturing it to order knowing we had finished goods stock to protect the customer's demand in case our experiment proved we could not make it in time. We found we could. Now, we had eliminated both the waste in order entry and the need for finished goods inventory at our customer's site and our site, for the most part.

Even more exciting, our experiment proved we could eliminate the local distributor's inventory and waste of picking job site orders by shipping from our factory directly to the job site. Eureka!

Build Consensus

The team was taught what consensus is and what it is not. Consensus, as we know it, means that everyone comes to a decision and commits to the decision. No underhandedness or resistance once the consensus is reached. Consensus does not mean each person feels the decision is the best. A good experimenter may actually work to disprove his or her hypothesis to more strongly test and explore alternatives. However, once consensus is reached, the team can trust that all move forward in the same direction and expend their Change Leadership energies on the next issues.

We had consensus with our customer and they had some work to do to build consensus with its local distributors to let us ship directly to the job site. Some did not buy in and continued to hold stock. This was acceptable, and we simply asked that they replenish what they sold and let us know if they knew of abnormally large site orders coming. I imagine many of these distributors eventually also started ordering and letting us ship direct.

By the way, I will mention now another part of the solution. Our customer was not ready to let its end-customers know that their competitor was making its products by seeing that the "ship from" address had my company's name. Just happening to be located in a small town and knowing the postmaster, we arranged a process to have our customer's name share the same address as ours. This allowed all of the carriers to ship from our address using our customer's name.

Train, Enable, Empower, Hold Accountable

Training in the Improvements

Training is the first step in getting people to know what we know. The good Change Leader is also a good trainer. Training should always start with an objective of skills desired by the student and knowledge attained. Using the vision statement protocol, we should envision a future state for the student and exert our energies in training accordingly.

Enabling others to participate in the change process occurs best after training. Engaging people in your improvement before they know the "end-in-mind" may actually backfire or create resistance to achieving your vision.

We simplified the information and product flow processes considerably, which made training new employees so much easier. The distribution centers at our location and the customer's now could use the space consumed by the $2 million plus inventory no longer needed.

Enable

Enable in this phase means to give the people the resources necessary to do the process the way it should now be operating. I have seen far too many solutions fall away when we did not enable the people in the process the time and resources needed to sustain the gains.

Standard work is another tool on the Roadmap. It is basically the right way to do a task. There is standard work for housekeeping, admitting patients, and a host of other tasks. People must be shown the instructions, or at least made aware that there is a right way to do work and a wrong way. Know the right way to sustain the gains and have more satisfied customers.

Empower

Empowering in the improve and control phase is critical to sustain. We were empowered to take orders directly and to ship directly. Empowerment comes with responsibility and this was a major risk to both of us. We used Failure Mode and Effects Analysis to think how our new processes could fail. We acted by putting in controls and real-time information to warn us of variation, and we controlled the processes. This is holding people accountable.

Hold Accountable

Everybody was sure that somebody would do it.

The process improvement team should be taught process control, enabled to measure the process as it flows, and empowered to make decisions within boundaries. The standard work used in training people in the change is also effective in holding people accountable. In healthcare, there have been several studies linking healthcare-acquired conditions, infections, let's say, to be caused by variations in how work is done. Evidently some are not following the standard work of those whose patients do not get infections. We need a way of knowing who is doing what to reduce the variation. Then, we ensure training is done well and the student has learned.

You might have heard of a Safety Culture. A subculture of a Safety Culture is a Just Culture. This is not a blame-free culture. If people come to work incapacitated due to substance abuse, the person should be held accountable. It is not society's fault and it must be dealt with. In the inventory story, we held our manufacturing and carriers responsible to make and deliver the right products to the right job site at the right time. We made sure everyone knew they could stop the process if something wasn't right and they were also held accountable to ask for help.

Lastly, our Roadmap helped us navigate the process improvement journey more quickly and easily. It is now time to celebrate. It may seem odd that we have "celebrate" on the Roadmap. It is not by mistake. We need to reinforce positively those individuals and teams who work to improve processes continuously. In America, individual certification is often desired. In other cultures, this may not seem for the good for the many. The process improvement leader should seek out what team members value. For many, it is simply a better work life. For others, it may be a little recognition. Whatever it is, don't forget to celebrate to tell everyone that process improvement is the behavior we reinforce.

Key Points

- Explore Together builds teamwork, reduces resistance, and should end with a better study than not exploring together.
- Explain connects the root causes found in Explore Together with the charter and project goals.
- Experiment is key to checking how countermeasures may improve a process or a design.
- Exploring alternative countermeasures and solutions may result in more improvement.
- Building consensus is vital and the Stakeholder Analysis may be used again to understand who might resist consensus.
- The control phase relies on people to be trained in the change.
- Standard work is an effective template to also hold people accountable.

Endnotes

1. Wikipedia: http://en.wikipedia.org/wiki/Abraham_Lincoln_and_slavery
2. Wikipedia: http://en.wikipedia.org/wiki/David_Livingstone
3. Donald Wheeler, *Experimentation: Understanding Industrial Experimentation.* (Knoxville, KY: SPC Press, 1990), 1–3.

Chapter 9

Utilizing the 3Ms: Measure, Manage to the Measure, and Make It Easier

Introduction

We are now ready to learn how to lead process improvement by remembering three important lessons. Process improvement that works and lasts requires:

- **M**easuring
- **M**anaging to the measure
- **M**aking it easier

Measure

Utilizing the first M is often enough to get an improvement started. There is a story of a manager writing a number on the floor, but saying nothing. People had no idea what he was doing. The next day, he wrote a different number, and again said nothing. Soon, someone figured out the puzzling behavior. He was writing the prior day's production output on the floor. Once the staff realized the "game," they worked together improving the process and beating the prior day's numbers. It became fun and the improvement started all because of a measure.

Practicing Measure

Try measuring as in the previous story and see how it works in your area. Don't manage anyone? This doesn't matter. Measuring works for anyone. For this exercise, try measuring something not working well in a common break area. Put a number on the wall of how many dirty dishes are in the sink left by others. Or, maybe put a sticky note with a count of how many times the coffee pot or water cooler are found empty. Use one of the charting methods we teach later in this book to share the measure daily and really have some fun with measuring. Let me know what happens at www.rpmexec.com.

How many times have you shared a measure with a team and heard, "I had no idea. If only we knew." For example, if you are in the healthcare profession, think of the top two or three outcomes of patient care for your organization. Mortality should come to mind if you are in an acute care hospital. Next, write down the measure of each objective. If you are struggling trying to figure out exactly the measure, that is not uncommon. I will cover the most common measures in healthcare because they are often not well understood.

Lastly, what is your current performance in each of the measures for each objective? I am not expecting you to have them all memorized, so look around for the measure to be posted. Struggling to figure where to look? Don't be alarmed. Workers can see the measures in a Toyota vehicle assembly plant, a consumer customer service call center, and a Best Buy store. They can see the objectives, the measure, and the current state daily. Your organization may not be there yet. You will know exactly how to achieve this for yourself and your organization and have them set up by the time you finish this book. The first M is the most important of the Ms. For without Measure, there is little to manage to, and one never knows if it is easier if we don't know from where we started.

Measurement is key to improvement. Measurement alone can often bring about change because it makes people aware of the need for change. A Change Leader can often get the change desired by simply doing the 3Ms. And the first M is not an option. Michael Porter and Robert Kaplan remind us of the management axiom, "What is not measured cannot be managed or improved," in their *Harvard Business Review* article, "How to Solve the Cost Crisis in Health Care," September 2011.[1] This axiom is a perfect lead-in to the second M.

Measurement matters. When clinicians see their numbers, they act to improve them, using their professional pride and competitiveness to find solutions.

Randall D. Cebul, MD[2]
Director, Better Health Greater Cleveland

Manage to the Measure

Simply measuring something and not managing based on the measure is fruitless. Example: We see hand hygiene charts posted quarterly on walls in the unit's break area. There is seldom any evidence that anyone pays attention to it. Often, the chart is dusty and not current. It is clear that the measure of hand hygiene compliance gets little attention and does not result in any significant change. Joseph Juran (twentieth-century management consultant) found the person doing work should be empowered in three abilities in his *Principle of Operator Self-Control*.[3] They include:

- The person doing the work has the necessary knowledge skills and tools to do the job.
- She/he has ability to regulate the process.
- She/he gets feedback on how they are doing.

Make It Easier

The greatest change will still fail if it is not easy enough to apply. "Water flows the path of least resistance." If it is easier to *not* change, change is destined to fail. The 3Ms are the most valuable three letters in process improvement. Doing all three Ms well is the best recipe for change to succeed.

I can tell you every change I have led where processes are controlled by humans succeeded because of the 3Ms. Whether it be improving customer service, eliminating wrong-site surgery, sustaining hand hygiene compliance, achieving record high on-time performance to demanding customers like Toyota and Big Box retailers, or preventing catastrophic vehicle failures, measuring, managing to what the measurement was telling us, and making changes easier.

Visual Management

Visualize your workplace. Look around your area for measures that tell you how the quality, safety, and productivity are right now. Like most, you may struggle. Try the computer at your station. Can you find any visual aids as to how things are managing now? How about a chart on today's sales. That, we probably have. That is a good example of visual management. Visual management is something that we can sense that tells us what is important and how we are doing, and where we want to be. Another example in healthcare is a monitor in the intensive care unit showing a patient's vital signs. It tells us in real time what is important, how the patient is doing, and goals or, at least, boundaries of acceptable status.

I work at Healthcare Performance Partners in healthcare quality and safety consulting and I love my job, my colleagues, and clients. Charles Hagood, Marshall Leslie, and my friend from working on hand hygiene compliance, Dr. Dave Munch, recruited me to join them at HPP, the world's foremost healthcare performance improvement consulting firm. Everything about HPP seemed right, especially how they treated their team and promoted the value of measuring early in the work. The entire HPP team promotes and requires the use of Visual Management in every project. Many of us have worked in high reliable organizations where we knew instantly how our customers were feeling, how the processes were working, if there were any quality issues, and we knew it visually. Having worked in high reliability organizations, I learned that real-time monitoring and process control is vital so that the frontline staff can intervene and prevent failures.

At Eaton Corporation, we made safety devices that had to be calibrated to prevent electrical shock. The circuit breaker is named a ground fault circuit interrupter. The product's purpose is to stop the electricity before a fault in the circuit allows electricity to hurt anyone. If the calibration is not done, the breaker may not function. What if one got past us into a box and was shipped to be installed in your home? Visual management was clear. If any breaker did not pass through the calibration system, an alarm would go off. Not next week, not tomorrow, but right now.

Measuring Example

Yesterday, I counted the number of pages I have written to see how I have progressed with this book. I counted the pages to manage my time to ensure that I finish the book on time for the publisher. After work, I read and write. I have written most of my working life, but started out more as just a reader. To write, I have to read because I am humbled each time I realize how much there is to know about just about anything. I have always used measuring when I read, too, come to think of it. I remember measuring the amount of books I read in early grade school per section. I wish I could remember the name of the reading series. It was set up to let one measure progress and I had fun managing my progress to get to the next series. Yes, as geeky as it sounds, I also measured and managed to the measure to compete.

Managing to the Measure Example

I really liked playing baseball, but I couldn't hit. Being the second shortest boy from first through eighth grade did not convince me that sports was my thing, either. I have to mention that reading was a big reason that my son excelled at hitting. I wanted to learn why I did not hit well and to see if my son could learn to be better at it than I. He led his age group in hitting virtually every year. Here is how my reading helped my son learn to hit. I read that Pat Murphy, coach of Notre Dame and Arizona State, had a baseball camp, so he taught my son how to hit. Okay, I set you up a bit on that story. I like to think that reading *Sports Illustrated* baseball and my working with Adam on the hitting drills well before Pat Murphy's camp helped at least a bit. Don't look for a book from me on baseball, though. Remember what I said about how little I think I know?

Make It Easier Example

Water flows the path of least resistance. Electricity flows the path of least resistance. People will often take the path of least resistance. I had a piano teacher who also believed people would take the path of least resistance until she had me as a pupil. I loved learning the piano in first grade until I discovered percussion around fourth grade. My interest in piano fell sharply as I took up drumming. I would not practice piano nearly enough and my teacher was becoming very annoyed with my lack of practice and obvious difficulty in playing the pieces. Finally, one day, she confronted me. Her words to me were, "Rick, isn't practicing easier than listening to me harp on you to practice?" She had a point. Practicing was the path of least resistance until I found an even easier path of least resistance. I quit piano. So, why not try finding the path of least resistance in process improvement?

I measure, manage to the measure, and make it easier to do anything that is really important to me. I have been married for over 30 years. I am delighted to have great clients and a place to work where I measure my contributions and what I learn daily. This book has been a work in process for several years, but it was not important enough until recently, and no one was measuring me on finishing it. The publisher and I both are measuring now. After measuring where I am in achieving the 250 or so pages to improve skills in process improvement, I think we are right where we need to be. The measure that I used is takt (German for pace or rhythm) time.

Takt Time: A Measure of the Pace Needed to Meet Customer Demand

My takt time to finish this book is two pages per day. Takt time is a good measure for writing a book and its value is found throughout healthcare. What is the pace that our manufacturing site needed to fill our customer's customer orders that shipped directly to the job site? What is the rate of patients, on average, a family practitioner needs to achieve to satisfy his/ her patients? What is the rate of production needed by your pharmaceutical company to avoid backorders? How can 167 prescription drugs be on back-order as was true in mid-2011? Maybe we could have measured demand or drug production better? Takt time is not the only measure, of course, but its value is often missed in healthcare—OR (operating room) scheduling, running labs, discharging patients, and much more.

Calculating the takt time in writing this book is easily done. Takt time is the ratio of the number of days I want to make available to write this book divided by the number of pages remaining. Example: 257 pages is our nominal page plan. I want to spend two nights and one weekend afternoon in writing. Let's call these sessions. The time available was 20 weeks, or 20 weeks × 3 sessions per week; 60 sessions divided by 257 pages demanded = 60/257 = a takt time of 0.233. This means I have to get a page every .233 sessions. This equates to about four pages per session 1/.233 = x pages/1 session. In other words, think of the publisher "pulling" four pages from me every session.

I, therefore, need to average four pages per session. Of course, some days I will do more and some days I will do less, but on average, I will get this book to you on time if I do 12 pages per week. Of course, there is a lot more to publishing a book than writing. Therefore, I create a team and we all measure progress every session to ensure we meet demand. Each of us must meet the takt time of 12 pages per week regardless of our roles. We manage to the measure when variation occurs, such as, we get an idea how we can help you learn the 3Ms by using a new experiment. This is when we decided to show you how impactful the 3Ms are with the public. What we find too difficult, we "make it easier."

Illustrating the book is a difficult task. My son, Adam, did some of the illustrations. We found that illustrations could not be done by one person at the takt time required. What do we do? Change takt time? Well, we only have two variables in the equation. Time available or the number of pages. We can't sacrifice the number of pages because we risk not meeting your expectations of the book. So, the only other variable is time available. We could try to speed up the illustrators, but quality may suffer. What is another way of making more time available? Time available is a function of two variables, actually. Time available = time to do a task × the number of resources doing the task. How about adding resources that increase the time available? Of course.

Determining the number of resources to meet the customer demand also can be found using the measure of takt time. If the illustrator can do two pages per session and we need four pages per session, then the number of illustrators we need is four pages per session needed/2 pages per person possible = two illustrators are needed to make takt time.

In our work with clients, we focus first on taking out waste before we suggest adding resources. One way to define Lean is using fewer resources for a given task. In reducing the wait time in support centers, we often reduce demand first because we find FAQs often are preferred by customer's who are on the Web frequently where they can easily access FAQs. In this case, we reduce the denominator: demand. We now use takt time to ensure the number of staff in the center is sufficient and how many are now required in the department. Therefore, we often reduce the numerator and denominator.

This is how we coach organizations to meet the demands and to reduce their backlog. And, just about every other issue in demand.

Measuring: The Most Important M

Measure—the most important concept in this book. Start measuring what is important, and that alone may be sufficient to lead change.

> I also share that, without measuring, little is achieved and even less sustained.

Honestly, what in the past has sustained that humans control? How many of your successes, whether it be organizing your desk, getting staff to wash their hands to training and promoting team problem solving has sustained without measuring? I am almost embarrassed to say that it is this simple to see a common thread. Yet, why do we have to reinvent this wheel repeatedly? Process improvement leaders and teams measure results. They measure not only the outcomes, they also measure the vital behaviors that lead to the desired outcomes, such as leading a perioperative team to measuring the behaviors up to and after the procedures.

Apply the First of the 3Ms and See the Value

Pick a task that you want to see occurring that is not at the performance level you expect. Choose a task that will give you data frequently so you still have time to learn the other two Ms instead of watching corn grow. In addition, choose one that you are not sharing the measure of performance to those doing the tasks or at least not in a timely manner to the task being performed.

We want a task where you can see failures occurring frequently so we can see the tremendous value in Measuring. If you cannot think of one, take hand washing using alcohol-based dispensers. Other tasks that might work for you are refilling the office copier with paper, opening the door for others, or something as simple as always greeting each other at the beginning of the workday before barking orders or requests. If you work alone, think of a task frequently done at home or at your local pub or community center.

Start with simply observing people doing the task inconspicuously to avoid influencing the behavior that you want to measure. I will use hand hygiene because it is needed everywhere and the events are easily observed. In addition, all of society will get a benefit—lower risk of infection. We can thank Dr. Ignaz Semmelweis again (see Chapter 3).

Setting Up Your Experiment

Purpose: Measuring if measuring has an impact on behavior.

Setup: Find an area where you can observe hand cleansing without being conspicuous. A high-traffic public area like a reception desk, patient rooms where the door is usually open, or a cafeteria are all good candidate areas.

Find a dispenser in a reasonable spot where people can easily access it (this is a hint of the third M: Make it easy). So, let us jump ahead and make sure it is convenient to do the task as we focus on the first M, Measure.

Measuring the Baseline

Measure the baseline to know if Measure has affected the rate of hand hygiene. Use the hand hygiene data collection sheet in Figure 9.1 that is also found in Appendix 6. Make as many copies as you wish to take with you to observe. Fold the template in half to make it even less conspicuous.

Create a measure: The simplest measure is often a count. For example, count the number of times someone refills the copier after using it versus having to refill it because it is empty. The count of how many times someone opens or holds open the door for another, or a count of people who say hello before discussing work. For hand hygiene, count the number of times someone does not wash upon entering and exiting a patient care area. A common issue in any workplace is leaving the task to search for supplies (Figure 9.2). (Do you see my point of this example?)

The team achieved exactly what it needed in a measure to show the problem: Nurses were wasting time leaving the room because of a lack of supplies where they needed them. Sometimes measuring can result in other wins. Some OR directors work to reduce the amount of times a door to an OR is opened. Opening a door allows air to exchange, which might allow pathogens inside the OR. This chart may lead the team to a reduction in surgical site infections.

The next simplest measure is to calculate a ratio using a count such as in Figure 9.2 and dividing the count by the number of times the task occurs. A ratio may be better when the number of occurrences varies significantly period to period. In the example of a chart for counts, it does not make sense to create a ratio because the data were gathered by each case. Figure 9.3 is a chart of the ratio of customers entering a cafeteria who washed their hands over the entire day. The number of customers varies significantly and a simple count might suggest compliance varies differently.

Hand Hygiene Observation and Contributing Factor Form						Date of observations:						Collected by:										
												Possible Contributing Factors to Washing										
						Observable												Observable by asking person				
Observation Number	Unit name (2 South, ITU, etc)	Circle time of observation (AM is 0801-1700, PM is 1701-0800)	Circle role of health care professional observed (RN=Nurse T=Therapy, HSK= Housekeeping, CATR=Catering, ThSf = Theatre Staff, ThPor=Theatre Porter, Phl=Phlebotomist, Con=Consultant), all others please identify in the comments section	1 Before Patient contact 2 Before aseptic task 3 After fluid risk 4 After Patient contact 5 After contact with Pt surroundings	Did person perform hand hygiene?	Dispenser location not in path of person or obstructed/hidden	Dispenser empty	Dispenser broken	Leaves patient room to use shared equipment	Hands full: Supplies/Equipment (e.g. food trays, lab supplies)	Hands full: Meds	Gloves - Did not wash before or after gloving	Urgency to act for patient safety concern	Person entering/exiting followed someone who did not wash	Frequent entry and exit	Admissions or discharge process	Isolation area (gown + gloves when required)	Lack of immediate feedback to person for hand hygiene compliance	Distractions/Forgets/Lack of knowledge/Chose not to wash	Perception that if nothing is touched in the patient care area hand hygiene is not necessary	Perception of skin irritation or dislike of alcohol based cleanser	Comments
1	2	4	5	6	7	8	9	10	11	12	13	14	15	16	17	18	19	20	21	22	23	24
1		AM PM	RN T MD Diet Rx PHL HSK CATR ThStf ThPor ODP Con	1 2 3 4 5	Yes No																	
2		AM PM	RN T MD Diet Rx PHL HSK CATR ThStf ThPor ODP Con	1 2 3 4 5	Yes No																	
3		AM PM	RN T MD Diet Rx PHL HSK CATR ThStf ThPor ODP Con	1 2 3 4 5	Yes No																	
4		AM PM	RN T MD Diet Rx PHL HSK CATR ThStf ThPor ODP Con	1 2 3 4 5	Yes No																	
5		AM PM	RN T MD Diet Rx PHL HSK CATR ThStf ThPor ODP Con	1 2 3 4 5	Yes No																	
6		AM PM	RN T MD Diet Rx PHL HSK CATR ThStf ThPor ODP Con	1 2 3 4 5	Yes No																	
7		AM PM	RN T MD Diet Rx PHL HSK CATR ThStf ThPor ODP Con	1 2 3 4 5	Yes No																	
8		AM PM	RN T MD Diet Rx PHL HSK CATR ThStf ThPor ODP Con	1 2 3 4 5	Yes No																	
9		AM PM	RN T MD Diet Rx PHL HSK CATR ThStf ThPor ODP Con	1 2 3 4 5	Yes No																	
10		AM PM	RN T MD Diet Rx PHL HSK CATR ThStf ThPor ODP Con	1 2 3 4 5	Yes No																	

Instructions:

1. Use a separate row for each entry or exit.
2. When known, check any contributing factor for each observation.
3. Emergency situations are EXCLUDED from the data collection process.

Calculate compliance for this sheet	Count of "Yes"		=		=
	Count of observations (rows used)				

Figure 9.1 Data collection sheet.

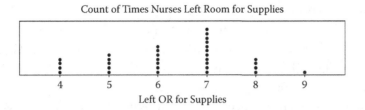

Figure 9.2   Chart of times nurses had to leave the OR for supplies.

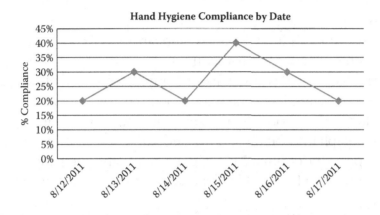

Figure 9.3   Hand hygiene compliance chart.

This chart is very effective in hand hygiene compliance because we count the times healthcare professionals washed compared to the number of times they should have washed. Figure 9.3 is an actual chart of hand hygiene. These data were collected before the hospital embarked on its hand hygiene compliance. The only chart the hospital had prior to this was compliance for the month. The chart in the past was shared only in monthly meetings and not on the floors or departments. Use the chart in Appendix 7 for your experiment.

Statistical Process Control Charting: Turning Data into Information

Another way to measure a process occurring every day is a statistical process control chart (SPC) (Figure 9.4). An SPC chart on hand hygiene compliance also alerts us to when compliance is significantly improving or worsening so we can celebrate or take action. We mentioned in the inventory case study how SPC highlighted the demand variation at our site and how little variation occurred when aggregating the total customer demand. We will learn how to use SPC in utilizing the 3Ms in Chapter 13. For now, just be familiar with how the same data can be shared. Managing to the measure is benefitted by charts such as these.

The average compliance is 0.62 or about 62%. Notice this chart has two other lines. The top line is an upper control limit. An upper control limit defines the upper range expected if the compliance continues as before. The lower control limit is the line marked "LCL." Statistically speaking, compliance for this data is not expected to be above the upper control limit or below the lower control limit. Seeing compliance above this line is improbable, but possible. The reason is that the lower control limit is based on what the compliance was in the past. If compliance goes below this line, this suggests something has changed beyond what is normal. Hand hygiene compliance lower than normal suggests exploring together and explaining the cause of compliance being so low. The same is true if compliance goes above the upper control limit. This is good news and the team should investigate to understand why hand hygiene is improving and ensure this change is sustained.

Peter Drucker (noted writer and management consultant) suggested that there are a few key methodological concepts adding value in charting.[4]

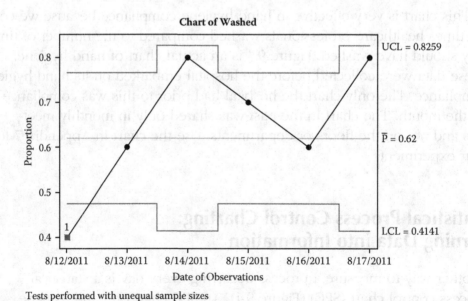

Figure 9.4 SPC chart of hand hygiene compliance using Minitab® software.

The key point is to transform data into information. Charts are a powerful method to show data as information. A control chart like the one shown in Figure 9.4 also shows fluctuations compared to what the process fluctuation is normally. Drucker added that the value of such displays of data is helpful. "As long as fluctuations stay within the normal distribution of probability … no action is taken. But the exception, which falls outside the accepted probability distribution, is information. It calls for action." There is no better method than SPC to show the fluctuations compared to normal fluctuations.

For your experiment, pick a time to observe people at times that represent what commonly happens. We can assume that the baseline time and then the times when you measure are similar with no other significant variable that may affect the behavior that you are measuring. Ideally, you can set a baseline and start experimenting all in the same session, but this is not necessary.

Now, create the chart to see if measuring has an effect. We created a chart for you. See Appendix 8.

Practice plotting the data as if you are observing, and scale the vertical axis for what you think the count or ratio will be. A good experimenter will make a prediction of the measure before actually observing. This is a good time to place wagers with those who are joining you in our experiment and have a little fun.

Sample Size

Determine a minimum time to observe. If you want to think in terms of sample size, here is a very important lesson all too often confused. Sampling is about representing the population. The sample size is about the confidence we have in estimating differences.

Some suggest that larger sample sizes better represent the population. I disagree. When we ask people to sample large numbers, the burden of data collection often results in them taking shortcuts to gathering the data to achieve the sample size. Sampling too many recently resulted in a hospital not getting the charts to the floor. The reason was it took so long to enter all the data that the team didn't have time to enter it. Maybe it would have been better to have less data to ensure charts are posted daily than to have no charts until much later while waiting on data entry. The desire for convenience overtakes the desire to represent the population across the variables that a sample should cover. I have seen people go to the biggest group, the biggest container, the highest volume time of day to get the largest sample in the least amount of time. Sample size gives us a level of confidence in our findings. There can be no shortcut to representing the population.

Hand Hygiene and the 3Ms

Recently our team began measuring hand hygiene on an inpatient unit. The observers were doing very well observing nurses, physicians, housekeepers, therapists, dietitians, and other healthcare professionals washing their hands. A ratio of 50% nurses, 3 to 10% were doctors, and a representative number of therapists were observed reflecting the balance of entries and exits to and from a patient's room by each caregiver. However, my team started having too much fun observing and wanted more observations. The last days of data showed a disproportionate number of nurses in the data. This particular unit had a well-trained nursing staff that washed at a rate above most hospitals due to its leader's coaching in its importance. The compliance rate started increasing only because the observations were not representing the rate at which each health-care professional was entering rooms.

Observe at the same time for the same amount of time on a day when the other variable that may affect what you are observing is usually a good practice. Do whatever makes sense to have the measurement be the only variable that changes between your baseline and when you start measuring.

Ready to Observe

You are just about ready to start observing. Make sure that there is an area to post your chart measure in full view of the person doing the task. It would be somewhat silly if the hand hygiene compliance was only shared off the floor with your Quality group and top leadership. (Oops, sorry if this is happening in your organization.) Think of this as yet another benefit of reading this book. No extra charge. Dr. W. Edwards Deming also promoted that the person performing a task should be allowed to know his or her quality and be his/her own inspector.[5] You may have a quick win if you are already measuring and posting the chart soon after the time of the data collection and the behaviors.

For a hand hygiene experiment, consider a dispenser on a stand immediately in front of the trays with an area to post a chart directly above the dispenser. These are readily available. Or, consider placing the dispenser on the wall with an area for the measure later.

Alternative Experiment

Replenishing paper in a copier is another good choice for experimenting. One way to fail is in those organizations where the copier is in a dark out-of-the-way place with walls already plastered with human resource mandatory postings on labor laws that no one ever reads. Make a data collection sheet and while you are at the copier, PLEASE refill it. Walk the talk!

Start observing. Plan your method of observation so you do not give away that you are measuring behavior. Now is probably a good time to share the story so often used in healthcare: the Hawthorne Effect.

The Hawthorne Effect

Between 1924 and 1933 at the Hawthorne Works outside of Chicago, experimenters gathered productivity data while changing the illumination level. The original researchers believed the changes in productivity were more a result of workers being studied than the changes in illumination. Therefore, the term *Hawthorne Effect* is used often to describe short-term improvements during observations that are not sustained after observation ceases. Hand hygiene compliance has increased initially during a healthcare organization's initiative only to revert to lower levels after observations have ceased. In our work on hand hygiene, we found that in the absence of an automated measurement system, the observation decreasing can correlate with a decrease in compliance. However, if the measurement from observation continues and is shared, compliance can be sustained. We did not observe compliance maintained when sharing the measurement ceased. Is a behavior changed and sustained because of just observation? Does it also need measurement? Or is the more important question, how can we maximize and sustain desired behavior change while minimizing both observation and measurement? Both are nonvalue-added to the patient and staff. The patient doesn't usually want to pay us to observe and record hand hygiene. But, that doesn't mean we should not do it. Some tasks are vital to support the value-added tasks, such as providing products and services. Although we prove the 3Ms are necessary to sustain gains in human controlled and variable processes, measurement is nonvalue-added and should be minimized as well.

I'll give you a solution. The design of a measurement system includes optimizing the measurement system for sustaining and improving behavior.

The study of reproducibility as a way of measuring the quality of the measurement system is the answer to knowing if the balance of observation with the 3Ms and sustained behavior has been achieved. Think of it this way: a department can earn the right to observe and measure itself in hand hygiene compliance when the hand hygiene compliance measured by the unit staff or physicians matches the compliance measured by a trained third party. Once the accuracy and precision has been reproduced, the amount of observation and measurement could be reduced. If the two groups measuring start to deviate, perform a measurement system analysis. The usual answer is to increase the observation and 3Ms until the desired accuracy and precision are reached again. This is also a good time to let the unit know what was learned and search for reasons and countermeasures to continue to decrease both observations and the 3Ms.

Desire to Increase Productivity

At the Hawthorne Works,[6] management wanted to increase productivity. The experiment was to be observed in real time by engineers and researchers and would record the productivity rate. Their experiment was to test if better lighting would increase productivity. The engineers began their baseline by going out to the factory floor and counting the production to calculate the productivity rate. The researchers noticed an improvement in productivity when the lights were brighter. Hmm, an increase in light increases productivity? Yes, they thought. Upon more observation, they wanted to validate that the lights levels would increase productivity. Therefore, they turned the lights back down to the original level. Lo and behold, productivity increased again. This was not what the engineers expected to happen. The conclusion from the experiment was that the variable that caused increases in productivity was the extra attention the workers were receiving by having the researchers out on the floor with them. Remember President Lincoln's practice of spending time with the troops in the field and how this experiment supports Lincoln's method. In Toyota and other facilities, they practice the same methods for similar reasons.

The Hawthorne Effect was born from this study. For years, we believed that productivity increases when workers are engaged and treated with respect. The Hawthorne Effect has been credited for changing from an autocratic "shut up and listen" culture to a true collaborative one in some healthcare organizations. In addition, productivity has gone up.

Utilizing the 3Ms by Changing the Measure

I can tell you firsthand how management interaction with employees in the process affects productivity. Around 1986, Alan Houser, Wayne Boatman, and I wanted to improve productivity in the plant where we worked. We had heard about how The Toyota Production System (TPS) and a Harley Davidson plant a few hours north of us had improved productivity and reduced inventory considerably by applying TPS. We started applying the concepts and found that they improved our quality and productivity. We did something else, though. We spent lots of time on the floor engaging workers in creating better flowing processes.

Bob Kayma and Ed Lechleiter were industrial engineers who helped lay out the first flow cells. They did something unheard of. They took teams of employees off the floor and out on the lawn to engage them in designing their own work area. We also had a big change for the workers that had us very anxious about resistance.

Incentive Piecework as a Measure

We knew that incentive piecework negatively affected quality. We needed to find a way to replace the piecework incentive with incentives that promoted quality and productivity. We tried autonomous work cells where employees were trained, engaged, enabled, and empowered to lead their small unit. Now, we had people helping each other by flexing to other stations, but the piecework incentive was not possible by individual. We had a dilemma. How do we equalize the pay for the extra value we were getting with these new methods? We sat down with the union and shared a lot of data and spoke to many workers. In the end, our experiment was to pay the team the average of what the group was earning on individual incentive. Naturally, some people lost take-home pay and some gained. We were surprised how little resistance we got.

Productivity went up to record highs despite eliminating incentive standards and without increasing total salary expense. We eventually eliminated the piecework incentive system. Many of the quality issues it caused by reinforcing only volume without regard to quality disappeared.

More on the Perverse Incentive Measure

Here is how perverse the incentive pay was. One person could make extra incentive pay by leaving out a few parts which allowed him to complete his task faster. Inspectors would later find the defects and then someone else would repair the devices, and they would be eligible for piecework incentive to repair the devices.

Measuring only good production versus total pieces leaving a bench also reinforced quality. Measuring only services and products that are valued is always the right thing to do.

Length of Stay is a widely used measurement in healthcare. For those that run hotels, it may seem quite odd that hospitals work to get their customers to leave. The simple reason is how hospitals are measured and paid. They are only paid for a certain number of days. It is in their financial interest, on the surface, to discharge patients. Some are learning now that the measure is reinforcing the wrong behavior if the standard is wrong. Hotels, on the other hand, work to increase length of stay because they are measured for room nights sold and get more revenue from customers for every day they stay.

How many times have we seen healthcare professionals focus on reducing length of stay (LOS) only to have readmissions increase? Watch what you measure; you may just get it. Isn't this the same issue we saw at the plant? Reinforce volume regardless of quality and one gets volume, regardless of quality. Reinforce turning beds, and one will get beds turned.

French Restaurant Dining

Dining in a French restaurant is an experience for first-time visitors from America. One will have a story about how leisurely and quiet and slow the experience is. What frustrates many Americans dining for the first time virtually anywhere in Europe is the experience of paying. You see, in Europe, your server will not deliver your check to you until you ask. In a restaurant in the United States, your server will often lay the check on your table before you finish your dessert. Servers are often annoyed when diners stay because they are measured on turning tables, and tips come from new diners, not diners sitting. In France and the United Kingdom, tips are truly optional because servers are usually paid for value delivered by the restaurant owner. Tips are often politely or rudely returned, in fact. We behave as we are measured.

The Hawthorne Effect Revisited

The end of the story at The Hawthorne Works is perhaps being rewritten. Someone claimed to have found the original data. The statistician reran the analysis and found a correlation with day of the week. Regardless, we will look at the role measuring productivity has on productivity.

Case Study in Timeliness in Sharing the Measure

How important is timing and frequency of sharing a measure? We found that in nearly every case, if you share the measure as frequently as the variation may occur, the faster the team can show improvement. Take, for example, the inventory case study. We went from monthly orders to multiple orders per day. The team on my shop floor could see orders as they came into the system. They then had much more planning time and could sequence their work with like products and save themselves wasted set-up time. Does a 20% improvement in hand hygiene compliance interest you? How about changing the culture in a large perioperative services unit in less than six months?

The 20% increase in hand hygiene compliance was appreciated at one of the world's finest hospitals, Cedars–Sinai in Los Angeles.[7] Jennifer Blaha is the master black belt (highly experienced performance improvement specialist) at Cedars–Sinai and wanted to see what the effect of simply increasing the frequency of posting hand hygiene compliance had on people's behavior. The unit was being observed daily, but the results were shared only monthly. The unit had achieved an increase in compliance, but had plateaued with a stable rate. The compliance was not increasing or decreasing. She began posting the hand hygiene charts in the unit weekly versus monthly, in addition to an elevator marketing campaign. Guess what happened to compliance? The rehab unit achieved and sustained a 20% increase in compliance.

Blaha also had begun posting the hand hygiene more frequently in another unit. While this unit also saw an immediate improvement in compliance, they were not able to sustain the performance. We wonder if the second M, Manage to the measure, might be needed. We will visit this again in the following chapters. Regardless, Cedars–Sinai went on to achieve record high hand hygiene compliance and has sustained these levels for over three years. Dr. Semmelweis would be very proud.

Key Points

- Utilizing the 3Ms goes hand-in-hand with being a change and process improvement leader.
- Charts are an effective way to share data and turn data into information.

- Simple charts can be all that is needed.
- There are more advanced control charts that give extra value to exploring and explaining and experimenting.
- Watch what you measure because you may get it. Perverse measures drive the wrong behavior.

Endnotes

1. Michael Porter and Robert Kaplan, How to Solve the Cost Crisis in Health Care, *Harvard Business Review* (September 2011).
2. http://www.qualityforum.org/Measuring_Performance/ABCs_of_Measurement. aspx
3. Western Electric History. Online at: http://www.porticus.org/bell/westernelectric _history.html#Western%20Electric%20-%20A%20Brief%20History
4. Peter F. Drucker, *Management Challenges for the 21st Century*. Copyright © 1999 by Peter F. Drucker. Reprinted by permission of HarperCollins Publishers. San Francisco: Jossey Bass Publishers, 1999).
5. Cedars–Sinai Medical Center, *Case Study of Hand Hygiene*. (Los Angeles: Cedars–Sinai Medical Center). With permission.

Chapter 10

What to Measure

Change Leaders, we know, have created a vision. They also have determined a way of measuring when the vision is achieved. This is an outcome measure relevant to the outcome desired from the change. Dr. W. Edwards Deming found that to achieve certain outcomes, especially those that occur infrequently or far in the future, it is useful and often necessary to measure the inputs. These inputs are the ones that need to change to achieve the outcome desired. Examples in every industry abound.

Hidden Factory of Rework and Swiss Cheese

Dr. Deming and James Reason help us know what to measure in process improvement. Dr. Deming coached process improvement leaders to measure the inputs to a process to achieve the outcome desired. A graphic may help you understand. We will use wrong-site surgery (WSS) and we use this frequently to achieve an understanding of why measuring the process is key to changing an outcome (Figure 10.1 to Figure 10.4).[1]

Eliminating WSSs is one of the best examples of needing to measure the process inputs that vary or may even go wrong. Fortunately, WSSs don't occur frequently enough to observe them. It is not practical to use the frequency of their occurrence to assess if changes have been successful in reducing surgeries that go terribly wrong. Even though WSSs are one of the top three most frequently reported sentinel events to The Joint Commission, some healthcare organizations have never had one. The Joint Commission creates standards for healthcare organizations and accredits them to receive reimbursement for Medicare and Medicaid.

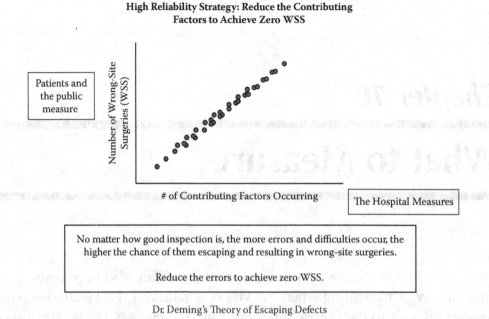

High Reliability Strategy: Reduce the Contributing Factors to Achieve Zero WSS

Patients and the public measure

The Hospital Measures

No matter how good inspection is, the more errors and difficulties occur, the higher the chance of them escaping and resulting in wrong-site surgeries.

Reduce the errors to achieve zero WSS.

Dr. Deming's Theory of Escaping Defects

Figure 10.1 Theory of escaping defects (Dr. W. Edwards Deming).

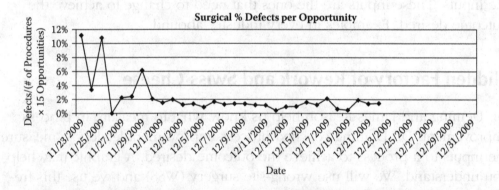

Figure 10.2 Chart of reduction in defects in surgical processes.

How do you lead a team to enact changes when the changes may never be seen in the outcome measure? Change the inputs. In Six Sigma, an equation often used describes what Dr. Deming did to improve the quality and safety in many different industries.

$$Y = f(x_1, x_2, x_3, \dots x_n)$$

where: Y is the outcome and the xs are inputs. The equation reads as: Y is a function of the xs. This equation is then used to teach teams that an output

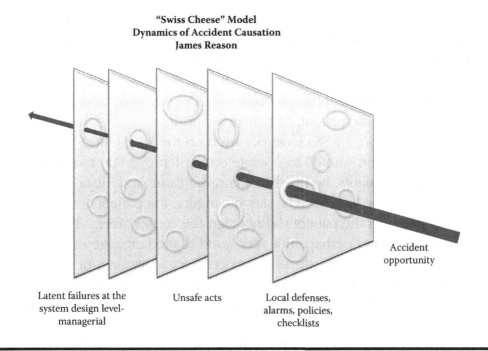

Figure 10.3   James Reason's Swiss cheese model of escaping defects.[1]

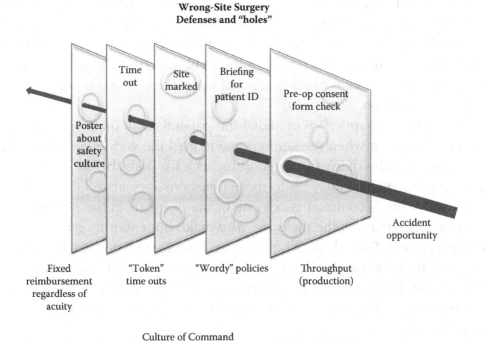

Figure 10.4   Swiss cheese model for WSS.

and outcome are a function of the inputs in the process that creates the outcome. In eliminating WSSs, we look at the processes from the physician's first decision to perform surgery until the last procedure in the OR has been completed. The *Y* is a successful correct site surgery. The inputs include the consent form (to document the procedure, site, and patient, and are signed by the surgeon and the patient, or patient advocate).

What can go wrong? WSSs have occurred on the wrong body part. In one case, the surgeon wanted to operate on the left eye. After seeing a number of other patients, he filled in a consent form, and mistakenly wrote the right eye, not the left eye. The day of surgery, the patient arrives and the hospital staff notices the patient did not sign the consent form. The patient, nervous, anxious, and perhaps not very good in the language of the form, signs as one signs the many documents necessary in signing for a mortgage. The surgeon may meet with the patient or not. Many hospitals don't require this premeeting. This patient may be one of eight patients he is operating on that day.

The surgeon may or may not read the consent form before he leaves to scrub. (Some surgeons mark the site for the procedure, some don't mark at all, and some patients have been told to mark themselves, causing confusion for all. In fact, a very popular talk show host jokingly suggested to patients that they should mark where the surgeon should not operate.) The OR team prepares the right eye based on the consent form and the surgeon walks in to the OR, performs the procedure on the right eye—the wrong eye—and leaves. The patient wakes in recovery and is shocked to find that the wrong eye was operated on.

How could this happen? Why didn't the patient speak up when signing the consent form or when the surgeon mentioned the wrong eye during the premeeting? Or why didn't the surgeon recheck his notes before performing the procedure? The answers to these questions vary across the WSSs we studied. What is common is not one of the hospitals in the system was measuring, managing to the measure, *and* making it easier to get the consent form correct. Even those who measured errors on the consent form, none were found to be sharing the measure frequently and managing to it. Fortunately, this is changing quickly. Again, the science of operating on the correct site is there, but the human element created the variability and wrong outcome.

Getting Started: Preparing for Change, Chartering, and Stakeholder Analysis (SHA)

Case Study: 3Ms Improving Surgical Safety

We have been measuring WSSs for a long time, and little has changed, despite the checklists and accrediting bodies with "Speak Up" campaigns. No one intends to do harm, but mistakes still happen. Success has been made, though, at Lifespan, Rhode Island's major healthcare system whose teams applied the 3Ms for process improvement.[2]

Dr. Mary Reich Cooper, senior vice president and chief quality officer at Lifespan and sponsor of our work, reports zero WSS since implementing the changes. The system had five wrong patient/site/procedure events in 2007 through 2009, according to Dr. Cooper. The team at Rhode Island Hospital (RIH) included Diane Skorupski, director of OR, Dr. Ed Marcaccio, Dr. William Cioffi, and every manager and staff person. RIH is the largest hospital in the state and a Trauma 1 hospital with over 25 operating rooms. My teammates were an OB-GYN physician, Dr. Erin Dupree, who is trained as a Lean Six Sigma green belt, and Kate Ranft, who was trained in change management and has a PhD in English. We worked with three Lifespan hospitals and researched everything we could find on WSS. We thank the states of Pennsylvania and Minnesota that had provided public information on occurrences of WSS.

The project at Lifespan was in a highly charged environment—leading change to reduce the risk of wrong patient and site surgery across the system. The stakeholder analysis template guided us in indentifying all stakeholders, prioritizing where resistance may occur, and developing strategies to engage stakeholders and manage resistance.

The Measure Is Invented

We started with measuring the number of WSSs, which included wrong patient surgeries that also had occurred. We found no measures currently in place. No one expected a chart measuring the number of WSSs. To Dr. Deming's point, measuring an infrequent outcome like WSS is not very useful. We dug deeper for other measures that might correlate with the errors in the past. We went to look for evidence of audits that might have recorded relevant measures. We held focus groups to learn the level of awareness of the staff and physicians in measures that might hint at issues. We not only did not find any measures, few of the staff remembers anyone gathering any information relative to WSSs. In fact, we found no ongoing measures within the hospitals of anything to do with quality and safety.

Let me be clear about Lifespan's measure compared to most hospitals and ambulatory surgical centers where I have worked. They are statistically no worse than many other healthcare organizations based on the number of procedures they performed. And, few others are measuring what we started measuring in Lifespan in 2009, the last WSS that Lifespan has had. I knew then that we could make a big difference in this very rare, but inexcusable, mistake. We use this case and their significant success in changing a culture and eliminating errors to learn process improvement's 3Ms: Measure, Manage to the measure, and Make it easier.

Measuring the Errors to Reduce the Risk of Wrong-Site Surgery

We had to find the defects along the way that may slip through defenses some day and result in a WSS. It is not one defect that causes these events. Often an interaction between two defects results in an error. We thought if we could apply Dr. Deming's methods to measure the defects, we would reduce the number of defective units, surgeries in this project.

Healthcare, like many organizations today, is complex. Complexity can be described by how many people, variables, environments, regulations, and reliability issues are present in the system. We had to find a way to focus on the vital few, or fewer in this complexity, and start measuring those inputs. A Failure Mode and Effects Criticality Analysis gave us the method to filter down to the vital variables to measure defects.

We found about 14 variables and some of these may seem quite trivial to those who are not involved with perioperative processes. In studying WSS, we saw that site marking, consent forms, and the energy it took to get staff and physicians to concentrate during the "time out" that should occur immediately before "knife to skin" are some of the 14. A time out is a method to get everyone to focus and inspect the site, side, patient, and other variables. It is the last chance to prevent an error. We created a data collection sheet to record the occurrence *and* quality of these variables. What we mean by quality is best described using an example.

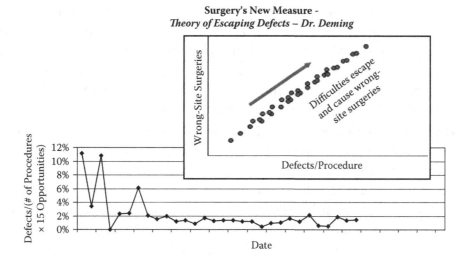

Figure 10.5   Surgery's new measure.

Culture is hard to measure, but we can measure behaviors. Is the culture in the OR conducive to people helping each other prevent defects? I have witnessed time outs done by a nurse in the corner and no one is paying any attention. At Lifespan, they got so mindful during time outs, they actually physically pointed and touched the site, just like two pilots who point and touch the dial to adjust altitude to ensure they are really concentrating on what they intend to do. Getting back to what we mean by the quality of an action, Lifespan would measure how many calls it took to get something to occur, such as a time out versus whether the action occurred or not. See the degree of difference? This gave Lifespan much more power in analyzing and improving.

We now chart in hospitals and ambulatory surgical centers similar charts like the one in Figure 10.5. Although not Lifespan data, this reflects the significant reduction in errors and defects possible. Measuring the defects and managing to them is exactly what Dr. Deming intended. Lifespan is leading the way in surgical process improvement to reduce the probability of a WSS.

Measuring the Quality of a Decision

At another health system, a process improvement team needed to correct poor decisions in assessing the risk of a patient falling. Some hospitals today have a "no restraint" policy. Restraints have been used for patients who may injure themselves getting out of bed. Hospitals with a no-restraint policy may provide one-on-one staffing to monitor the patient. If they cannot assess the fall risk well, they may not provide the staffing, which could result in a fall, or they may be wasting resources providing one-on-one staffing. Measuring the quality of judgment is yet another reason to utilize the 3Ms. We will cover how to measure judgment in Chapter 12.

In his book, *Essence of Decision*,[3] Graham T. Allison relates the problem in the quality of a decision when the leader is surrounded by "yes men." Leaders benefit from advisors who will voice disagreement, as was the case in the Cuban Missile Crisis. Allison questions if Khrushchev's advisors did not disagree with his decision to place a nuclear missile so close to the United States knowing the risk during the Cold War of a nuclear crisis. In healthcare, patients want to trust the surgeon and are in a very strange environment, and often don't voice disagreement. We will come back to how process improvement teams can improve the culture where people are comfortable in challenging others, even charismatic leaders who may have the authority to fire. There are solutions, and the 3Ms guide teams and leadership in improving cultures as well as processes and outcomes.

Practicing Measuring

Let's practice measuring an outcome that is easier to measure and see the effect from changes you will make. Pick an outcome that you can measure frequently in a day and which provides an opportunity of seeing the tasks that lead up to the outcome. Some ideas include the time it takes getting visitors to where they want to go. The outcome is getting them to the correct place in your building or via the phone the first time with no wrong turns or mistakes. Another metric might be arrival in the least amount of time given the pace the visitor wants to travel. A good outcome metric in this last scenario might be the seconds elapsed from the time the person needs help until the person is where she wants to be. Note that the time is when the visitor first needs help, not when we recognize we need to help. Outcome metrics should be customer-centric, not business-centric. Tasks along the way may start with recognizing that someone needs assistance.

Staff in hotels, Disney properties, and hospitals seems to do this better than just about anyone else, I think. I see housekeepers, nurses, receptionists, volunteers, and executives stopping whatever they are doing to help a visitor navigate an often confusing path to where he or she wants to go. I have seen CEOs speaking with other executives stop dead in their tracks to help someone with directions. Other tasks can be pointing out the signage, contacting others by phone, writing directions, etc.

Setup

Set up a table to record the outcome metric and input metrics each time a visitor needs help. Record the data in a reasonable increment. For the scenario above, minutes might not be granular enough to see changes. Time can be aggregated up, so maybe start with measuring any time metric in seconds. Another metric might be whether an error in direction is made. A count of errors gives us both a time and a defect metric. Let's keep this first practice simple and record the number of wrong turns or mistakes the visitor makes in getting to the destination and the errors in giving direction and signage that was not understood by the visitor. A simple interview with the visitor usually works to get this data without being too obtrusive. The visitors may actually be impressed with your effort to improve what we have all needed—getting directions in your building or neighborhood. I even have trouble finding the way out of my family physician's office treatment room area. See Figure 10.6 for a data collection tool. I include a larger one in Appendix 8 for your convenience.

Visitor (Remember patient confidentiality rules, so use something like a number or destination)	*Outcome metric: Number of wrong turns in getting to the destination*	*Errors in giving direction (count the times that you change your instruction, regardless of reason)*	*Signage: Missing, wrong, confusing, too many signs, blocked*	*Visitor taking a wrong turn (turning differently than the directions that you gave or the signage directs)*
1	4	2	1	3
2	1	0	3	1
3				
4				
5				

Figure 10.6   Data collection for directions.

After recording your data on a reasonable number of events and probably discovering some other "opportunities" to improve during this little exercise, analyze the outcome and input metric data.

- Total the count of input errors for each visitor assisted.
- Compare the number of errors for outcomes when the visitor reached the destination correctly the first time with the number of errors made when the visitor did not reach the destination so well.
- Do you see more errors for the bad outcomes? This simple exercise illustrates the Theory of Escaping Defects. What if we would have had no input errors? The outcome is self-evident, of course, but even reducing the errors getting the visitor to the destination increases the probability that the visitor will reach the destination correctly the first time.

Any quick wins? Just by measuring, we often get some great ideas in what to improve. Perhaps a sign would be a little clearer? Or a map in your pocket to give to visitors or to help you give directions? Measuring has so many benefits to process improvement. Why does anyone resist it?

Please share your experiment with me at www.rpmexec.com, and I will share with others, giving you credit. We can keep it confidential, if you prefer. Regardless, I hope you see the difference in measuring inputs and outcomes and how reducing the errors in the inputs can have a favorable effect on outcomes.

A Change In One Area May Affect Other Areas

We need to be aware that measuring several outcomes may be necessary, depending on the project. An improvement in one area seldom occurs in a vacuum. It may have an effect elsewhere. Therefore, we need to consider measuring the outcome we expect to change and outcomes that may change because of changes made. We need a counterbalancing metric when a singular focus on one metric may result in an unfavorable change in another metric. A balance is needed. In an Agency for Healthcare Research and Quality (AHRQ) study of High Reliability Organizations,[4] the following statement was made:

"Anything can be measured and measures can be quite simple, but sometimes multiple measures are essential to track system performance."

Inventory Management

Inventory management is an example of when we may need to measure two or more outcomes. Organizations often experience waste when supplies run out. In one hospital, a person had to leave the OR an average of seven times per patient case to get something outside the OR. Sometimes the most common supply, such as saline to irrigate an incision site, is in short supply. We often find that someone was charged with reducing inventory, which is quite easy. The outcome is easy to measure, too, and is usually the amount of money in inventory.

In inventory reduction projects, I have seen people go after the big dollars with arbitrary goals, such as to reduce the amount of inventory dollars by 50%. The team may have looked at the items with the most dollars in inventory and translated the goal to be a 50% reduction in count to get to the 50% reduction in dollars, euros, pounds, or whatever the currency is. The team identifies an item and then cuts the inventory in half. You know that there is something missing here. One should measure how many are needed and at least another variable, the responsiveness of the supplier to replenish, before changing the amount in inventory. So, here we have four measures at a minimum:

■ Inventory investment (count, and maybe currency)
■ Demand quantity
■ Frequency of replenishment
■ Time to replenish

Did you think of another critical metric? Outcome metrics should be customer-centric. Does a patient really care how many pounds of saline are on the shelf? What do patients care about? That the OR team has the saline when they need it. Thus, we have a "balancing" outcome metric that process improvement leaders who are successful often measure. Service level *and* inventory reduction should always be measured together. These are classic balancing outcome metrics that process improvement teams need to understand and are confident enough to use. Sometimes resistance will come based on the measures. Not all of them will be politically correct, but that doesn't mean you should completely ignore the metric. The number of times a surgeon is late for a case is a sensitive metric. A good process improvement leader can minimize the resistance to get the measurement working for the organization.

Measure What the Customer Measures

A good rule of thumb is to measure whatever your customer measures. Resistance will come soon and strong if the measure you are using in process improvement is not appreciated by the stakeholders. As much as I respect a physician I worked with, he and I continue to have different views of what to measure in surgical safety. He wanted to measure the number of surgical cases (a case is defined as all procedures performed in a single trip to the OR) that had zero slips, lapses, and mistakes. I wanted to measure and share with the client the number of slips, lapses, and mistakes. I could estimate the average number of cases with zero defects by dividing the number of slips, lapses, and mistakes by the number of cases. We both knew that this was not precise because a large number of defects in any one case results in the average number of zero defect cases being lower than actual.

Calculating the number of cases with zero defects takes a lot more effort in recording because we have to record all defects for each case versus simply measuring the number of defects for the day, or whatever period is used to chart the defects. This goes back to the issue of not getting a measure for hand hygiene from the hospital that collected lots and lots of observations because we did not make it easy enough to measure. My other argument for not focusing so much on the number of zero defect cases is an argument of customer-centricity. I don't think a patient values as much a metric about how many defect-free cases the surgery center has had. He cares that there are no errors, or zero defects along the way. It would be foolish to expect inspection to catch all errors.

I would think of James Reason's Swiss cheese model when I am going in for surgery because I don't trust the defenses, knowing defects happen. And, the type of defect means a lot to me, if not more than the number. I will choose a surgeon who has forgotten to wait until everyone is silent when he is doing a time out over a surgeon who has marked the wrong incision site.

Base the Measure on Correlation with the Outcome

What we measure should be based on importance to the outcome. This is the key point to customers as well as teams. The energy to reduce resistance also can be better applied by the leader if the importance to the outcome of each metric is estimated. If I am getting resistance on how to measure something that we think might be important, that is one thing. But if I am getting resistance in measuring a primary function, I am willing to devote more energy to reducing that resistance.

Now is a good time to add another benefit of the 3Ms, specifically, Make it easier. I hinted at this benefit earlier when I discussed trying to measure defective cases and how hard it is to collect the data to calculate the percent of defective cases. Make it easier to measure, for if measuring is too difficult, the person leading the team and team members will meet with much resistance. How many times is measurement not achieved because the resistance to the effort to measure is the argument? In Chapter 11 on how to measure, we will make it as easy as we can to measure. Just because something we know is important to measure is hard to measure, this doesn't mean we shouldn't measure it. Mike Fenger, formerly the Chief Quality Officer and my boss at Motorola, taught us all that even though it may be hard to measure, keep trying to find a way. Dr. Deming acknowledges numerous times that what is most important may not be measurable. That doesn't mean it is not important. And, it doesn't mean the leader is off the hook to measure. We must find a way to measure.

High Reliability Organizations: What Do They Measure?

Zero failures reaching the customer are one measure. We'll share more after some definitions. Executives are talking a lot about High Reliability Organizations (HROs). Everyone seems to want to become one, whatever they think HROs are. I think healthcare should become an HRO, too. So, what is an HRO? What do they measure? What can a process improvement leader do to help his/her organization become an HRO?

Let's give credit to authors who have studied companies and industries that many refer to as HROs. My favorites are James Reason, Karl Weick, Kathleen Sutcliffe, the Orladys, David Marx, to name a few. We would be remiss for not mentioning Dr. Deming, Dr. Shewhart, Sakichi Toyoda, Taiichi Ohno, and companies; and SKF, a Swedish manufacturer that pioneered many of the concepts HROs practice today. Let me add the U.S. Navy and United Airlines, which has not had a pilot-caused error fatality since 1978. United Airlines pioneered the team-building technique named Crew Resource Management (CRM) in the aviation industry.

Weick and Sutcliffe[5] believe HROs are mindful of variation occurring and ways failures occur and, thus, are more able to prevent accidents than those who are not mindful. They find five key elements of being mindful. Using healthcare examples, they include:

Sensitivity to operations. Preserving constant awareness by leaders and staff of the state of the systems and processes that affect patient care. This awareness is key to noting risks and preventing them.

Reluctance to simplify. Simple processes are good, but simplistic explanations for why things work or fail are risky. Avoiding overly simple explanations of failure (unqualified staff, inadequate training, communication failure, etc.) is essential in order to understand the true reasons people are placed at risk.

Preoccupation with failure. When near misses occur, these are viewed as evidence of systems that should be improved to reduce potential harm to patients. Rather than viewing near hits as proof that the system has effective safeguards, they are viewed as symptomatic of areas in need of more attention.

Deference to expertise. If leaders and supervisors are not willing to listen and respond to the insights of staff who know how processes really work and the risks patients really face, you will not have a culture in which high reliability is possible.

Resilience. Leaders and staff need to be trained and prepared to know how to respond when system failures do occur.

Should we measure the organization's mindfulness if it is that important? How do we measure mindfulness? Should we measure the five elements and consider mindfulness an outcome to a greater outcome, which is safety? Do HROs measure the elements?

In our reliability and safety work we definitely measure the five elements. Role playing, "war games," and other exercises help us become more mindful, and practice is important. Pilots spend a lot of time in flight simulators experiencing errors and defects for a couple of reasons: (1) they learn how to counter the issue, and (2) they become more mindful of the issue.

Measuring these specific considerations, general orientation, impact on processes, and ultimate outcome is what Dr. Deming intended as his theory of Escaping Defects. We can use the $Y = f(x)$ equation again. Exceptionally safe, consistently high quality of care = f(specific considerations, general orientation, impact on processes). If you want it, measure it.

Note: For use in this book, suffice it to say a process improvement leader will do well measuring these if charged with leading his/her organization to become an HRO.

Many of the specific initiatives described below include descriptions of how progress was measured over time.

A Safety Culture and How to Measure

The aviation industry has its HROs. Even though lives have been lost, the volume, complexity, and uncontrollable factors, including weather, make air travel arguably safer than most other modes of transportation. The culture in HROs is a "safety culture." Reason, in his book, *Managing the Risks of Organizational Accidents,*[1] shares what a safety culture is and its four critical subcomponents:

- A reporting culture
- A just culture
- A flexible culture
- A learning culture

The interaction of these four subcomponents equates with the term "safety culture."

I don't know how to measure culture, but I have measured the behaviors in reporting, judging, and coaching, flexing with variables that occur prior to failures, and behaviors of instructing and coaching. These cultures are pervasive in HROs. These behaviors are seen in HROs every second of the day. The people in HROs behave this way regardless if someone is watching. They manage to the measure. Any behavior that is not safe is managed. That is Managing to the measure. HROs also make reliability easier and easier as they get more reliable. An HRO is a continuous improvement organization at its highest level of meaning.

Measuring the Inputs versus Just the Outcomes

Reason finds that measuring the intrinsic safety of a system is not best done measuring outcome data. A better method is to measure the process. As in our work in reducing WSSs and catastrophic failures in vehicles where the events rarely occur, outcome data is an unreliable method because it is too late and too infrequent. As Dr. Deming shared, the way to prevent bad outcomes is to measure the process variables that correlate with outcomes. Control these variables, and one controls the outcomes. Think of these as the vital signs. Vital signs are those measures that can predict health. Improving the vital signs improves the outcome.

An outcome desired by many improvements, regardless of industry, is financial gain. Notice that the financial metric follows the outcome and process metrics. These efforts and measures all have an impact that can be translated into money. For instance, reducing medical errors saves the patient time and money and, sometimes, her or his life. Reducing this most common error also reduces the healthcare organization's costs, and may even save its existence when the cost of litigation and lost revenue is too great for the organization to survive.

Therefore, a leader's greatest convincing argument is often to translate improvements in process metrics and outcomes into financial impact. A leader is wise to always consider financial impact, even if she decides later not to mention financial impact. A leader may actually increase resistance if he tries to use money saved as the reason to reduce errors in surgery. Others may be so enraged by mentioning financial impact when the true purpose of the change is to protect patients and staff, they may rebel and not even start the change process.

In many changes, the financial impact is a leader's tool and he/she should use it. The cost of healthcare today is one of the biggest issues in America, the United Kingdom, and across the globe. We have to change to something different because we can't continue to go deeper into debt and receive the same amount of care. Presidential candidates have used healthcare's financial implications as a reason for change.

Measuring the Culture

I have never found a means to measure culture directly. But we have successfully measured behaviors in the OR and relevant behaviors before and after surgery. Those behaviors were measured for every case and every procedure within the case, and immediate feedback was given by many to correct the behaviors before they resulted in failures.

There are stories of surgeons becoming angry and throwing knives. I have never witnessed such an event, but I have heard from many experienced and reputable surgical team members that these events have occurred. I have also heard that little, in fact nothing, had been done to address these behaviors in the past in some institutions. These are the same institutions where no measurement or recording of the event probably took place. To change to a culture of safety, we decided to measure the four subcomponents of a Safety Culture.

The WHO (World Health Organization) Surgical Safety Checklist[6] is a valiant attempt to reduce the risk of error in surgery. There are three process steps measured in the checklist.

- The "sign in" step includes measuring if the patient and the surgeon are in agreement on the surgery to be performed and if the staff is aware of possible risks, such as allergies to medicines.
- The "time out" step is arguably the most important step to measure in the prevention of wrong patient, wrong site, and wrong procedure. The behaviors expected inside the OR are often predictable during the time out. The time out's purpose is ensuring the team, the correct patient, procedure, and site are known before the surgeon makes the incision or entry. If the culture is one of teamwork, the time out will have all members paying attention during this very quick, but very effective minute spent.

  If the culture is one of top-down, authoritative, and limited value of teamwork, the time out may not even occur. A circulating nurse may be responsible to ensure the surgeon performs the time out and this nurse may be berated for reminding the surgeon to perform the time out. I have seen in even the finest hospitals a surgeon totally dismiss doing the time out while the circulating nurse goes through the motion of a time out in the corner of the OR. Measure these behaviors, and manage to these measures, and make it easier for the surgical team to perform the time out correctly, and wrong-site surgery can be eliminated. Rhode Island hospitals have not had a WSS since enacting a checklist that not only measures if the time out was done, but how well everyone behaved during the time out. If the surgeon required several prompts by the staff to do the time out, these prompts were measured, charted, shared with leadership, and addressed with the surgeon.
- Debriefing: A powerful communication and learning step. The military will debrief after war games and battle to become more mindful and improve.

Total Quality Measurement System for Perioperative Process. Preop and OR Critical-To-Quality Factors

Preop site mark (surgeon's initials) on or as close as anatomically possible to the surgical site upon arrival in OR
Surgeon-initiated time out independently without prompt
Surgeon initiated time out after prompt from a team member
Surgeon initiated time out after more than one prompt from a team member
Surgeon refused to do the time out after prompt
Surgeon refused to do the time out after prompt and the situation was escalated up the chain of command
Did not initiate a time out and was not prompted by a team member
Team members ceased conversation independently without prompt
Team ceased after prompt by a team member
Team ceased after more than one prompt from a team member

Figure 10.7   Measuring behaviors to measure the culture.

The checklist and job aids created for each role on the surgical team made it easier to do the right thing. An example of how to measure behaviors in seen in Figure 10.7. The desired behavior is listed first. Subsequent rows show an increasing degree of undesired behaviors. The mildest nonconformance usually is that the behavior is missing initially, such as the surgeon initiating the time out, but begun after one prompt by a team member. The most severe behavior is refusal to do the behavior and no member prompting the behavior. No one speaking up is considered worse than the responsible person refusing, despite a team member reminding the person. The reason is that besides the responsible person refusing, the reporting culture, as mentioned by Reason as practiced by HROs, is also missing.

A National Transportation Safety Board (NTSB) presentation includes this quote from the Honorable Jim Hall, former Chairman of the NTSB[7]: "We've found through 30 years of accident investigation that sometimes the most common link is the attitude of corporate leadership toward safety."

We used data from past failures across U.S. hospitals that publicly reported to reduce the resistance to change. The NTSB also considers a corporate culture to be triggered at the top of an organization and measured at the bottom.

President Franklin D. Roosevelt's First Inaugural Address

The only thing we have to fear is fear itself.

Franklin D. Roosevelt[8]

Leaders recognize the fear of change and address it head on. Franklin D. Roosevelt in his inaugural address before he took the oath of office as president of the United States during the depths of the Great Depression (1933) spoke this famous line often quoted by process improvement leaders: "So, first of all, let me assert my firm belief that the only thing we have to fear is fear itself—nameless, unreasoning, unjustified terror which paralyzes needed efforts to convert retreat into advance." How many times have you found resistance to change when those resisting don't even know the reason for their fears? Or, their information is false?

FDR goes on: "In every dark hour of our national life, a leadership of frankness and vigor has met with that understanding and support of the people themselves, which is essential to victory. I am convinced that you will again give that support to leadership in these critical days." Again, we repeat the need for process improvement team leaders to be frank with the people, and the people will understand and lend support to the changes necessary. "If they know what I know, they will feel like I feel, and they will do as I do." FDR continues, "With this pledge taken, I assume unhesitatingly the leadership of this great army of our people dedicated to a disciplined attack upon our common problems. This Nation asks for action, and action now." A process improvement leader informs his/her "army," engages her stakeholders, acts, and acts now, not later.

So, how do we measure risk that leads us to realize fear, and reduce the very fear that creates the resistance to change, and especially the paralyzing fear of change? The next chapter answers that question.

Key Points

- Measure the input variables, the xs, to improve the outcome.
- Balance measures to achieve the right change, not to sacrifice one outcome for another.
- Measure the five elements of mindfulness and manage to the measure.

■ High Reliability Organizations measure and operate on mindfulness and measure and manage to the behaviors that are safe.
■ Making it easier to be mindful and build a safety culture is key to achieving a safety culture.

Endnotes

1. James Reason, *Managing the Risks of Organizational Accidents.* (London: Ashgate, Publishing Limited, 1997). Printed with permission. Mary Reich Cooper, M.D., Lifespun.
2. Used with permission, Lifespan, Dr. Mary Reich-Cooper.
3. Graham Allison, *Essence of Decision: Explaining the Cuban Missile Crisis,* 1st ed. (New York: Little Brown, 1971).
4. AHRQ, *Becoming a High Reliability Organization: Operational Advice for Hospital Leaders.* Online at: http://www.ahrq.gov/qual/hroadvice/hroadvice.pdf
5. Karl E. Weick and Kathleen M. Sutcliffe, *Managing the Unexpected Resilient Performance in an Age of Uncertainty.* (New York: John Wiley & Sons, Inc., 2007). Printed with permission of John Wiley & Sons, Inc.
6. http://www.who.int/patientsafety/safesurgery/ss_checklist/en/
7. http://www.ntsb.gov/doclib/speeches/sumwalt/SCEG_pre.pdf
8. http://historymatters.gmu.edu/d/5057/

Chapter 11

Measure Risk to Achieve High Reliability

High Reliability Organizations (HROs) measure risk. Then, they prioritize the risks and act to prevent failure. The tool they use is aptly named, Failure Mode, Effect, and Criticality Analysis (FMECA). FMECA was originally documented in 1949 by the U.S. military. (FMECA can be found in MIL Spec MIL-P-1629.)[1]

Measuring Risk

Resistance can come from fear. Fear may come from what the change brings to the person resisting, to the future, to the organization, to the patient or customer, or to any other stakeholder.

The National Transportation Safety Board's vice chairman, Robert L. Sumwalt, summarized the NTSB's findings in over 30 years of accident investigations. *"The safest carriers have more effectively committed themselves to controlling the risks that may arise from mechanical or organizational failures, environmental conditions, and human error."*[2]

FMECA is a reliability evaluation technique to determine and measure the effect of system and equipment failures. Although the FMECA is an essential reliability task, it also provides information for other purposes. The use of the FMECA is called for in maintainability, safety analysis, survivability and vulnerability, logistics support analysis, maintenance plan analysis, and for failure detection and isolation subsystem design. This coincident use must be a consideration in planning the FMECA effort to prevent the proliferation of requirements and the duplication of efforts within the same contractual program. These failures were classified according to their impact on mission success and personnel/equipment safety.

There are two steps to a FMECA:

■ Failure mode and effects analysis (FMEA)
■ Criticality analysis (CA)

We will concentrate on the FMEA because it is one of the first tools in designing a process or product and the foundation of FMECA. The FMEA's purpose is to measure risk, prioritize that risk, and then prevent failure with an action plan and control plan. FMEA is a process improvement team's tool to engage the stakeholders in the change. FMEA is the culmination of the thoughts of the stakeholders and subject matter experts of how a system can fail the effects of those failures, and the priorities in making the changes. FMEA is also a leader's tool to improve a change and the change process. Stakeholders engaged in completing the FMEA may well discover potential failures in the change. The FMEA is assisting the leader and the stakeholders to reduce the potential failures in the change.

The FMEA Form

Look at the FMEA form in Figure 11.1. The form is well known in HROs and virtually every company in the auto industry, aviation, aerospace, electrical safety, nuclear, as well as many other industries. I will explain FMEA and how it measures risk and prioritizes risk by explaining each column of the FMEA form. FMEA is a measurement tool for change. Measuring outcomes and inputs are easy in the FMEA. Notice the column for the input. This FMEA form makes it easier for you and your team to connect how the inputs and outcomes are related. Not every FMEA has a column for the input, and there are variations to FMEAs, but this FMEA form will look familiar to anyone who has used FMEA in healthcare, automotive, aviation, NASA, and the nuclear industry. Not listing the inputs misses a chance to "connect the dots" of inputs failing and resulting in poor effects (outcomes). We have clearly identified the connectivity of inputs to the possible outcomes via each row on the Excel® file.

Failure Mode and Effects Analysis

System or process name:				Process Owner Name:				Prepared by:			
Core team member				Date latest version:				FMEA Date (Orig)			
Process Step or Function	Input	Potential Failure Mode	Potential Effect(s) of Failure	S E V	Potential Contributing Factors to Failure	O C C	Current Process Controls Prevention	Current Process Controls Detection	D E T	R P N	
Include step from Process Map in all rows for sorting	Include input from Process Map in all rows for sorting	Failure symptom evidence in the output	Impact on the customer requirements	How severe is the effect to the customer?	Causes to input failure. Add row for each cause within step/input	How often does cause or FM occur?	Existing controls that prevent the cause or the Failure Mode	Existing controls that detect the cause or the Failure Mode before defects escape	How well can you detect cause or FM?	Risk Priority #	
1											
2											
3											
4											
5											
6											
7											
8											
9											
10											
11											
12											
13											
14											
15											
16											
17											
18											
19											

Figure 11.1 The FMEA (failure mode and effects analysis) form.

The Process Step or Design Function

The FMEA begins by identifying a system and then subsystems listed in the header. The perioperative process in healthcare could be such a system with intraoperative processes as a subsystem. Within the process are steps. In a design effort, the process step column converts to a function of the design. A piece of imaging equipment has one primary function and that is to develop an image. We will stay with the example of perioperative services to explain the FMEA process and form. I will use an input that was a contributing factor in 60% of the wrong-site surgeries (WSS) we studied—site marking. Site marking is to identify on the patient where the incision is to be made.

Input, Failure Modes, Effects, Causes, and Scoring of Risk

The next column lists the inputs to the process. In our example, we will consider site marking as a critical input to preventing an incision in the wrong area. We list "failure modes" in the next column. A failure mode is how a failure of the input is evidenced. A common failure mode for site marking is not marking the site. It is important to list all failure modes for each input. Another failure mode for site marking is marking the wrong limb. The failure effect is the outcome that goes wrong—wrong-site surgery, in this example. The next column is the first of three measures, what this book is about. Severity is a measure of the impact the failure mode has on the customer or patient in our example. The higher the severity to the patient, the higher the severity value. There are tables that healthcare organizations may use to calibrate the severity measure with a 9 or 10 reserved for catastrophic failure. (See Appendix 9 for tables that you can use or modify.)

Catastrophic failure is a loss of personnel and or equipment. The next column lists the potential causes for the failure. Again, we may have multiple causes for each failure mode. The team should exhaust all causes knowing that a prioritization will occur in the FMEA process to focus on the vital few causes. The second measure, occurrence, is in the next column. Occurrence refers to the frequency of the cause occurring resulting in the failure mode. Data are sometimes available and should be used in FMEA. However, FMEA is to be used first in designing a process so data won't exist. Comparable relevant data should be used, however subjective it may be, and replaced as data becomes available. A high occurrence relative to the entire FMEA for this system refers to a cause that more frequently occurs relative to other causes.

Existing Controls

The next two columns are related. They are to list any controls in place that will prevent the root cause resulting in a failure mode and, thus, an unfavorable effect. Often, the FMEA will have nothing in this column because no control exists to prevent failure. The next column is more likely to be populated, especially in healthcare, where often inspection is the only control in place. We can't always control a surgeon's marking of the site if we are in the OR setting up a case. However, the team can detect and control the process by requiring the surgeon to mark the site prior to the patient entering the OR. The last of three measures, Detection, is the FMEA's way of measuring the ability of detecting if a root cause occurred that may result in a failure mode and unfavorable effect. This measure often confuses people doing FMEA for the first time. The lower the ability to detect that the root cause has occurred, the higher the detectability measure. The reason it is higher is that an unfavorable condition will have a higher number as in occurrence and severity.

Risk Priority Number (RPN)

Now, for the Risk Priority Number (RPN), the Value that measures the risk of the combination of the severity, occurrence, and detect ability of the cause, failure mode, and effect. The higher the RPN, the higher the risk.

I also have a column to list how we might detect variation in the input. The detection column is one of the three characteristics used to calculate the Risk Priority Number. Detection is often the most important variable in the RPN in healthcare. The severity and occurrence may be the same for different cancers, but cancers with tests that can identify them, have a lower RPN because the Detection value is lower. Remember, the easier it is to detect an input starting to fail, the lower the detection value. Heart disease can be cured if inputs going wrong are measured (detected) and caught in advance. Diet, smoking, obesity, cholesterol, and other inputs once measured can be used to detect heart failure risk. Modifying and controlling these inputs can prevent heart disease and even cure it in some individuals. template we use to better connect inputs to outcomes. The inputs are what may vary and fail. Again, improvement comes from managing the inputs and to prevent failure.

At the Corporate Initiatives Group responsible to consult in quality, we launched a quality improvement campaign named "Quality Vital Signs" under the direction of Mike Fenger, chief quality officer. Motorola Solutions leads the world in the sales of First Responder communication devices, such as police and fire radios. If you work in a hospital, police force, firehouse, or any number of First Responder organizations, chances are your staff uses Motorola devices, whether it is for clinical reasons or simply to trigger staff to bring more supplies. The former Motorola Automotive unit is where we turned around the quality of OnStar® for GM using FMEA extensively to create highly reliable communication devices.

FMEA for IT

Even IT (information technology) in Motorola Automotive began using FMEA. Bill Cooper, IT manager for the Automotive Group in Seguin, Texas, and I led teams in design and manufacturing to improve the quality of automotive safety products including OnStar and BMW Assist™, a similar system to protect occupants of vehicles via communication of critical parameters and accident information. We were working to reduce zero kilometer failures of the OnStar device. Zero kilometer failures are failure modes that occur before the vehicle leaves the factory. You can imagine this is embarrassing to any supplier and highly frustrating to the vehicle manufacturer—GM and BMW were threatening to develop other suppliers—and Motorola was at risk for the first time since developing Telematics®, the technology that makes OnStar and BMW Assist work. The engineers had used the FMEA to design the product and the processes to make OnStar. They had submitted the FMEAs to GM and BMW prior to shipping the first devices years ago. However, it is clear the FMEA and subsequent design and process improvements missed something.

Data Can Be a Component In Today's High Tech Equipment

The team discovered that data errors occurred within the device causing the failures. Data in a Telematics device is a critical "component." I put component in quotes because components prior to microprocessors being installed in devices were seen as screws, metal, electrical resistors, etc. In Telematics, data allowed the device to function. An example of data working as a component was the "wake up" feature. Data in this feature included the identity of the vehicle where the Telematics unit was installed. If the data that identified the device was faulty, say it was actually another device and thus another vehicle, the intended device may not wake up and function.

One function is to contact the police if an accident occurred. Help may not arrive, or as quickly, if the device does not function. But, there never has been a FMEA on data components

I asked Cooper to bring the FMEA to the team so we could learn about the failure modes and potential causes of the effect of data components being wrong and not waking up the device. He looked a bit embarrassed. He knew what I didn't know. FMEA was not required by the manufacturers for data components and IT had never done a FMEA for any reason, despite the fact that data downloaded into a Telematics unit is as valuable as the hardware that holds the data. In fact, Cooper coined the term *data component*, which is commonly used today in Telematics, to elevate the importance of designing a device that has a process to download data into it to function.

Why wouldn't a designer want to use the same proven method of using FMEA that has improved the quality and safety of everything from the simplest devices to space travel. I don't think it is any coincidence that the group that makes First Responder radios and other safety equipment is also the business that helped develop Six Sigma in the 1980s when its quality started to suffer. This business unit is by far the market leader still and has now also won the Malcolm Baldrige Award. It was the first time Motorola won and when Six Sigma became widely known outside of MOT.

FMEAs Don't Always Prevent Catastrophic Failure

You may know that NASA and its partners used FMEA extensively and used them on the same systems that experienced catastrophic or mission-ending failures: Apollo 1, Apollo 13, and the space shuttles, Challenger and Columbia. What experts know is that without FMEA, we never would have had the many successful missions. In a *Wall Street Journal* article by Betsy McCaughey,[3] she countered a Medicare study and an editorial by another author *suggesting that many surgeries on older Americans are wasteful because "32% of elderly American patients undergo surgery in the year before they die." McCaughey added, "That's like saying Babe Ruth struck out 1,333 times so he must have been a poor ballplayer—even though he had a .342 lifetime batting average."* NASA engineers describe rocket launches as sitting on top of a controlled explosion. Space travel is not without risk and the safety record is as high as it is because of tools like FMEA that measured the risk, prioritized actions, and then used measurement of the input variables to know when to act to prevent failure.

The space shuttle Challenger disaster highlighted the value of FMEA. The failure was technically a result of leakage eroding an O-ring, allowing gases to escape and ignite. Scientists and engineers had identified the risk of cold ambient temperatures allowing conditions resulting in the erosion of the O-ring. What failed that day was the ability of engineers and management to stop the launch despite knowing the risk. One could suggest it was what every Change Leader has to overcome—resistance. Resistance was from the decision makers to listen to the engineers that the input ambient temperature had varied that day to a level never yet seen at launch. The engineers had measured the amount of O-ring erosion after each launch knowing from the FMEA that there was a probability of erosion that could result in catastrophic failure. They had correlated ambient temperature to have an effect on the amount of erosion.

3Ms Lesson: Must Manage to the Measure, Not Just Measure

The Challenger disaster is a 3Ms lesson. Measurement had occurred. NASA and Morton Thiokol engineers were measuring the amount of erosion of the O-ring and measuring the ambient temperature the day of launch. What failed that day was the second M, Manage to the measure. The measures were disregarded by management. Despite clear evidence that colder temperatures increased the risk of O-ring erosion with a possible effect on personnel and vehicle loss, NASA management failed to manage to the measure. They launched—and the shuttle program's first catastrophic failure occurred. NASA ultimately used the third M—Make it easier for engineers to be heard and management to make the correct decision to launch. A panel was set up to make it more difficult to make decisions to ignore valuable tools like FMEA and measurements of inputs that may vary beyond limits.

HROs have hundreds of FMEAs amounting to thousands of ways a system can fail. FMEA is used so pervasively in HROs that one cannot use a fastener in a safety circuit breaker without having a FMEA on the risks of that fastener failing. The FMECA, according to the original documentation in the military, "is an analysis procedure, which documents all probable failures in a system, determines by failure mode analysis the effect of each failure on system operation, identifies single failure points, and ranks each failure according to a severity classification of failure effect."[4]

We find no sense in talking about something unless we specify how we measure it; a definition by the method of measuring a quantity is the one sure way of avoiding talking nonsense ...

Sir Hermann Bondi[5]
in Whenever You Can, Count, by Sir Francis Galton[6]

The risk of a change, or not changing, which is more appropriate for a book on leading change, is measuring the potential impact on achieving the mission and staff safety. Yes, the leader often reduces resistance to change by informing stakeholders the risk and impact to them if change does not happen. Paralyzing fear must be addressed, and the FMEA is a way to inform and engage stakeholders to reduce fear that often comes from an inability to measure the impact.

Facilitating a FMEA

Leading FMEA is easy once one gets some practice. Judging what is an input versus a failure mode versus an effect and cause can be difficult. I help you by adding definitions on the FMEA form provided. You also can ask an experienced facilitator to get your team started. One is of great benefit to get the team going if everyone is new to FMEA. The facilitator can leave after the team shows confidence and competence. "Calibrating" the team by giving some examples relative to the process always helps.

Judging the RPN is a function of judging the severity, occurrence and detection. I include tables in Appendix 9 that can be used as is or modified.

The next lesson in measuring is how to know if change is really occurring. This is most critical. This gives the leader and the stakeholders confidence that change is happening.

Key Points

- Failure Mode and Effects Analysis is an important and valuable measuring system.
- FMEA prevents failures by thinking how a system can fail, acting to prevent failure, and controlling the system to sustain function and performance and minimize risk.

■ FMEAs in healthcare are just starting whereas they are extensively used in HROs.
■ FMEAs must be shared; people must manage to what they suggest—manage to the measure; thinking about risk without acting is not worth much except sleepless nights.
■ FMEAs are relatively easy, but can be time consuming without strong facilitation.

Endnotes

1. http://www.assistdocs.com/search/documents_details.cfm?ident_number=86479
2. http://www.ntsb.gov/doclib/speeches/sumwalt/SCEG_pre.pdf
3. Betsy McCaughey, "Cooking the Books on Grandma's Health Care," *Wall Street Journal*, Nov. 1, 2011.
4. *Potential Failure Mode and Effects Analysis (FMEA) Reference Manual*, 4th ed. (Chrysler LLC, Ford Motor Company, General Motors Corporation).
5. *Sir Hermann Bondi in Relativity and Common Sense* (1964). Online at: http://www.todayinsci.com/QuotationsCategories/M_Cat/Measurement-Quotations.htm
6. James R. Newman, *Commentary on Sir Francis Galton,* quoted in *The World of Mathematics,* Vol. II. (New York: Simon & Schuster, 1956), 1169.

Chapter 12

Measurement as a System

You, in this country [the USA], are subjected to the British insularity in weights and measures; you use the foot, inch and yard. I am obliged to use that system, but must apologize to you for doing so, because it is so inconvenient, and I hope Americans will do everything in their power to introduce the French metrical system. … I look upon our English system as a wickedly, brain-destroying system of bondage under which we suffer. The reason why we continue to use it, is the imaginary difficulty of making a change, and nothing else; but I do not think in America that any such difficulty should stand in the way of adopting so splendidly useful a reform.

Baron William Thomson Kelvin (1824–1907)[1]
British physicist, mathematician, and engineer

Overview

Quite a relevant quote for our subject, I think. Making it easy to measure is to change to the metric system. The metric system's common denominator of 10 seems so much easier than the English measure divisible by 12 for feet to inches. The reason we haven't switched despite over 40 years of saying we should is the resistance to change. Maybe we could apply the learning from this book to finally convert to the metric system? Remember what we taught in chartering about a SMART goal? Is this really attainable? Who wants to lead this change?

This chapter helps ensure that the measures you are taking are correct. This is not the easiest chapter to read due to its sometimes technical nature. Please read the first few pages to understand what a measurement system is. Then, you may want to skim through the balance of this chapter for now to appreciate the value when you really need it later. This is a "how-to" book and this chapter will deliver its value when you have a variable that you aren't quite sure how to measure or you are concerned about the quality of the measurements you are taking. The next chapter on how to measure is very much dependent on the concepts and techniques covered in this chapter. Don't be embarrassed by someone finding error in how you measure.

Measuring outcomes and process measures is sometimes easy and begins with having a measurement system that already exists. So often it seems that there is no measurement system and the team must lead the creation of one. Don't worry, we will teach you step-by-step how to use an existing system or make one. Examples of measurement systems include errors in admissions documentation, inventory time supply, sales, margins, call wait time, hand-off communication quality, and countless more measures.

Designing a measurement system starts with a purpose. The charter taught earlier clearly defines the purpose, so please consider starting with the chartering process to design a measurement system. The charter walks us through the process of defining clearly the issue, the outcomes and process variables, and the metrics needed to measure changes in the outcomes and process variables. We even have a goal that further connects the issue with the measurement system.

Measurement as a System

What is a measurement system? Let's define it word by word. We have covered the word *measurement*. A system is a network of components that work together to achieve a function. In a measurement system, the components work together to assess a variable. Think of a measurement system we have all experienced. A gas gauge as mentioned in the first chapter is a very common one. Is the gas gauge a high quality measurement system? Has it seemed that the gas is being consumed faster when the gauge is under a quarter of a tank? If so, you may question the quality of the gauge thinking that the car is not consuming gas at a faster rate when the tank nears empty. In fact, you may think the gauge should show a slower rate of consumption because gas mileage is highly dependent on weight. With less gas, the gauge should reflect a slower rate of emptying. These questions are why we need to be able to assess the quality of a measurement system. Change is difficult enough, but if your resistors question your measures, you have a much more difficult leadership challenge. A good measurement system is everything needed to measure accurately and precisely.

Measurement System Analysis (MSA) Critical in Utilizing the 3Ms

The last thing you want in leading change is to have your first M, Measure, to be wrong. Critics and resistors of change will often question measurements to stop or slow change. The leader and team members need to know the value of analyzing measurement systems and ensure that the measurements are correct.

Have you also thought about doing an MSA on your favorite restaurant's wait times for a table? What is the process that they use to estimate the wait times? In America, I have seen signs that suggest patrons leave if others are waiting. In the United Kingdom, I think it would be considered most rude for a restaurant owner to post such a sign. What is the impact of such a policy on estimating wait times?

We should do an MSA before we start measuring anything of importance. There are even legal consequences if the measurements we proclaim in advertising or research are not correct.

Analyzing a Measurement System

Let's analyze a measurement system we have all experienced, and maybe questioned its quality. Every measurement system is composed of a measuring device and something to measure. Some are more complicated than this with multiple components. A blood pressure measurement system as shown in Figure 12.1 has these components:

- Patient
- Nurse or other qualified person trained in taking a measurement
- Arm cuff
- Finger cuff
- Meter

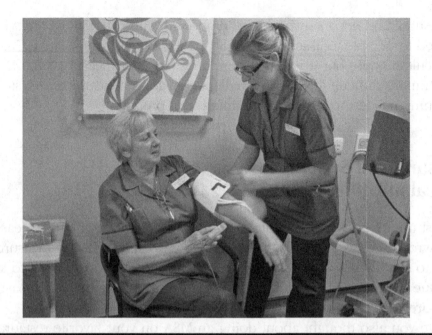

Figure 12.1   Components of a measurement system taking blood pressure.

- Electrical power
- Procedure
- Stethoscope, optional, in this system

Each of the components is necessary to measure blood pressure. There are multiple ways the measurement can be inaccurate. The patient's blood pressure also may change between readings, but if the change in readings is not the patient's actual pressure changing, we have variation in the measurement system. This is an error in the measurement system. Any variation not attributable to the item or service being measured is an error.

Qualities of an Acceptable Measurement System

No two things are alike, but even if they were, we would still get different values when we measured them.

Donald J. Wheeler[2]
Author, statistician, and expert in quality control

A quality measurement is one that measures only what is being measured. The measurement system itself should not influence the measurement. Have you stepped on your bathroom scale, read the measurement, stepped on it again and the scale shows a different weight? Did your weight really change that much in the two seconds between each weighing? The variation in weight is a result of a lack of quality in the measurement system. A quick way to lose credibility in healthcare is to have a bad measurement system.

We step on a scale to weigh ourselves; we don't like the answer, so we weigh ourselves again. What are we thinking? If we don't like the answer, we blame the measurement system. Do you weigh yourself twice if you first get the weight you expected or desired? Probably not. This practice is very common in healthcare. Perhaps you had a nurse taking your blood pressure and she decided to retake it. A common reason a person takes the blood pressure reading twice is because the person felt uncomfortable with the earlier reading and retook it. Did you ever wonder why they never seem to retake a measurement if the measurement is within an acceptable range, yet they seem often to retake a measurement when it is not within range? What makes them think that if the measurement system is flawed the first time for an unacceptable or border line measurement that the second measurement will be more accurate and precise?

During my last annual physical, this very thing happened to me in my blood pressure result. The nurse took my blood pressure. It was a bit higher than we both expected, having reviewed my chart. She dismissed it as perhaps I was a bit anxious, announced the doctor would be in shortly, and left. My doctor reacted to the blood pressure similarly. My doctor retook my blood pressure knowing now that I was anxious, and it was significantly lower than what the nurse measured. The doctor said all is well and chalked it up to a bad measurement system. Did my blood pressure really change, in fact go down, knowing that the anxiety would have only increased my blood pressure more? There are several components to most measurement systems, and to get a high-quality measurement, we need to be able to identify any component that causes variation in measurements.

Attributes of a Measurement System

A quality measurement system has fundamental characteristics. They include:

■ The ability to differentiate differences in what is being measured. Think of using a yardstick to measure the thickness of a piece of paper. This is not a very good discrimination.

- Location variation can be described as the accuracy of a measurement system. Location is how well the measurement system assesses the location of the true value. If the true average gas mileage is 20 miles per gallon, a good measurement system would locate the gas mileage around 20 miles per gallon, not 15 or 25.
- Width variation is another fundamental characteristic and it is considered the precision of the measurement system. If each time we step on the bathroom scale we get a different reading above and below the true weight, we see poor precision. The repeatability of the measurement system each time we measure is not very good. If one person measures my blood pressure and gets a different reading than a second person, they are not reproducing the same value. This is poor reproducibility. The measurement should represent what is being measured and have enough precision to differentiate changes in what is being measured.

The best way to understand location and width variation using the terms *accuracy* and *precision* is described below.

Accuracy

Accuracy is the measurement system's ability to find the true value. If a measurement system is not accurate, it is said to have a bias.

Bias

Bias is a measured value consistently lower or higher than the true value. Weighing yourself at home compared to the value at the doctor's office? A measurement process is biased if differences exist in the average of the measurements made by different persons, machines, etc., when measuring the identical characteristic. The average of measurements is different by a fixed amount.

In taking blood pressure, if the systolic pressure is actually 127 mmHg, and the measurement system gives a systolic of 126 or 128, it may be considered accurate. If the system gave a reading of 140, we would say it is not accurate. The difference between what is actual and what is measured is important enough.

Precision

The precision of a measurement system is its ability to discern differences in what is being measured. If the systolic blood pressure is rounded off to the nearest 10, such as reading 120 or 130, we might consider that this system is not as precise as one that reads to the nearest mmHg.

Repeatability

Repeatability is the ability to consistently get the same value on the same service or product using the same measurement system. If I measure your blood pressure twice with all the same conditions within a very short time frame, I should get the same blood pressure reading. If I get different blood pressures, I have not repeated the measure well and, thus, there is a repeatability error in the measurement system.

Reproducibility

Reproducibility is the ability for two different measurement systems to achieve the same value. Poor reproducibility is when two different people or measurement systems, such as an automatic blood pressure reading system, get different blood pressure readings that should not be different.

The MSA methods differ based on the type of data. I will teach you a way of measuring the quality of a measurement system for both types of data—and the simplest MSA for the discrimination needed. We apply what we teach: Make it easier.

Variables type data, also known as continuous type data and discrete or attribute data (discrete data's other name) are the two types of data.

Designing a Measurement System

> It is really just as bad technique to make a measurement more accurately than is necessary as it is to make it not accurately enough.

> **Arthur David Ritchie**[3]

Inputs	Process Map Steps for Measurement System Design & Analysis	Outputs
Customer CTQs Development needs	Purpose for measuring and standards	Purpose
Similar systems DOEs FMEAs	Determine environmental factors that may influence measurement system	Completed FMEA with action plan for influences
Similar systems Standards Expert advice Suppliers of systems	Design measurement system	Design
Standards Higher discriminating/quality measurement system	Calibrate system	Calibrated MS
Trained belt/expert Operators expected to use MS MSA methodology	MSA	Acceptable MSA Unacceptable MSA
Training plan Control plan	Train operators	Operators capable System capable
Measurement system Process or product	Implement	Truth in measurements
Standards Stability & Linearity cycles MSA	Control Plan	Calibration plan MSA Plan

Figure 12.2   Measurement system design and analysis process.

Figure 12.2 describes the process of designing a measurement system. The steps in the design flow down from the top middle columns. The inputs show what is required in the design and the outputs demonstrate what each step delivers. The team could benefit from this map if it has to design a new system or wants to understand the components.

Performing a Measurement System Analysis (MSA)

Conducting an MSA is important for the team. Change is difficult enough sometimes without having your credibility questioned. Sometimes the MSA is as simple as validating that the start and end times are well defined.

MSA helps determine if the measurement system is capable of:

- Classifying good from bad
- Measuring process improvements

A team wants to measure the average wait time for patients who come to the Emergency Department (ED) on the weekend to ensure staffing levels are sufficient. The first step in a MSA is to know the purpose and then to define the boundaries of the measurement. We often measure elapsed times and the MSA should define when the timing should start and when to "stop the clock." In this project, the team defines the clock start time to be when the patient signs in and stops when he/she is seen. Some of you are questioning if this is a truthful way to measure wait times. You might be thinking that it is not fair to stop the clock only when a physician sees the patient. Some of you are comfortable to define the wait time as between sign-in and triage (triage is French for separate or sift). Triage was used in World War I by French doctors to separate patients into one of three categories:[4]

■ Patients that would live, regardless of what care is received.
■ Patients that will die, regardless of what care is received.
■ Patients, if treated immediately, may have a better outcome.

Triage is a process in many EDs between the sign-in process and being seen by a physician to quickly route the patient for safe care. A patient with chest pains may be immediately routed for tests, as an example. If the purpose of your project is to ensure an early judgment of the care a patient may need, triage may be the best process to measure the end time. Know the purpose of your measurement to make the right decision.

MSAs Can Be Really Easy

Your MSA in this example is fairly easy and starts with getting consensus with your sponsor when the clock should start and stop. You may also want to ensure how granular your measurements should be to discriminate differences in wait times. Perhaps rounding to the nearest minute in ED wait times that are now taking up to 20 minutes is granular enough. A statistic that is useful in an MSA, to judge if the measurement system is good enough to assess how well a process is performing to what is required by the patient, customer, or process owner, is % Precision to Tolerance (%P/T). I will show you how to use this and other useful statistics to assess the quality of your measurement system and when to use each one to ensure your measurements are truthful.

After you apply the 3Ms and performance improvement and get the wait times down to three minutes, your MSA may suggest measuring in seconds to continuously improve your process. This is when the MSA statistic, % Precision to Total Variance (%P/TV) or % Contribution is the correct statistic to use. Once the ED wait times are better than what the patients demand, the MSA statistic described earlier, %P/T is less relevant. We now need to be able to measure improvements regardless of patient expectations.

An important MSA for any company can be in its supply chain responsiveness. Procurement may be receiving complaints from the staff that they are running out of supplies. The procurement team may study the supplier response times. The procurement team may believe the suppliers' response time is too long. The team may find purchasers didn't realize that the requested receipt dates set by the computer add an extra day due to batch processing.

Inaccurate Measurement Systems Can Lose Customers

Not knowing your capacity in surgical services or radiology or any number of services may result in your staff turning patients and high margin customers away. Turning away doctors who want to use the services of your healthcare organization can be a big loss to your margins. This can often be a failure of the measurement system. A CEO of a large hospital recently heard that his staff turned away two prospective professional football players who needed tests as a condition of their contracts. These football players were already well known and a football player can be a significant user of healthcare services for many years. They also tend to be able to pay. You now know the CEO's concerns and reason for change.

This issue was not just in the hospital's lab and test services. I saw firsthand how a measurement system's inaccuracy and lack of precision almost resulted in two surgeons being told the surgery center could not accommodate their requests for OR time. The hospital staff looked at their paper-based scheduling system and both read that the recovery areas were too full to allow any more surgeries to occur. They were about ready to turn away the business. Instead, they looked at a new scheduling system that had just been put in place and saw that there was plenty of recovery space to allow the surgeries to occur. Of course, there could be other remedies to allow the surgeries if the recovery area was the constraint, but our point is the measurement system was flawed and in the busy day, people were turning patients away due to the measurement system they had. This system had two flaws. The system was not accurate or precise. Accuracy and precision are two first tests of the quality of a measurement system.

A Measurement System Using Actual Data by Surgeon and by Procedure

The hospital team found that the system could not accurately estimate time for patients who required multiple procedures. The system would add the full time for each procedure as if the procedure required patient positioning and other setup that is not necessary once the surgeon has started one procedure. What would show as three hours to do two procedures might only take a few more minutes after the first procedure, say a total of 100 minutes to do both procedures. Thus, there was a significant amount of time available. What is even more complicated, there are two groups of staff making decisions if time is available. The first group receives booking requests from the surgeon's office and tries to estimate the time procedures take and also ensures that the surgeon has the allotted reserved time, called a "slot" or "block time."

They know the measurement system, the computer-generated total time for both procedures, is flawed. So, they become the measurement system trying to estimate the time to know if the next question, if the surgeon has enough block time, results in enough time available. The block time practice is very common in surgery centers. We also find that the block times are often not used and not made available to other surgeons who may be looking for time to do surgeries. Not making a good estimate of the time required for procedures is described as being inaccurate. The times are inaccurate estimates of the total time required for both procedures. Next, we will describe how a lack of precision can describe a measurement system's quality.

The standard times in the scheduling system were rounded up to quarter-hour increments. If a procedure took 5 minutes, the system might round it up to 15 minutes. The original intention might have been in the patient's best interest. It may be better to tell the surgeon that there was not enough time versus allowing the surgery and then not having sufficient space in recovery when the surgery is complete and needing to transport the patient to another area to recover. Good intentions overriding improving effort to improve a poor measurement system, however, are not in the patient's, surgeon's or hospital's best interest. Measurement systems need to be accurate and precise in healthcare. High Reliability Organizations (HROs) know this and ensure their measurement systems meet their quality requirements. Measurement systems must be designed to meet the quality requirements.

This is how the hospital team improved the measurement system. The first step was to find all the elements of the measurement system. A critical element is the data used to estimate the average time each procedure took by each surgeon. The average time for the same procedure performed by two different surgeons can vary by over 100%. No one knew where the original estimates came from, and we believe they were standards supplied by the software firm in who knows what country and by what type of surgery center. We were fortunate to have the actual times for each procedure and combination of procedures for most surgeons. This helped us improve the accuracy of the scheduling system immediately. Eighty percent of the cases that had multiple procedures had data on the total elapsed time of the case.

We wanted to improve the precision as well as the accuracy. Resistance was heavy in the scheduling department. Previous attempts at getting the informal leader to try new ways had failed. I call these attempts, "drive-by change attempts." Sometimes we test the waters for how much resistance we can expect by suggesting a few ideas as we walk by or through a department and see the reaction. When a team hears, "Oh no, that won't work," during these drive-by change tactics, we know change will come with more difficulty.

We started to improve the precision of the measure of how long a procedure might take by calculating the variance of each combination of procedure and surgeon. Using the variance, we were able to more precisely estimate the time most cases would take if we wanted to schedule the OR and recovery area with enough time for 95% of the occurrences. We found even with this estimate, the software estimate was still considerably higher than what the surgeon needed.

This measurement system is already much more accurate and precise just by improving one element in the system, the data. To test the new system, we used an actual day's schedule when they were very busy. We simulated the recovery area needed using the new measurement system and found it measured what really happened very well. We now knew we needed a process to take new bookings and find ways to achieve higher capacity so we did not turn any business away. The schedule is visual and easy to read (Figure 12.3).

Another component in many healthcare measurement systems is us, the human. If we were not around to hear the two staff fretting about telling a surgeon they were too busy, they confirmed they would have turned business away. This is a leader's dilemma and one that frustrates anyone who has a good idea, and yet some don't use it. How do we get the human element in a measurement system improved?

	Time	Trolley Bay 1	Trolley Bay 2	Trolley Bay 3	Trolley Bay 4	Trolley Bay 5	Trolley Bay 6	Trolley Bay 7	Trolley Bay 8	Trolley Bay 9	Trolley Bay 10	Trolley Bay 11
	7:00:00	1A	2A	4A	5A	6A	7A			Patient 13		
	7:10:00											
Trolley	7:20:00											
Chair	7:30:00											
Overnight	7:40:00											
	7:50:00											
	8:00:00											
	8:10:00											
	8:20:00											
	8:30:00											
	8:40:00											
	8:50:00											
	9:00:00											
	9:10:00											
	9:20:00											
	9:30:00											
	9:40:00											
	9:50:00											
	10:00:00											
	10:10:00											
	10:20:00											
	10:30:00											
	10:40:00											
	10:50:00											
	11:00:00											
	11:10:00											
	11:20:00											
	11:30:00											
	11:40:00											
	11:50:00											
	12:00:00											

Figure 12.3   Measurement of bed availability.

Drawdown

Drawdown is another military invention, I hear. I am not sure where it was first coined, but it is often the only way to get people to make the change. I was a Lotus 1-2-3® user for many years. Lotus 1-2-3 is a spreadsheet application and it revolutionized using math and making charts. Anyone working with numbers and needing to make charts who had a PC in the 1980s probably was aware of Lotus 1-2-3.

Then, Microsoft started selling its spreadsheet application, Excel®. Eventually, my company's IT group tried to get us to choose Lotus or Excel. One can imagine the resistance in shifting. I was very happy with Lotus, even after trying Excel, and I was running a site that demanded focusing on customers and my employees. Doing spreadsheet work was a part of my work life, but definitely it was just a tool to allow me to focus more on customers and employees. Why should I switch when there would be time wasted learning Excel? What is the third M? Make it easier, right? It wasn't easier to use Excel. It sure wasn't easier to have to learn the same functions in Excel when I already knew how to do everything I needed in Lotus. Did anyone ask me what I thought?

Over time, the IT group lobbied and eventually got the company to make Excel the standard. That meant that all of us "Lotus Lords" who knew Lotus like the backs of our hands had to switch. The IT group couldn't get everyone to voluntarily switch, and they implemented a change management technique called drawdown. They took Lotus off our machines to force us to change to Excel. Drawdown is the term for when a leader reduces or decreases the resources, such as in a troop drawdown in a foreign country. The drawdown will result in a change because the old method is no longer available. This forces people to change to the new way, or new location using the troop drawdown technique. I want to be clear here. I use drawdown as the last resort, preferring to get people to change willingly. But, not all change is favorable for each individual, as we taught in the first chapter. Sometimes a Change Leader needs to invoke a drawdown for the benefit of the organization. The good news is that Excel wasn't all that bad. That one spreadsheet software fortunately became the standard so everyone could communicate and share.

There is another lesson here. Even a good change will result in resistance on minor issues with the change. For example, I still struggle with the changes in charting in the 2010 version of Excel, as do many of my colleagues. I think Excel could use this book and the 3Ms. I don't think they did a very good job leading us to the new changes in this version. They were evidently concerned enough that they provided an application that tells you how to do a feature based on the screen navigation for the prior version. Unfortunately, they didn't do a very good job communicating how they did this. I also don't think they measured client satisfaction with the new methods. Otherwise, they would have done something differently.

Measurement Systems That Add No Value to the Client

Are you also annoyed at Microsoft's error message that asks if we want to send information to Microsoft now that their software and/or system just failed? You have seen the box with a blue margin on it after your application has crashed. It starts with the words "Please tell Microsoft about this problem. … We have created an error report that you can send to help us improve Microsoft Office Outlook. We treat your report as confidential and anonymous." Of course it is anonymous. They don't want to give you access to them. Did you ever wonder what happened to customer service phone support? At the bottom, we are asked to send or not. Here are just more keystrokes and wasted time they push onto me the customer to help them measure their lack of reliability. My takt time had to be revised, too, which we discussed earlier. I lost four hours of work due to MSWord® crashing. I had four hours less time available while the page counts went back up for the pages I lost. When the numerator goes down, which is the time I have available, and the denominator goes up because the page count increased back to before the crash, takt time must be even faster than just losing the four hours. Takt time, as you can see, is another measure for the lack of quality. Rework costs both time and supply.

Calibrating a Measurement System

Most measurement systems include a process known as calibration. Calibration "tunes" the measurement system to meet accuracy and precision require-ments when the measurement system is first put in use and to maintain its accuracy and precision. Our bathroom scales are often not accurate because calibration is needed. I know some people purposely don't calibrate their scale at home because of change; they don't want to admit they need to change their diet and way of life, maybe? For years I would set (calibrate) my wristwatch to be about five minutes early. This is another example of inaccuracy. The precision was good because it was able to discriminate in seconds as well as I needed, but it was not accurate to the actual time.

Calibration also has been used to help teams improve processes. When people don't seem to appreciate the reason for change, the team may recali-brate their thinking. An example is in the time customers are waiting in line. This can be a very relative measure, by the way. Does it seem longer to wait 5 minutes on the phone for customer support than a 10 minute wait at your favorite attraction at a Disney park or your favorite table at a restaurant? Do you feel differently about an estimate of time waiting for a service if the time you actually wait is less than the prior estimated wait time? In Failure Mode and Effect Analysis (FMEA), we discussed rating the severity of a failure mode. We calibrated the team's measurement system of severity by having them find the most severe failure mode and giving it a high value. This was to calibrate their ratings to equal or less severe failure modes relative to the most severe. I had to recalibrate a factory manager one time who dismissed as unimportant a late shipment saying, "this happens all the time." My recalibration of his attitude was done with data proving otherwise and consequences to us if late shipments continued.

Statistical MSA Methods

In this section, we are going to use statistics to analyze measurement systems. Again, keep the MSA as simple as necessary for the need for location and width variation. However, there are many instances that a more statistically derived MSA benefits the team. A good measurement system appropriately approximates the true value or reference value and is trusted. Just doing an MSA often reduces the resistance to the story the measurement system will help you tell in your process improvement work.

Categories and Types of Data

Measurement system analysis techniques vary based on the categories of data and types of data one is wanting in the measurement system. The categories include:

- Quantitative (numerical responses)
- Qualitative (categorical responses): Variables for which an attribute or classification is measured

There are two types of data within the quantitative category:

1. Continuous (variable data). Any point on a histogram is possible, such as when decimal subdivisions are possible:
   - Data that indicates how much or how many
   - Variable data can be subdivided into finer increments of precision:
     a. Time (seconds)
     b. Speed (feet/minutes)
     c. Rate (inches/time)
     d. Dimensions (millimeters)
2. Discrete (attribute): Numerical responses from a counting process where not every point is possible on a histogram:

- Good or bad counts
- Number of machines working
- Shifts of overtime scheduled
- Counted things (# of errors in a document, # units shipped, etc.)
- Percent good or bad (% derived from counting)

Qualitative (categorical responses): This includes variables for which an attribute or classification is measured:

- Yes or no
- Good or bad
- Meets the standard, or doesn't

Checklists as Measurement Systems

Many checklists used in aviation, aerospace, healthcare, financial services (including tax preparation), and automotive use a yes or no response option. A checklist is often qualitative based on the binary response option. More difficult surveys may use a degree of response, such as a survey that asks to judge satisfaction in a service based on a scale from 0 to 10, with 10 being highly satisfied.

MSAs can be very difficult for qualitative data. Judging the staff's friendliness is a judgment call with a hard-to-define standard. Remember, measurement is a way to compare something to a standard. In 2013, America's Centers for Medicare and Medicaid Services (CMS), which is a major payor to hospitals for healthcare reimbursement, is basing some of its reimbursement on a patient survey. The questions from the survey are seen in Figure 12.4 as well as the process measures. Note that CMS is using process and outcome measures in its system to reimburse hospitals in the future. This reimbursement practice based on quality and outcomes is a major change in healthcare that has few equals in other industries. The measurement system has gone through extensive analysis and is still debated.

Every one of the Hospital Consumer Assessment of Healthcare Providers and Systems Survey (HCAHPS) questions is a qualitative measure. Doing a measurement system analysis on such data is fraught with chance for error. Healthcare organizations (HCOs) that can do MSAs on this type of data may be well ahead of others who don't understand MSA. For instance, understanding the elements that affect a patient's judgment, such as how staff can affect the patient's measurement of services, can create variation in the

TABLE 4—ACHIEVEMENT THRESHOLDS THAT APPLY TO THE FY 2013 HOSPITAL VBP PROGRAM MEASURES

Measure ID	Measure description	Performance standard (achievement threshold)
Clinical Process of Care Measures		
AMI–7a	Fibrinolytic Therapy Received Within 30 Minutes of Hospital Arrival	0.6548
AMI–8a	Primary PCI Received Within 90 Minutes of Hospital Arrival	0.9186
HF–1	Discharge Instructions	0.9077
PN–3b	Blood Cultures Performed in the Emergency Department Prior to Initial Antibiotic Received in Hospital.	0.9643
PN–6	Initial Antibiotic Selection for CAP in Immunocompetent Patient	0.9277
SCIP–Inf–1	Prophylactic Antibiotic Received Within One Hour Prior to Surgical Incision	0.9735
SCIP–Inf–2	Prophylactic Antibiotic Selection for Surgical Patients	0.9766
SCIP–Inf–3	Prophylactic Antibiotics Discontinued Within 24 Hours After Surgery End Time	0.9507
SCIP–Inf–4	Cardiac Surgery Patients with Controlled 6AM Postoperative Serum Glucose	0.9428
SCIP–VTE–1	Surgery Patients with Recommended Venous Thromboembolism Prophylaxis Ordered	0.9500
SCIP–VTE–2	Surgery Patients Who Received Appropriate Venous Thromboembolism Prophylaxis Within 24 Hours Prior to Surgery to 24 Hours After Surgery.	0.9307
SCIP–Card–2	Surgery Patients on a Beta Blocker Prior to Arrival That Received a Beta Blocker During the Perioperative Period.	0.9399
Patient Experience of Care Measures		
HCAHPS	Communication with Nurses	75.18%
	Communication with Doctors	79.42%
	Responsiveness of Hospital Staff	61.82%
	Pain Management	68.75%
	Communication About Medicines	59.28%
	Cleanliness and Quietness of Hospital Environment	62.80%

Figure 12.4   CMS process measures for healthcare (HCAHPS).

measure. I can affect the way people rate my training by how I discuss the survey that they will get. Just by asking people to fill in the survey, I can change the measurement of my services. A classic example is a hotel survey. Who fills in a hotel survey? More than likely, it is someone who has had a horrible experience. If I can get more guests who are delighted with my services to fill in the survey, I can change the measurement, even though I did not change the service quality.

We will talk more about such effects, called bias, when we discuss sampling error. For now, just understand that there are two categories of data, with different types of data. MSAs need to be done on all data, regardless of category and type, but we will need different MSA approaches for each.

Granularity

Granularity is another variable in measurement. Granularity refers to the degree of discrimination in the data. Let's understand discrimination first to understand granularity.

Discrimination

Discrimination is the capability to detect and indicate even small changes. Examples include:

- Swim event stopwatch times for a grade school compared to the timing required for an event in the Olympics. In the grade school event, seconds may be granular enough. In the Olympics, the measurement system is able to discriminate between 10,000 of a second.
- Days of inventory versus weeks on hand. Days are more granular.
- Dollars versus cents
- Well-trained or competent

For quantitative data meeting the continuous- or variables-type data and width variation is critical with high granularity desired, a Gage Repeatability and Reproducibility (R&R) measurement system analysis may be the best.

Overview of Performing a Gage R&R

A good way to do a Gage R&R without a computer is to follow these steps:

- Gather a sample, or determine how to gather a sample, that represents the population that the measurement system is expected to assess. I suggest including a range of samples representing both extremes of the population. An example is if you want to measure the time in the ED from sign-in through starting the triage process. Take an example when the waiting room is empty and a time when the waiting room is very crowded because the times may be very short and very long.
- Have two people with watches that can measure in seconds and are reliable (many Smartphones have stopwatch functions) positioned so they can see the patients from sign-in until they are seen in triage.
- Ensure each person measuring knows when to start and stop the watches and have them practice on measuring patients in the environment. Correct any confusion.
- Determine the most representative sample, such as time of day, staffing at nominal levels (levels that meet requirements), and that will span the range of times needed to be measured.
- Have each person time at least five patients, if possible, from sign-in until they are seen in triage by a qualified person.
- Compare the times recorded by each person. Calculate the differences in each measurement. Judge if the differences between each observer are acceptable for the accuracy and precision needed.
- If not acceptable, determine the reasons why and correct. Trial and correct until accuracy and precision are achieved.

For most situations, this MSA will satisfy the quality in your measurement system needed.

MSA for Blood Pressure Reading

Cardiologists have a number of "tricks up their sleeve" in taking blood pressure. By taking the blood pressure standing up versus sitting down, a cardiologist can measure certain conditions. Taking the blood pressure in each arm also can detect issues. The measurement technique in taking blood pressure can change the value of the pressure significantly. Some experts suggest that blood pressure readings should be taken while the patient is seated and has rested for two minutes or more. Seldom do these conditions occur. So, what is the quality of the measurement in these situations? Is the quality sufficient? These are the issues in measuring blood pressure. The person taking the reading, the time the patient has rested, and the equipment are elements of the measurement system. All can affect the quality of the measurement.

When the granularity of measurement needed is low, a simpler measurement using two measurement systems may be enough. In the swim example, having two parents clock the swimmer and compare the two measurements may be enough to have confidence in the measurement system. There isn't a need to calculate the average and variance. If the two times are close enough for determining a winner, the measurement system is good enough. Periodically, someone should check the watch and method used to ensure stability over time.

MSA for Attribute Data

- How do we assure one person judges a good result correctly?
- Can we use measurement systems analyses to certify a person is ready for a role where judgment is required?
- How does a person being surveyed agree with herself over time? Under different conditions? Against an expert?
- These scenarios demonstrate why measurement systems analysis is needed for even attribute-type data.

Attribute Agreement Analysis

For qualitative data, there is a technique named Attribute Agreement Analysis (AAA). It is a statistical technique like those mentioned above, and may be the best MSA when judgments must be correct and to a standard.

An example is judging the level of care placements for psychiatric and addiction services for both adult and child/adolescent populations. A Level of Care Utilization System (LOCUS) was invented by the American Association of Community Psychiatrists and used in healthcare to measure the risk of harm. An example of the judgment criteria for a moderate risk of harm follows:

Moderate Risk of Harm

- Significant current suicidal or homicidal ideation without intent or conscious plan and without past history.
- No active suicidal/homicidal ideation, but extreme distress and/or a history of suicidal/homicidal behavior exists.
- History of chronic impulsive suicidal/homicidal behavior or threats and current expressions does not represent significant change from baseline.
- Binge or excessive use of substances resulting in potentially harmful behaviors without current involvement in such behavior.
- Some evidence of self neglect and/or compromise in ability to care for oneself in current environment.[5]

The Soft Drink Challenge with AAA

Here is a fun way to learn AAA. Can your measurement system differentiate between two sodas? You are the measurement system; many people claim to be able to measure the difference. Try it and report the results on my Web site www.rpmexec.com (the instructions are included in Appendix 7).

See Figure 12.5 for an example of the output.

An AAA tells us not only where the errors are, it suggests where to improve the measurement system.

- Poor repeatability (within appraiser)
- Poor reproducibility (between appraisers)

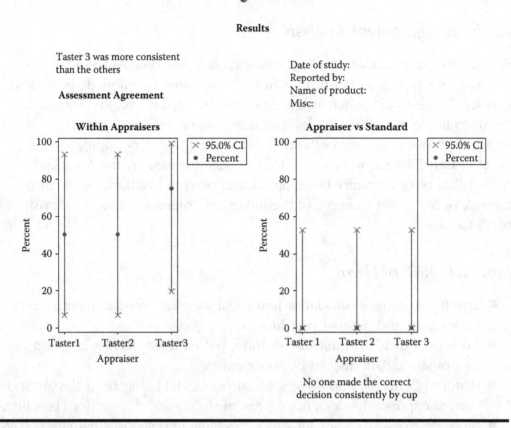

Figure 12.5   AAA for drinks.

■ Poor accuracy (wrong decisions)
■ How do we improve our taster's ability?

The way to test a person's measurement quality in attribute data, such as risk of harm, is to set up scenarios spanning the range of risk and asking the person to determine the risk of harm. A standard is needed to know if the judgment is correct. Another statistic in an attribute agreement analysis is the repeatability of the person. Good repeatability is the person making the same judgment, for the same scenario, more than once. The same situation may not be identical to mask similar scenarios. If the person judges the same situation differently, the measurement system is flawed and one needs to find the contributing factors and correct them. Repeat the AAA until the person correctly judges.

Stability

Stability is another variable in measuring that we need to understand. Stability is getting the same measurement on the same exact service event or product over time. Any difference in measurement of the same event or product is a result of an unstable measurement system. In measuring our weight over a year's time, the scale may give us different readings. If we did not actually gain or lose weight, the scale has introduced error, or variation, in the measurement. The scale may have gone out of calibration because dust has collected over time and made the sensors less sensitive. Correcting poor stability is often achieved by recalibrating. In measuring anything over time, it is a good practice to check the calibration. A Change Leader's practice should be to check the stability of the measurement system before claiming victory.

Linearity

Linearity is a measure of the difference in accuracy or precision over the range of the measurement device. Examples include the ability to measure:

- Long-cycle events and short-cycle events equally as well. The ability to measure the time patients wait in ED when the wait time is short and extremely long.
- Large objects and small objects
- Customer satisfaction in Asia and South America

Overview of MSA for Continuous Data and High Granularity

Gage Repeatability and Reproducibility (Gage R&R)

This method is very powerful in assessing the quality of a measurement system. This MSA methodology also guides teams where the MSA might be improved by tests of the characteristics.

However, it is most useful when you have:

- Continuous data
- High granularity and high discrimination required
- MSA is highly dependent on the quality of the characteristics (discrimination, stability, linearity, accuracy, and precision)

$$\sigma^2 \text{ Total variation} = \sigma^2 \text{ What is being measured} + \sigma^2 \text{ Measurement system}$$

$$\sigma^2 \text{ Measurement System} = \sigma^2 \text{ person measuring} +$$
$$\sigma^2 \text{ Measuring equipment} +$$
$$\sigma^2 \text{ Measuring technique} + \dots$$

■ The team is trying to improve the strength of an electrical disconnect using a male and female plug much like the extension cords you use at home. Too much force risks cord breakage and electrical shock. Too little force is associated with nuisance disconnects and possible electrical arcing resulting in fire.
  − The measurement system is a "pull" test where the amount of force (continuous data) is measured until the two plugs disconnect.
  − Seven samples are selected that represent the variation expected from the manufacturing process.
  − The team is concerned that the tool used in measuring pull strength is not always giving correct readings.
  − Calibrate the gage, or assure that it has been calibrated.
  − Select the parts to measure (usually 5–10) from the "normal" process.
■ Select the people measuring (usually two to three) to measure the parts. (Each person will measure each part at least two times to test repeatability).
■ Set up your schedule to measure by person. Be sure to randomize.
■ Have them measure the samples according to the random order.
■ Analyze the data to determine the statistics of the MSA described next. These include:

  % Contribution, %P/TV and %P/T

■ Analyze results and determine if improvements are needed to assure a quality measurement system.

Precision to Tolerance: (%P/T)

Knowing Good from Bad[6]

To determine if the measurement system is capable of accepting or rejecting what is being measured according to the specifications:

■ However, the spec width may be too tight or too loose.
■ Calculates *percent of the tolerance (as indicated by the customer!)* taken up by measurement error
■ Desirable to have the %P/T <30%
■ Usually expressed as a percent and called the "% Tolerance" in Minitab®[7]

Percent to Total Variation %P/TV

For process improvement beyond just knowing if product or service is good or bad:

- Includes both repeatability and reproducibility
- Minimal to have the %P/TV <30%
- Desired is <20%
- Usually expressed as a percent and called the "% Study Variation" in Minitab software

The %P/TV is the better measure to use for process improvement because it will detect changes in the process, not just how well the service or object being measured meets customer specifications.

% Contribution

% Contribution is the best for understanding the performance of the measurement system. % Contribution addresses what percent of the total variation (as indicated by the process) is taken up by measurement error.

- Includes both repeatability and reproducibility
- % Contribution should be less than 9%
- Desired is <4%

The % Contribution is perhaps even better than the % P/TV because the contribution is a more understandable measure of the variation caused by the measurement system.

Remember, measurement systems *must be analyzed before* spending much time collecting data. Too many times people collect data, sometimes spending money and time, only to find the measurement system is flawed. It is important to use the measurement system analysis that best fits the accuracy and precision and purpose.

Using Minitab in Measurement System Analysis for Gage R & R

One way of performing a Gage R&R study is to use a computer and statistical software like Minitab. Minitab is a common software application and makes doing a Gage R&R much easier. I include an example of a Gage R&R in Appendix 11.

Sampling

Sample selection is very important. Sample during normal production to capture total range of process variation. Be cautious of data from systems if you did not measure the data that went into the system. Know exactly how the data was gathered, sampled, if any data was omitted or edited, etc. An MSA is absolutely necessary for any data. The MSA does not have to be arduous.[8] Just analyze the system to make sure the data are truthfully representing what you are measuring, and accurate and precise enough to help you make decisions. Don't even think about *not* validating your measurement system, it could be very embarrassing.

Should I Measure 100% or Sample?

Let's answer using examples of projects almost every hospital has tried—measuring the wait times patients experience in an ED (aka ER or emergency room). First of all, let's understand what a population and sample are. A population is the entire set one wants to understand. A sample is a portion of a population.

We are sitting in the lobby and measuring the time it took for every patient to be seen. This is measuring the population. We measure every patient that comes in, day and night. Perhaps we have other things to do, yet we still want to estimate the average wait time. We could go to the ED once an hour for 10 minutes and measure the time for any patient who enters during that 10 minutes. We, of course, would not be measuring every patient (the population), assuming patients arrive when we are not in the ED. To know all wait times in an ED population would be to measure every patient that enters the ED, every hour, every day. Sampling would be to measure less than the entire population of patients. Writing the words "entire population" is redundant because I could have just said population. But, I want to stress the definition of population as everyone or everything, and a sample is less than the population.

Sampling Quality

Sampling quality is simply determined by how well the sample represents the entire population. The most common question I get is: "How many samples do I need?" This is not the most important question. The answer is *to represent* truthfully what you are measuring.

Sample size is important to achieve the confidence we want in our decisions. Often, we want to compare two groups to see if there is a difference.

In reducing catheter-associated urinary tract infections, we may want to compare two standards of care. We take samples from both techniques of care and then analyze to see if there is a lower rate of catheter-associated urinary tract infection (CAUTI) in one technique compared to the other. Sample size is important to estimate the confidence we have in the outcome if there is a true difference. A good rule of thumb is to gather at least 30 samples from each group to be compared. If we want to study the difference in CAUTI between treatment A and B, we would gather 30 samples of treatment A and 30 samples of Treatment B. Most important still is if we represent both populations of patients and techniques.

Key Points

- Measurement Systems Analysis is critical to ensure the measures we are using are correct.
- Your MSA should be kept as simple as needed to have confidence in the measure. Don't over complicate your MSA.
- MSAs are based on data types. MSAs for continuous-type data are different than methods for discrete-type data.
- Minitab and other software make doing more complex MSAs very easy.

Endnotes

1. William Thomson Kelvin, Baron, Science quote on the metric system (4), *Journal of the Franklin Institute*, (Nov. 1884): 118, 321–341.
2. Donald Wheeler, Experimentation, Understanding Industrial Experimentation, SPC Press, Knoxville, TN, 1990.
3. Arthur David Ritchie, *Scientific Method: An Inquiry into the Character and Validity of Natural Law,* (London: K. Paul, Trench, Trubner & Co., 1923), 113.
4. M. Chipman, B. E. Hackley, and T. S. Spencer, Triage of Mass Casualties: Concepts for Coping with Mixed Battlefield Injuries, *Military Medicine* (1980) 145 (2): 99–100.
5. LOCUS is used with permission by the American Association of Community Psychiatrists. Online at: http://communitypsychiatry.org/aacp/contact.aspx
6. Potential Failure Mode and Effects Analysis (FMEA) Reference Manual, 4th edition, Chrysler LLC, Ford Motor Company, General Motors Corporation.
7. Used with permission, Minitab. www.minitab.com
8. Jeffrey Bauer, *Statistical Analysis for Decision Makers in Healthcare,* 2nd edition, (Boca Raton, FL: Taylor & Francis, 2009).

Chapter 13

How to Share and Communicate Measurements

A picture is worth a thousand words.

Charting

Managing to the measure is often facilitated by graphically displaying the data. There are a number of charts that can help the team share what is happening. We will cover two of the most valuable charts:

- Pareto charts
- Charting: Statistical Process Control

Pareto Charts

Pareto charts are bar charts that display the most frequently occurring variable to the far left, and bars are displayed in descending order. A helpful feature of Pareto charts is a cumulative percentage line. The bars show the variables in the order of importance and the cumulative line allows the reader to assess how many variables make up x percent of the total. (See Figure 13.1 for an example of a Pareto chart of the reasons for not washing hands.)

The most frequently noted contributing factor in this hospital for not washing hands is that the person is distracted or forgets to wash. The

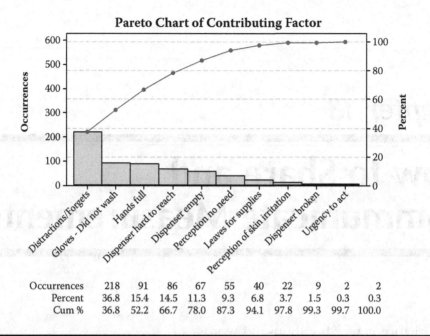

Figure 13.1   Pareto chart of reasons for not washing hands.

second most frequent contributing factor is the frequency of entering and exiting a patient's room. If we wanted to reduce 80% of the contributing factors, we can use the table below the Pareto Chart, or use the cumulative line to find where 80% of the contributing factors noted are located. In the chart, we see that only five contributing factors make up 78% of the occurrences. If we were to eliminate these five factors, we would eliminate 78% of the occurrences when we did not wash our hands.

A Pareto chart helps the Change Leader focus on the vital few issues, instead of wasting time on all possible factors. The measurement system used in determining the occurrence of each factor is very important. Teams will use Pareto charts often in a complex change to continually focus the stakeholders and prove to resistors that progress can be made.

Pareto to Reduce Resistance

I use Pareto analysis to reduce resistance. I was getting resistance from a group to use the 3Ms to improve staff satisfaction. They did not want to measure the outcome, believing it was too difficult to measure staff satisfaction frequently. I asked them to list the reasons why it was difficult to measure employee satisfaction every day. We counted the frequency or number of people who listed each contributing factor and arranged the reasons in descending votes. The top reason was that some felt this wasted time and a person would not give us different readings. What the people did not realize is that we planned to sample only a portion of the population of staff. Therefore, no one person would get surveyed more than once a quarter. The next frequently noted reason is the time was too great to survey so frequently.

We suggested that the team simply ask how likely the staff member would recommend working at this organization to family, friends, and colleagues. The second question simply asked why the person rated their desire to recommend or not as they did. If they gave an answer, they could again do a Pareto chart and focus precisely on the contributing factors that, if eliminated or reduced, would improve staff satisfaction.

Pareto Analysis is a simple tool that can focus a team on the critical few issues. It also can reduce resistance by helping resistors see that often what they are resisting may not occur very often at all. A Pareto chart is a snapshot of a system at a point in time. What a team also needs is a chart that shows the system through time.

Statistical Process Control Charts (SPC)

An SPC chart helps you, your friends, and relatives feel that the navigation device in your vehicle operates correctly. SPC has been credited with helping turn Japan from a country shipping junk to one that is shipping some of the finest quality goods ever. It is often viewed as a chart, also known as a Control Chart, SPC chart, Run chart, and various other names. It is one of the simplest charts to use. Let me repeat, it is one of the simplest charts to use for those of you who think or hear that SPC is too complex for your organization.

More importantly, it is the correct chart to use in performance improvement (PI), which is too complex to not consider using SPC. We'll see why, and, I will teach you how to measure using a control chart even if you don't have a computer. Learning it with pencil and paper (make it easy again, by supplying the paper) is the best way. Pencil and paper may be all you use in creating your SPC charts. The results can be all you need.

First SPC Chart: May 1924

The first SPC chart was shared in May 1924.[1] Western Electric, a manufacturer of transmission systems, wanted to improve its reliability. Western Electric found that relying on inspecting final product to sort out defects was not reliable. Despite having a department of engineers for inspection, failures in electrical transmission systems continued to occur. Western Electric at the Hawthorne Works (Cicero, Illinois) relied a great deal on inspection; they had an engineering inspection department. This is where Dr. Walter A. Shewhart (American physicist and statistician) worked. He wanted to improve the quality at Western Electric and find an alternative to relying on inspecting. Inspecting wasn't catching all the quality issues and it was very costly. He was looking for a method to know when a process was starting to vary, go out of control, before defects were made. Once made, despite inspectors, defective product made it underground only to fail and cause service disruptions and costly repairs.

High Reliability Organizations (HROs) and SPC

Stop and think how many times in your organization you heard of the need from high reliability organizations (HROs). At this time I want you to think back to Dr. Ignaz Semmelweis's story (Chapter 3) and how it ended for him. He proved beyond a doubt that his change to washing hands led to the desired outcome, but his Change Leadership was weak and the system went back to its old ways and mothers died because of the lack of sustained change. Dr. Shewhart also proved beyond a doubt how to improve reliability and reduce the waste of inspection. The end of his story, although not as grave personally as Dr. Semmelweis's, proves the need for Change Leadership because his techniques also took some time to catch on.

Many resisted, and in healthcare I see this resistance every day. This resistance slows the increase in reliability, adds to costly inspection, and who knows how many lives have been lost for not using his technique that we will cover now. What Louis Pasteur did to convince people that Dr. Semmelweis's discovery was the right thing to do, Joseph Juran, Dr. W. Edwards Deming, and Bonnie Small did for Dr. Shewhart's discovery. You might know Juran's contribution was to engage every employee, even the shop floor employee, in learning this technique. Dr. Deming emphasized the leader's role in quality as well as training everyone in Dr. Shewhart's technique.

Small, however, may deserve much of the credit for turning Western Electric's processes into more reliable processes. It took 25 years from when Dr. Shewhart in May 1924 sent a memo to his boss with a diagram that came to be known as a control chart, to more widespread use of control charts. This is the story of Small, straight from the Western Electric company Web site,[1] a company now known as Alcatel–Lucent.

> At Western Electric, this expertise on quality was communicated to the shop floor—most dramatically by Bonnie Small who joined the Hawthorne quality assurance department in 1940. Her experiences there during World War II convinced her that Shewhart's abstract ideas alone were of little help to newly hired workers, so she set out to translate the ideas of Shewhart into practical methods. After joining the Allentown Plant in 1948, Small assembled a committee of quality professionals throughout Western Electric to write a handbook for the factory. This handbook represents the confluence of Western Electric's long-standing traditions of quality control and of education and training. Much of the material for the book was based on Western Electric training courses given to managers, engineers, and shop floor people from 1949 to 1956. The *Western Electric Statistical Quality Control Handbook* appeared in 1958, and has been the shop floor bible of quality control throughout the world ever since. It remains in print, available from the company today.

One of the answers to achieving high reliability follows. I dare say, without this technique, your industry will never achieve high reliability. I am not talking just about using this technique inside the walls of your organization, either. This technique is needed throughout the value stream, including at suppliers, equipment manufacturers, components, and distribution. This technique was used to improve the reliability of answering phones, in shipping on time, in ensuring the safety of residents when an electrical ground fault occurred, and in redesigning the perioperative processes aiding in the elimination of wrong-site surgeries (WSSs). Its uses are endless. It is easier than you think to apply as I show you now. And, if you think Toyota does not take advantage of it, read on.

The "Swiss Army Knife" for Process Improvement

There is not a more powerful chart in a leader's repertoire than an SPC chart. From Dr. Shewhart's first control chart in the 1920s, control charts have been used by HROs ever since, although control charts were not widely known outside of Western Electric until World War II. These charts are so valuable that some customers require evidence of a controlled process before buying the first product or service from that process. This chart fits medicine like a glove. How many times have you come up against resistance because the change you wanted wasn't evidence-based? How many times have you struggled to convince a stakeholder that what he or she thinks is improvement is only random variation and there is no trend? Have you ever wanted some proof that what you asked for isn't out of the ordinary? That your supplier should have anticipated your demand and been ready to meet your request? Most important in HROs is the ability to prevent failure. This chart can do all this and more.

This same chart is so versatile and has so many benefits, I call it the "Swiss army knife" of process improvement and Change Leadership. Yes, Change Leadership benefits from it. If you think that change management is measurement-averse, it often is, but great Change Leaders utilize the 3Ms and this chart very well. Although Abraham Lincoln did not have the benefit of leading with this chart, we know he constantly measured his generals' progress, managed to the measure (he replaced many generals until he found one that could move the measure), and made it easier for his generals to know his vision and his direction and he empowered them to make it easier for them to lead.

This chart can not only show the status as it is occurring, but it can be used in a Measurement System Analysis (MSA) previously covered to show the quality of the measurement system. SPC can tell us if a change is actually occurring or if the measure simply is from normal common cause variation. Another benefit of the SPC chart is to show capability of a service or process before and after a change is made.

Figure 13.2 is an example of an SPC chart of hand hygiene compliance. I also include a template in Appendix 8 that you can use in your organization. Hand hygiene is not just a healthcare industry task to measure. If you want to reduce the risk of colds and the flu in your family, measure hand hygiene and manage to it. Make it easier by providing your family alcohol-based hand cleaner, too.

Please look at the chart as I explain its features in a quick overview now and in more detail in later paragraphs. The hand hygiene compliance for August 12 was 20%. Compliance for the next day, August 13, was 30%. A line connects the compliance for each day. The line in the center of the

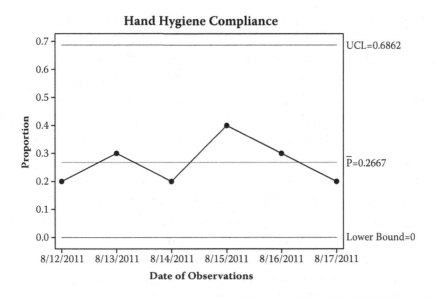

Figure 13.2 Hand hygiene compliance in a unit. UCL stands for Upper Control Limit. X stands for Mean. LCL stands for Lower Control Limit.

two horizontal lines is the average of the compliance across all six days. Therefore, the average hand hygiene compliance is immediately evident by looking at this line and reading the value, which is 26.7% (.2667).

The other two lines are called control limits. They represent the "tails" of the distribution of the data. One would expect that the hand hygiene should be between these two lines most of the time. One would not expect in a stable environment that the hand hygiene compliance will fall below the lower line. A stable process is one where there have been no significant changes to the process. If the compliance went lower than the lower control limit, we have reason to conclude there might be something special happening that day. The same logic works if compliance breaks through the top control limit. We would not expect a day when hand hygiene exceeded .686 or 69%. If it did, the team is wise to practice the second M, Manage to the measure. The team should immediately go out to the process and invite people to explain why the hand hygiene was so good when compared with prior days. The team wants to reinforce these behaviors to sustain the higher compliance.

Components of the SPC Control Chart

SPC charts have common components, but not all SPC charts share all common components. Here are the most common:

◾ Data points representing a statistic that you want to chart. In the case above, we are charting by day the proportion of times healthcare professionals wash when they should have washed. These points also could be a single number, such as the number of defects in a surgical process, a range, or a mean of a sample taken from the process at different times.

◾ An SPC chart is usually a time series chart. That is, the bottom scale is in order of time. Data are plotted from the earliest time period to later time periods.

◾ Parameters: Three lines are usually charted. They include:

  – The mean line (center line) using the data points from the chart for a period of time that represents the period that you want to use in calculating the central tendency. Often, the control chart uses every data point on the chart to calculate the mean line.

    • A useful option is to use the SPC chart parameters to show a difference before and after a change. We do this by calculating the mean line with only the data points before the change, and then recalculate the mean line with data points after the change. We will show an example later.

  – Upper control limit (UCL, sometimes called a "natural process limit") that indicates the threshold at which the process output is considered statistically "unlikely" to be above. This line is typically at three standard deviations (or an estimate) from the center line.

  – Lower control limit (LCL) that indicates the lower bound of where points are likely to fall above in a stable process.

Control limits have nothing to do with what the customer requires. It is not your goal. Think of control limits as the "voice of the process." Specification limits can be the "voice of the customer." Please don't confuse the two.

Specification limits could be added to the SPC chart, but we must be very clear that these are not control limits. I have learned to emphasize this many times to ensure people do not confuse control limits with customer specifications. Because of this confusion, I resist adding customer specifications on a SPC chart until I am confident people understand what the control limits are.

Control and Out of Control

Statistical Process Control is an apt name for a control chart because the chart is able to tell if the process, that is, a statistic from the process, is in a state of control. A process in which its control chart shows only data falling between the control limits and doesn't show trends or patterns, is said to be a process in control. Another word for control is *stable*. A chart that has points falling outside the control limits, or has patterns or trends, is said to represent a process out of control, or unstable. Processes that are in control exhibit common cause variation. A process that is out of control has special cause variation. Special causes, such as when a team implements a change that really improves a process, are what makes a stable, in control chart showing only common cause variation to go out of control. Do you see the chain of events and understand the terms now? Let's take another scenario to practice better understanding SPC.

Case Study

Call Center Wait Times

We start a new call center and the wait times vary tremendously as the support staff and technical engineers who provide support work out the kinks in scheduling. We find that on days when the more junior technicians normally don't work, the control chart of wait times goes out of control. The wait times are under the lower control limit. We know there is a special cause because the chart went out of control. Going out of control is not necessarily bad, or unfavorable. In fact, we want the chart to go out of control when we make a change. Another name for change is a *special cause*. A leader might find using the term *special cause* easily understood early in the change process. Later, when the team is charting the process being changed, the special cause will be seen and celebration may be in order. Remember Small's contribution to this wonderful tool. Make it practical.

Here is how practical it can be. Now, if you have Minitab® and know SPC like the back of your hand, I want you to relax a bit here. I want others reading about SPC for the first time to not resist learning this tool, and taking a bit of liberty with statistics. Close is better than not doing SPC at all. Even Dr. Shewhart and Dr. Deming considered control charting to be more a rule of thumb, heuristic, versus a pure statistically perfect method.

Using a Simple Histogram to Create SPC Chart Parameters

Estimating the control limits is done several ways, but an approximation of a variance statistic to calculate control limits is much better than not setting control limits at all. For more on this subject, read *Understanding Statistical*

Process Control, by Don Wheeler and David Chambers.[2] Wheeler was a student and worked under Dr. Deming for 21 years and has advanced Small's work in making SPC practical for any industry. Plot the wait times on a histogram. The way to do this is to create a simple chart with the expected range of wait times on the bottom scale, the x axis. List the lowest expected time on the far left and the highest expected time on the far right and write values in between these two values along the bottom. Next, plot the wait times observed by making an "x" above the wait time on the x axis. If you get two wait times of the same time, put one x above the other, and so on. Eventually, the data will form a "mountain" or perhaps a few mountain peaks. Draw a curve that best fits the top of each column of xs. Extend the curve to the left and to the right following the shape of the curve. These are the "tails" of the distribution.

A histogram is simply a graphical depiction of the data. It shows the central tendency where approximately half of the data is to the left and half is to the right. The histogram also shows the spread of the data. The width of the curve you drew shows the spread or variation. The histogram also shows the shape of the data. If the data looks like a "bell" with one pronounced peak symmetrical to each tail, we call this a normal distribution. Many times we might see two peaks. This is commonly seen when we have two different processes being measured or data from two shifts of workers or any number of possibilities. If the chart has more than one peak, I need you to stop here and first find out why you have two peaks. Once you understand why and find the reason for two different "populations," you are probably better off to create two SPC charts. I explain how next.

To create your SPC chart, look at where the central tendency of your data lie. This wait time on the x axis will be your average line. This line is often colored green in software. To estimate your upper control limit, simply go out to the right of the histogram and estimate where about 99% of the data will be at or below the wait time shown on the x axis. Use this wait time for your upper control limit. Do the same on the left tail to estimate where the first 1% or less of your data are and use that wait time on the x axis as your lower control limit. *Voila*. You now can draw your SPC chart in time series on the x axis and start plotting the wait times in times series order. It is a good rule of thumb to wait until you have 25 or more samples before creating your histogram.

Post your SPC chart with a footnote on how you estimated your parameters and start measuring and managing to the measure. Include the SPC interpretation chart that I supply in the book alongside your SPC chart and start watching what happens. Let me know how it goes at www.rpmexec.com

Practicality is the friend of process improvement and perfection is often the enemy. Is this technique that much worse than what these people do in Excel® with imposing a trend line and making statements that there are significant trends? Of course it isn't. I would rather have people use this technique over the Excel trend line any day. Dr. Deming grew tired of people tweaking processes suggesting there were trends when in reality there was simply common cause variation. If anything, go try this method with relatively normally shaped distributions and test the sensitivity of the parameters knowing the actual standard error of the mean and other more precise statistics used to calculate the SPC control limits. (See Figure 13.3 for a comparison of parameters using a histogram and using software.)

Interpreting SPC charts

The leader and team can take advantage of a special cause happening to understand the process of better scheduling. If the chart was displayed the next day, the team would have seen something special happened the day before when the chart went out of control. Still fresh in their minds, someone might have suggested that yesterday was the day that the less experienced technicians didn't work. Further investigation as to why new technicians might be correlated with out-of-control wait times may have exposed that the Web site update on call center work times was changed.

This bulge of customers calling at the same time would have explained why the wait times were longer than the days before the Web site change. Aha! The SPC chart triggered us to look for a special cause and a solution now is self-evident—schedule the junior technicians evenly across the week and stagger the start times and post on the Web site. (See Figure 13.4 for how to interpret in-control and out-of-control SPC charts.) This easy-to-read chart is useful to display with SPC charts for people in the process of managing their processes.

The chart in Figure 13.5 shows how the SPC chart can alert us that the process has changed. It is very clear now that we have made an improvement in hand hygiene because the process is out of control. Out of control is exactly what we wanted. Out of control means we made a change that had an effect.

We calculate the parameters (mean and control limit lines) using the baseline data. We now "lock in" these parameters knowing we have changed

Summary for Measurements

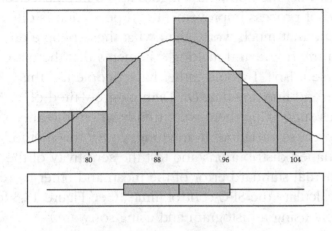

Anderson-Darling Normality Test	
A-Squared	0.23
P-Value	0.798
Mean	90.512
St Dev	7.974
Variance	63.588
Skewness	-0.041802
Kurtosis	-0.738376
N	42
Minimum	75.000
1st Quartile	84.000
Median	90.592
3rd Quartile	96.475
Maximum	105.000
95% Confidence Interval for Mean	
88.027	92.997
95% Confidence Interval for Median	
88.000	93.967
95% Confidence Interval for St Dev	
6.561	10.168

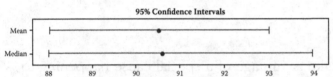

95% Confidence Intervals

Chart of Measurements

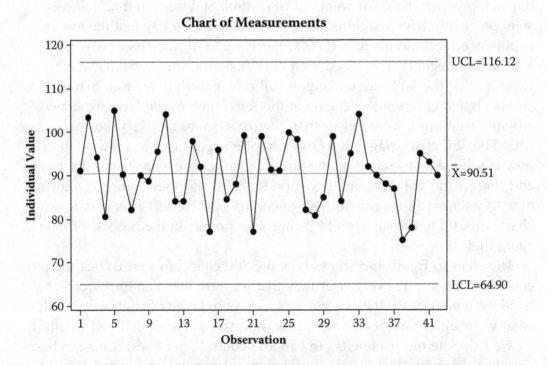

Figure 13.3 Comparison of estimating parameters using histograms and SPC software.

SPC Interpretation

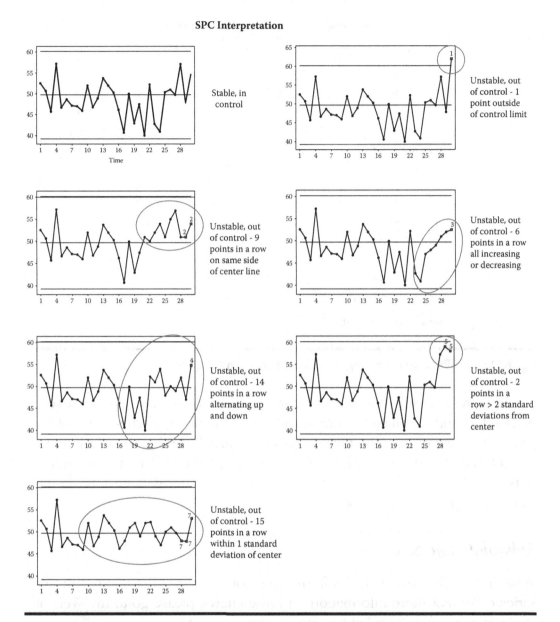

Figure 13.4 Control chart control and out-of-control examples.

the process. The changes we made were training everyone in hand hygiene, adding dispensers to make it easier to sanitize, putting up posters reminding everyone the importance of cleaning, stocking rooms with common equipment and supplies, and putting computers in each room so nurses don't have to waste time exiting the rooms so often to get dressings and do their charting. We plot hand hygiene on the same chart with the parameters, not recalculating every time we add a new day and see what happens.

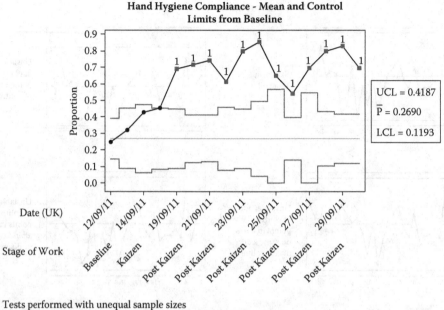

Figure 13.5 SPC chart showing out-of-control from baseline.

In Figure 13.6, we show the three major stages of our process improvement effort and calculate the mean and control limits by each stage. This gives us a view of how the three stages compare. Note that the chart is in control in all three stages. Although there is not enough data, two points, in two of the stages, we are more interested in the later data and if it is showing improvement and stability.

Reliability and SPC

Reliability engineering benefits from some control charts that are not in time series order. For more information on these charts, please go to my Web site at: www.rpmexec.com\reliabilityengineering

Additional features found on some SPC charts include:

- Upper and lower early warning limits, drawn as separate lines, typically two standard deviations above and below the center line.
- Stages where special causes are known and the parameters are recalculated to show how the process has changed. (See above when we recalculate the parameters to show a "before and after" effect.)

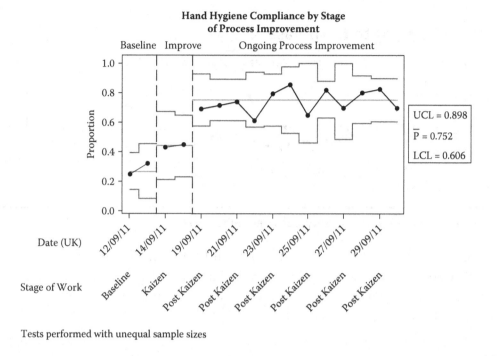

Figure 13.6   Showing stages.

SPC Is Often Preferred in Managing to the Measure

The SPC chart is the preferred method of Managing to the measure. Simply writing comments, questions, and suggestions on the chart demonstrates that you, the leader, are measuring and value the input of the team. This is so simple, yet so powerful. Try making a note on the charts every day that they are posted. On days where there was an attempt to improve the process, note the attempted special cause, and stay tuned to the chart to see if the change has created an out-of-control situation. If, and when, it goes out of control, reinforce the team in acting. The Progress Principle can be seen having an effect. Make sure to reinforce progress toward the vision.

An example of how to manage to the measure using the SPC chart is seen in Figure 13.7.

Prove Change Really Occurred

The team can use the SPC chart to prove change really occurred. If the team eliminated or reduced the effect that the top contributing factors had on

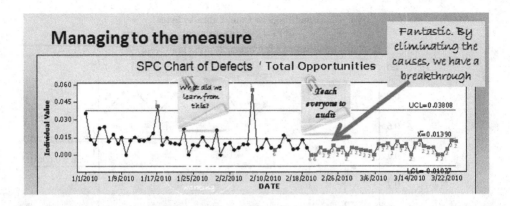

Figure 13.7   Notes made on surgical safety SPC chart.

people washing their hands, the team would know if they really improved hand hygiene when the SPC chart showed a trend of points above the upper control limit. The Pareto Chart and SPC are like peanut butter and jelly. They go so well together.

Change Management without SPC?

There are some process improvement programs that don't cover charting, and definitely not statistical process control. The better ones tag team with an instructor or firm that teaches Lean Six Sigma, or at least the fundamentals of quality. I don't know why any change management consultant would position his or her firm on the premise that creating consensus on a need, molding a vision, and getting teams together magically makes change and then makes change last. I do know such efforts can fail to make change happen. "If you want it, measure it" evidently isn't believed by change management instructors who dismiss the value of measuring. I have heard many excuses why measurement is not taught in some change management initiatives. The worst excuse is the one that is most counter to the philosophy of change management. That excuse is that control charting is too difficult for the people. Isn't a mantra of Change Management a belief in people development and abilities?

Frontline Workers Have Been Using SPC Since the 1920s

Dare someone to prove that SPC is too difficult for frontline workers to use. Remember that Bonnie Small and Joseph Juran successfully taught SPC to factory workers in the 1940s. I started teaching SPC in 1982 to factory workers, some of whom didn't have a high school certificate. I have witnessed tens of thousands of dollars spent on change management programs, and thousands of hours learning change management without measuring, managing to the measure, and making it easier. After a couple of years with one of these initiatives, not one change could be attributed to the investment. This came from one of the Change Masters, herself. Not even the culture significantly changed. Reporting did not increase, there definitely was not a just culture, and no one felt safe despite all the leadership chatter on growing a safe culture.

What did change were results from teams who measured, managed to the measure, and made it easier for people to do the right thing. One of the subcultures required for achieving a safety culture is a culture of reporting. SPC is a way to report. Even a line chart would be useful. Even better, SPC shows when change really is occurring. It gives evidence to a team that they are making progress, and when they are not, so they try new ways.

I believe if you achieve the skill in using control charts, you will use SPC. Even if you approximate the control limits, or use the rules of a Run Chart explained next, you will do better than those who talk about change, but refuse to measure the impact. SPC is a tool that should always be in "your back pocket." I haven't left home without it since 1980 when I first learned it.

Run Charts

One physician uses run charts that are similar to SPC charts. Run charts and SPC charts are a leader's friend because they prove if trends are occurring, if the process is in control, and if changes are having an effect. The difference between run charts and SPC charts is mostly that run charts don't have control limits. Therefore, run charts are not as sensitive to special causes from large variations from the norm. For some practitioners, they find using the same interpretation rules as SPC charts for trends and patterns gets them the information they need without calculating control limits. Run charts made more sense before computers when control limits were an added calculation. Computers today are located almost everywhere and software calculates the parameters easily and accurately.

Your organization may already have software to create SPC charts. If you are a healthcare firm accredited by The Joint Commission, I know you do. My team, with the help of Susan Swarts, provided a free SPC feature in the hand hygiene feature. It was that important to me to make it easy for all of our clients. The National Health System (NHS) in the United Kingdom makes an SPC application available to anyone with an NHS email address. What a wonderful gift. The Institute of Healthcare Improvement (IHI) in America provides free training in Run charts and SPC charts.[3]

There are applications that run in Excel to make control charts and my favorite quality improvement software and the choice of many Lean Six Sigma practitioners is Minitab. I list several sources in the Appendices and challenge you to try creating an SPC chart now. Go to www.minitab.com,[4] download a free 30-day trial, gather some data in time series order, and make your first SPC chart. I even include screen navigation instructions on how to make an SPC chart. For data, go to my Web site and download the data. I include the answers as well as the SPC chart for you to compare yours to mine.

Even Run charts are better than using a line chart in Excel. Above all, don't even think about using the Excel trend line feature, unless you know how the trend line is calculated.

Now that we know SPC, we can better Manage to the measure.

Key Points

- Statistical Process Control Charts are the "Swiss army knife" for process improvement.
- Managing to the measure is much more effective with SPC because we know if there has been a real change in a process.
- SPC also can be an early warning of a process or function starting to vary. SPC helps prevent failures, if used in a timely manner.

Endnotes

1. Western Electric History. Online at: http://www.porticus.org/bell/westernelectric_history.html#Western%20Electric%20-%0A%20Brief%20History
2. Don Wheeler and David Chamber, *Understanding Statistical Process Control*, 3rd ed. (Knoxville, KY: SPC Press, 2010).
3. http://www.ihi.org/offerings/VirtualPrograms/OnDemand/Run_ControlCharts/Pages/default.aspx
4. www.minitab.com

Chapter 14

3Ms: Manage to the Measure

If you cannot measure it, you cannot control it.

John Grebe[1]

Fine, fine; don't do anything to patch it up. The way things are going, gangrene will set in. Then we can amputate and clean up the problem once and for all.

John Grebe[2]

Managers taking action was more effective than their communicating about actions taken … Managers would be well advised to take action—preferably substantive and intense action—in response to frontline workers' communications about problems.

Anita L. Tucker and Sara J. Singer[3]

The Scoreboard

The 3Ms are not worth anything if no one sees the measures. Imagine walking into a sports stadium after the event has started and hearing the crowd cheering. What's the first thing you look for? The score. What is one of the biggest pieces of equipment in even the largest of stadiums? The scoreboard. If you want to see what just happened on the field, what do you look at? The scoreboard. Why do we make it so difficult in our organizations to see the score? Where is your score posted? When was it posted? Yesterday? Last month? Last quarter? Would you value seeing the score in the sports stadium three periods later than the one you are watching live? Before we get too down on how poorly our scoring systems are, though, let's realize that in our ICUs (intensive care units) we have scores showing a patient's vital signs, everyone who needs to see the "score" can see; some "scoreboards" even have alarms in case a vital sign is varying. And, they are in real time. So, maybe the question is: How do we scale up from where we have been keeping score for years? I will share some tips that you can use right away, especially now that you have made your first Statistical Process Control (SPC) chart.

Visual Management

Visual management is an appropriate term for the second M. Managing to the measure is making the measure visible to the people in the process. The takt time and performance to takt time is often displayed for all to see. I already shared with you that in one organization in the 1980s, any person in the facility could see all key measures in near real time. Some organizations have gone far beyond visual management for internal use. They post their measures on their Web site and in their organizations to be completely transparent. High Reliability Organizations (HROs) have a safety culture, and we know that a subculture necessary for a safety culture is a culture of reporting. A leader may use public reporting to help reduce the resistance to change.

Dashboards are another term that fits the bill. Think of the dashboard in the car. Within the dashboard are measures that are critical to the safe function of the vehicle (Figure 14.1).

There is a gas gauge, a speedometer, mileage, and an indicator for your headlights displayed on virtually every car's dashboard. What would be in your dashboard? Your supplier's?

Until GPSs (global positioning systems), there was not a visual management gauge for the primary outcome metric for why we use a car, interestingly enough. I guess we didn't need one because we could look out the window to see that we reached our destination. Now, we have a visual and a voice telling us" "You have arrived at your destination." The value of a GPS is the guidance we get along the way to our destination, our desired outcome. This is the same reason we measure the inputs that drive the outcome

Figure 14.1 Car gauges.

desired in our organizations. We measure the number of slips, lapses, and mistakes, as James Reason[4] lists, in our process to reduce the bad outcomes. We measure the vital signs of a process to predict the probability of poor outcomes. A reporting culture is one in which people are willing to report their slips, lapses, and mistakes. The benefit is to achieve a Learning Culture, another subculture to a Safety Culture.

What to Expect Short Term and Long Term from Measuring

We need to understand that even SPC charts are a means to an end. Once a process has become stable and capable, the work is not over. There is a way to reduce and even eliminate the need to continue to measure. The way is to assure stability and capability and robustness to variation. Mistake-proofing is one way to achieve all three, and thus eliminate the need to continue to measure. After all, if there was no way for the inputs to vary, and the outcome was acceptable, measure has done its job and may be reduced to a level just to make sure variation does not return. An example of mistake-proofing in your car is the inability of shifting from park without your foot on the brake. As long as the process that installed these safety devices is mistake-proof, there is little need to measure the quality.

For many processes, we are a long way from such control and performance. Nonetheless, as improvements occur from the third M (Make it easier) and the control and capability increased, the frequency of first M (Measure) may be gradually reduced. This, in turn, may reduce the frequency to manage to the measure, the second M (Manage to the measure).

Instructing and Coaching

Managing to the measure requires both instructing and coaching. It is cruel to expect people to change before they have been taught what the change is, why it is occurring, and what their role is in the change. We did a Stakeholder Analysis as one of the first steps in process improvement. Now is a good time to "dust it off" and refresh it. Managing to the measure is both a coach's tool as it is an instructor's tool.

The role of the instructor is to share with others how to do a task to achieve the outcome desired. The measure is how the instructor can assess if the student learned. The measure also is how the coach knows skill and progress is gaining.

Training within Industry

Learning how to instruct is a good way to learn how to Manage to the measure. Training within Industry (TWI) has been credited with much of the success among the allies in winning World War II. The situation in the early 1940s was dire. Men went off to war and left a vacuum of talent in the factories to provide equipment and munitions to support the men overseas. A commission reached back to research work started in the 1920s to improve the method of instructing workers, women, to be exact, who would replace the men in the factories. The method they discovered evolved into TWI.

There are four steps in TWI. They include:

■ Job Instructions (JI)
■ Job Methods (JM)
■ Job Relations (JR)
■ Program Development (PD)

Job Instructions

If the worker hasn't learned, the instructor hasn't taught.

There are two steps in Job Instructions for the instructor:

■ How to get ready to instruct.
■ How to instruct.

TWI breaks each step into tasks. The term *Standard Work* is often used in Lean Six Sigma and borrowed from The Toyota Production System.[5] Taiichi Ohno gives TWI credit for the basis for Standard Work.

- How to get ready to instruct:
  - Have a timetable for you to instruct and the student to learn the skill.
  - Breakdown the task into the right way and with key points.
  - Have everything ready to teach and do the task correctly.
  - Have workplace properly arranged.
- How to instruct:
  - Prepare the student to receive the instruction: Put them at ease.
  - Present the task to learn: Tell her, show him, illustrate, ask in small doses.
  - Try out his performance: Have him perform the task and verbalize why he is doing what he is doing. Ensure he states key points.
  - Follow up: Ensure the student knows who can help if needed, not just anyone who may give wrong instruction.

We can practice Job Instructions skills using the charts. Practice instructing how to use a chart to Manage to the measure. Follow the instructions in Job Instructions just as they are written. You might instruct them how to read the chart, how to know when it is in control or when it is not, and what might be a useful comment to post on the chart to show you care and want the team to succeed in process improvement.

After instructing and observing the person Manage to the measure, ask your pupil how you did as an instructor. If we make it easy to learn, we will utilize the 3Ms faster and better.

Job Methods

Listed below is a practical plan to help you produce greater quantities of quality products in less time by making the best use of the manpower, machines, and materials now available.

Step 1. Break down the job:

1. List all the details of the job exactly as done by the present method:
   a. Be sure details include all:
      i. Material handling
      ii. Machine work
      iii. Hand work

Step 2. Question every detail:

1. Use these types of questions:
   a. Why is it necessary?
   b. What is the purpose?
   c. Where shall it be done?
   d. When should it be done?
   e. Who is best qualified to do it?
   f. How is the best way to do it?

Step 3. Develop the new method:

1. Eliminate
2. Combine
3. Rearrange
4. Simplify

Step 4. Apply the new method:

1. Sell your proposal to your boss
2. Sell the new method to the operator
3. Get full approval of all concerned on safety, quality, quantity, cost
4. Put the new method to work

One can see that the Job Instructions and Job Methods are very similar to what many call Lean. That is no coincidence. Japan was taught by Americans using TWI after the war. Not all credit goes to either country. It is surprising to me how we again are reinventing these materials for a third or fourth time. TWI actually evolved from work done in the World War I.

Job Relations

Job Relations is the third part of TWI. It starts with the quote: "A supervisor gets results through people."

Our Change Leadership principles follow closely the Job Relations methods including engaging the workers who do the work, training them, and enabling them in process improvement.

Program Development

According to TWI, Program Development is about problem solving. Its steps include:

- Spot a production problem
- Determine a plan to study it
- Get a plan into action
- Check results

This is very much why the 3Ms work. Program development is about using measures to help improve a process.

Standard Work to Manage to the Measure

The article in Figure 14.2 (from one of the original TWI government brochures) explains about hospitals and how TWI was valued in healthcare.

What many of you know as Standard Work started out as shown in Figure 14.3. How to make it easier to do the right work the right way is shown clearly in this layout. Note the term *Key Points*. It is no coincidence that I use Key Points at the end of every chapter to help you capture the essence of this book. The instructor will ensure that the tasks are done correctly and also ask the trainee to state the key points to ensure the student knows the importance of the work.

HOSPITALS in various parts of the country are finding that the Training Within Industry program of the War Manpower Commission holds a great deal of value to them. This program was first described for hospitals in an article by Ellen Aird entitled "You Can Keep Employes," published in The MODERN HOSPITAL for December 1942.

Figure 14.2 Training within Industry (TWI) in hospitals.

CLEANING AN OCCUPIED ROOM

STEPS	KEY POINTS
1. Clean rug with carpet sweeper. Clean with vacuum cleaner once a week. 2. Dust floor with dry mop.	1. Do not bump bed or furniture with cleaning tools, as this annoys the patient and mars the furniture. When vacuum cleaner is used also clean the floor with it.
3. Dust all furniture. 4. Dust windows, sills and window shields, wood work and hardware. 5. Clean face bowl and plumbing. 6. Empty and clean wastebasket. 7. If there are dirty spots on floor, wipe them up with wet cloth. 8. Wash floor every other day, except in unusual cases, which might require washing the floor every day.	3. Be careful to dust all hidden corners. 4. Wash when needed. 5. Dry all nickel or chrome plate. 8. When rug is vacuum cleaned, also wash the floor. This makes the patient feel the room is thoroughly cleaned.

Figure 14.3   Standard work for cleaning an occupied room.

In Figure 14.4, I include an actual Standard Work form on the same task in the 1940s. We might be a little more conscious these days about hand hygiene, but the similarities are striking.

Utilizing the 3Ms has been going on for years as evidenced by these 1940s articles. Measuring is mentioned throughout the four steps, Managing to measure is in all four steps, and making it easier is what Program Development is about.

Coaching is Key in Managing to the Measure

I wanted to share some tips on coaching with you. Instructing is necessary to get the skills learned, but coaching is what gets process improvement occurring and with sustained gains.

- Teaching is the Job Method. This is part of standard work.
  - A checklist in the cockpit is an example of Standard Work. But, it does not alone guarantee performance.
  - Instructing is not enough to change behaviors.
  - Coaching is required to achieve the performance after instructing.
- "In the moment" or "Just In Time" coaching is much more effective than "a week later" coaching.

Standard Work Procedure - Cleaning Occupied Room						Pod or Area:			
Process Name:		Cleaning Occupied Room				Signoff or initial acknowl-edgement		Recorded by:	Revision Date:
Key		Safety	Critical	Quality Check		Supervisor names			
		⬛	△	◆					
		Time (seconds)							
Step #	Process Steps	Time (seconds)	Key	Safety Equipment Required	Moment	Layout and Graphical Job Aid			
1	Park trolley outside patient room								
2	Knock on door and enter		⬛	Sanitize	1				
3	Ask if service is required								
4	Sanitize and glove		⬛	Sanitize	2				
5	Empty bin from room and bath to bag at entrance								
6	Clean bathroom								
7	Use chemical to clean surfaces								
8	Wash sink, shower, and by toilet								
9	Wash floor to dry								
10	Deglove & Sanitize hands		⬛	Sanitize	3				
11	Reglove & Sanitize hands		⬛	Sanitize	3				
12	Clean bedroom, dusting high and low, surfaces, etc.								
13	Pick up bin to sluice								
14	Deglove and Sanitize hands		⬛	Sanitize	3&4				
15	Pick up towels using shoulder to open cabinet door								
16	Bring linens to room and store								
17	Complete vacuum								
18	Sanitize hands		⬛	Sanitize	5				

Figure 14.4   Standard Work in the twenty-first century.

Just-In-Time coaching can only occur in the process or with real-time measurement shared remotely. A Change Leader must be an instructor and a coach. One can't coach correctly if the coach does not know the right way to do the task. Instructing without following up to observe the person doing the task will not guarantee the reliability and quality of the performance. Everyone needs a coach, even star musicians and athletes have coaches. Executives wanting to improve often have coaches.

Now is a good time to remind one of the Progress Principle[6]: "Of all the things that can boost inner work life, the most important is making progress in meaningful work." A coach carves out progressive goals for the person he is coaching. If we want people to some day accomplish the remarkable, we should instruct and coach them on the fundamentals. An example is when I instruct people in how to do the 3Ms. I teach them the three Ms with the overview slide listing examples. I teach them the key point of each M, which is included in the title immediately following each M. Next, I have them practice the 3Ms with a relatively simple example in class or, even better, an example in his or her work area.

Coach's Playbook

At Motorola, we helped each coach create a playbook. The playbook lists standard work for routine and regularly occurring tasks. The playbook can even have alternative plays based on variables that change. Interestingly, the quality program was named, "Quality Vital Signs."

A coach needs to manage by walking around and engaging the people in the process. Instead of telling people what to do, a wise coach listens, observes, and asks the right questions at the right time to engage the person's intellect and get feedback on how well the instruction given earlier has been absorbed.

The coach should lead off conversations with a question how things are proceeding. The performance to the key measures is what the coach is expecting to hear. By asking how things are going, the coach is looking for the person to demonstrate performance and issues using the measures. The dashboard is a wonderful method to show the coach how the process is running.

Again, TWI has the same message we teach today (Figure 14.5).

Key Points

- Managing to the measure started with the charting skills being built.
- The SPC chapter gave us powerful and easy to use charts to know what we can do as managers to build on the success and to support the teams.
- Training within Industry is clearly the parent of Standard Work and how we instruct workers today. TWI had extensive reach into healthcare as well.
- Coaching is vital to managing to the measure. A little common sense and the Golden Rule go far in helping us become better coaches.
- The key aid is the measure allowing us more confidence in how things really are.

(1) Knowledge of the Work — materials, tools, processes, operations, products and how they are made and used.

(2) Knowledge of Responsibilities — policies, agreements, rules, regulations, schedules, interdepartmental relationships.

These two knowledge needs must be met currently and locally by each plant or company.

Such knowledge must be provided if each supervisor is to know his job and is to have a clear understanding of his authority and responsibilities as a part of management.

(3) Skill in Instructing — increasing production by helping supervisors to develop a well-trained work force which will get into production quicker and have less scrap, rework and rejects, fewer accidents, and less tool and equipment damage.

(4) Skill in Improving Methods — utilizing materials, machines, and manpower more effectively by making supervisors study each operation in order to eliminate, combine, rearrange, and simplify details of the job.

(5) Skill in Leading — increasing production by helping supervisors to improve their understanding of individuals, their ability to size up situations, and their ways of working with people.

These three skills must be acquired individually. Practice and experience in using them enable both new and experienced supervisors to recognize and solve daily problems promptly.

Figure 14.5 Coaching in TWI.

Endnotes

1. Ray Boundy and J. Laurence Amos (eds.), *A History of the Dow Chemical Physics Lab, The Freedom to Be Creative* (New York: Marcel Dekker, 1990, 53).
2. Ray Boundy and J. Laurence Amos (eds.), *A History of the Dow Chemical Physics Lab, The Freedom to Be Creative* (New York: Marcel Dekker, 1990, 180).
3. Anita L. Tucker and Sara J. Singer, "Going Through the Motions: An Empirical Test of Management Involvement in Process Improvement," *Harvard Business Review* (April 2009).
4. James Reason, *Human Error*, (Cambridge, U.K.: Cambridge Press, 1990).
5. C. R. Dooley, Report III: Vocational Training, International Labor Organization (Montreal, 1946).
6. Yasuhiro Monden, *The Toyota Production System*, 2nd ed., (Norcross, GA: Institute of Industrial Engineers, 1993).

Chapter 15

3Ms: Make It Easier

Performance Improvement in Making It Easier to Change

If change was easy, you wouldn't be reading this book. The "laws" of process improvement follow other laws as we have witnessed with electricity and now from Sir Isaac Newton, who is considered one of the most important scientists of all time. He studied motion and developed three laws. Newton's First Law of Motion[1] is often paraphrased in Change Leadership to explain resistance. We think it has a dual value. Besides referring to a body at rest, we think his law supports the benefits of a culture of continuous improvement.

> Newton's Law I: Every body persists in its state of being at rest or of moving uniformly straight forward, except insofar as it is compelled to change its state by force impressed.

The process improvement leader simply presents the force to help people change, whether the change is to start moving or to change direction.

Newton's second law is easier to understand if we understand his third law first.

> Newton's third law: To every action there is always an equal and opposite reaction.

Let's say that you want your son and daughter to become more active. You find them too often sitting in their rooms watching TV and you are concerned about the lack of exercise. You decide that you want to be a Change Leader and lead them to engage in a sport or play a musical instrument. You literally have bodies at rest, in your view. You try to pull them off the floor to go outside with you. You pull, and they pull back. Resistance. If they are the same size as you, the resistance is considerable. Now, let's add the second law and relate it to how a Change Leader can use these three laws of motion to lead change easier.

Newton's second law is that the acceleration of motion is ever proportional to the motive force impressed, and is made in the direction of the right line in which that force is impressed.

Newton explains that the forces may be:

■ Equal
■ Opposing

However, the acceleration of change on the two bodies is dependent on the mass of the bodies. In other words, when the kids are young and small, mom or dad can change these bodies at rest into bodies in motion much easier than when they outgrow the poor parents.

Case Study

Store Staff Spending Time with Customers

Relating this to change in the workplace, we want to change a worker's behavior with customers. Managers want to increase the face-to-face time retail workers spend with shoppers. They believe this change will result in more satisfied shoppers because customers may feel their store cares more than the store's competitors. You, the manager, find the clerks everywhere except with the customers as they browse and often struggle to get assistance. You find your staff running to the back getting supplies, chatting at the desk, and in meetings that you set up. To make the change easier, we suggest applying process improvement to the first and third issue. Process improvement could include eliminating the reasons that the supplies aren't where they are supposed to be or in sufficient quantities. The third issue could be caused by other changes going on that you want them to know. These are legitimate reasons, but even legitimate reasons may be a force that is keeping your next change from happening. A process improvement team or manager must often choose timing of changes so changes do not create a resistance themselves from overburden.

Once we have the first and third issue resolved and resistance to change reduced, let's focus on the second issue: chatting at the desk.

Job Satisfaction

Before we show how Newton's laws can help teams improve a process, let's realize that this book has actually given you tips on making change easier throughout. Remember the "Hawthorne Effect?" Let's use it to answer if a customer's level of satisfaction improves with more attention: Even though the study measured productivity, perhaps satisfaction with the job actually improved productivity first. Applying this same idea with workers, will the staff be more satisfied and "productive" with productive meaning the amount of time spent with customers if their manager spends more time with them? Try this in leading your next change and see if simply spending time with the stakeholders reduces the resistance and gets the change you are looking for occurring. Now let's go back to our example using Newton's laws in leading change.

You walk to the desk and see staff searching the Internet on the computers. You start with an icebreaker to create a safer culture for reporting and chat a bit. Next, you share with them the benefits you believe occur for the customers and themselves if they spend more time with customers on the floor. You purposely pause to let them respond and watch for nonverbal communication to understand their receptiveness to this conversation on change.

You get some remarks about how they normally walk among customers, but customers don't want to be bothered. And, you discover that they are often going to the back of the store to get new batteries in their handheld scanners used to check availability for customers on the floor. You promise to get someone down from IT to help fix this issue. Even then, they share that they like to sit at the desk where they have access to the faster computer to check inventory and can print options for the customers, which they can't do out on the floor. Voila, you are finding that this change is going to be tougher than expected because there are a number of valid issues that make this change more difficult than simply walking around.

We realize again the benefit that Abraham Lincoln found in his principle to "CIRCULATE among followers consistently." And, as I have shared with you, "If we know what each other knows, then we'll feel like each other feels, and we will do like each other does." In Toyota, they have the saying, "Go to the Gemba." Translated, this means go to where the work is. The value of being where the work is in invaluable in process improvement.

The change that you wanted the clerks to make—spending more time with customers—has been resisted for valid reasons. The forces acting on the clerks to not be on the floor was greater than the force from others to be on the floor. In fact, it was impossible to fully serve customers when the handheld computers don't operate. Any force that a manager would apply without helping them with time and support to solve these issues would have been met with an equal and opposing force. And, for this action there would always be an equal and opposite reaction. The staff outnumbers the managers, so the mass of the group being greater than the one manager would result in the acceleration of the manager being greater than the bodies at rest behind the desk.

Making Change Easier Is What We Need to Do

What would make it easier for the staff to spend time with customers? This entire book is about this chapter, "Make It Easier." Let's start from the top: the Roadmap for a Change Leader and process improvement leader. This chapter will walk you through the entire book of key points. We will use the Roadmap to guide us. By the end of this chapter, I think you will have the knowledge to utilize the 3Ms for Process Improvement and more confidence from practicing it with me (Figure 15.1).

The issue is to improve the process so staff spends more time with customers. Let's get started at the top left of the Roadmap.

Roadmap to Performance Excellence™				
PDSA	What are we trying to accomplish?	How will we know when a change is an improvement?	PDSA Cycle - What are the possible solutions and how do we implement the best solution?	How do we maintain the gains we have achieved and standardize?
Lean Six Sigma	Define the issue What does the customer value?	Measure the current state	Measure /Analyze for	Improve and Design Achieve flow and let the customer pull	Control
Change Leadership	Prepare for change - Train, Envision, Engage, Enable and Empower	Explore Together	Explain	Experiment, Explore, Build Consensus	Train, Enable, Empower, Hold Accountable	Celebrate

Figure 15.1   PDSA Lean Six Sigma and Change Leadership Principles.

Prepare Stakeholders for the Change

Train

Training them in the value of spending time with customers begins the preparation phase. The best way to train is to be a role model and show them the behaviors for which you are looking. Go to the floor and observe the staff. If possible, do it as a team and have everyone observe and record what facilitates spending time with customers and what detracts. If the staff is trained in Value Stream Mapping or SIPOC mapping (Supplier, Input, Process step, Output, Customer), use these mapping techniques to see the issues more clearly. Regardless, use the time to train them in the behaviors for which you are looking.

Envision

Envisioning the future is key to starting change; a future when staff is able to spend time with customers due to a reduction in wastes and quality issues. What are those variables that prevent staff, who trained extensively with often great hardship, from spending time with customers? We should create a vision where staff members value spending more time on the floor assisting customers. Help them envision "what's in it for them," not just what's in it for the customer and other staff.

Engage

Engaging the staff in the change is the only polite and effective method and so often ignored. You already incorporated engage by observing with them in their environment and by listening to them. My, how often I wish people wanting to lead change would listen instead of talk. My father was a car salesman all my life. He was the leading salesperson for the dealership where he worked. What did he do better than others? He listened and knew when to quit talking. It just wasn't from my observations of my dad that I learned to listen.

I was in high school and went to a large party at my classmate's father's gas station. At the party, I overheard a mailman who evidently just bought a car from my dad. He said, "That (expletive deleted) Walt Morrow wasn't saying a thing and I basically sold myself the car." My, the power of silence.

My mom tells the story of how my first-grade teacher told her I was not engaged in class. The teacher suggested I might be "slow," a term used in those days suggesting I was not very smart. She may very well have been correct, but my comment was, "I know the answers. Why does she (the teacher) have to know I know the answers?" I would relearn the power of listening, which should be coupled with silence many times over my career in leading process improvement. If I could suggest only one thing to most consultants, it would be to listen.

Enable

Enabling the people in improving their work delivers more and better improvement. Teach them how to eliminate, or at least reduce the issues that prevent them staying on the floor. We have shown that change can happen with very simple tools and methods. Change can be accelerated and even enhanced by using Lean and Six Sigma methods. I have taught and launched Lean Six Sigma and Change Leadership across the globe for Eaton, SKF, Motorola, United Airlines, The Joint Commission, and many healthcare organizations with Healthcare Performance Partners. All of these programs have sustained. I am very proud of the people and my staff and the thousands of people who learned these performance improvement methodologies and continue to apply them to enact change.

Empower

This is a key differentiator in programs that sustain. Too often management talks a good game and offers training and cheerleading, but to make change happen, someone has to do something. It is much better to empower people in process improvement.

There is one change management practice developed for, and now sold by, a large company that purposely denies the people on the team the ability to execute. This company has used the program internally for years and also consults other companies in change management using the same name. However, I find a significant difference in one aspect between what they do inside the company and what they teach others. Externally, they have this odd rule to not allow the person with the authority to be part of the team investigating and developing improvements. The person with authority is brought in the last day for the final report out to listen to the team's recommendations that they explored together. This is absolutely counter to empowerment and continuous improvement. I can tell you this was not the practice used when I supplied products to this company and worked out solutions with the company's team. I, as the decision-maker for my company, and the decision-makers at this company, participated in investigating and developing and approving solutions frequently. We, the people in the room, were empowered to make the decisions and execute. Of course, there are always exceptions, such as when the decision-maker might not listen to the team, but this is not the rule and really points to a bigger issue that needs addressed. The manager of this decision-maker should coach the person how to participate in team problem-solving and monitor until behaviors are learned and practiced. The other off issue with this change management program as delivered by its consultants at outside companies is the almost total disregard to measurement.

Explore Together

We now explore the contributing factors that are the reasons we need change. The team is trained, the vision is shared, the team is engaged, enabled, and empowered. Discovering the contributing factors to a problem is the better way to change than jumping to solutions. Jumping to solutions without knowing the root causes often fails because one is acting blindly by forcing countermeasures onto unknown, or at least, questionable root causes. The first M, Measure, pays off in the Explore Together phase. Measuring the current state using Value Stream Maps or SIPOC maps with data helps in Explore Together.

I don't remember a single group who did not benefit from exploring contributing factors together. I often hear, "I had no idea that happens the way it does." This shared discovery is a wonderful team-building and process improvement method. It can pay dividends for the next change. Observing and listening is easier than the stress of talking over everyone, which may be caused by a Change Leader who is unsure and a bit anxious. When I coach process improvement leaders, I watch for leaders talking over people and I look for the root causes of this rude and wasteful practice.

Going back to our story of getting staff in your store to spend more time with customers, we often find no one trained, envisioned, engaged, enabled, empowered, and explored together the change. We told you the end of this story in Chapter 1. The change to Computers on Wheels (COWs) failed because there was insufficient to nonexistent:

Training
Envisioning
Engaging
Enabling
Empowering
Exploring together and explaining the issues

In this case study, the team needs to explain the issues of why staff was not spending more time with customers. The good news is this hospital's staff members are getting training, envisioning a brighter future, and enabling managers and staff to work on process improvement. They are engaged, empowered, and exploring better ways to assist customers and improve the staff's inner work life

Many organizations in healthcare, aviation, and other consumer industries have a long way to go to get the 3Ms working for them. In healthcare, the patient satisfaction measures are required to be only sampled instead of asking everyone. This leads to a nonresponse bias. Worse, the results are far from timely with some not available until a year after the patient's experience. There are some simple fixes to this delay. One specialty clinic asks 100% of its patients at discharge the likelihood to recommend its organization to a relative or friend. The Wellington Hospital in the United Kingdom recently received a very high score from its surgical patients in the "likelihood to recommend" question. The general manager is one of the best in process improvement. More projects have been sponsored by her than any other GM. We think there is a correlation.

Satisfaction and Loyalty Measurement

The "likelihood to recommend" question has become almost universally adopted after Fred Reichheld's and Rob Markey's book, *The Ultimate Question*.[2] A supporting system also Manages to the measure every day using the responses from the prior day. The results are posted and visible by not only staff, but also the patients in one clinic. Third, the clinic practices the third M; they make it easier to help the nurses help the patients by empowering them to provide services to patients, even if the requests are somewhat out of the ordinary for a cancer clinic, such as acupuncture. The Facilities Department employees get measured on repairs. Their responsiveness and quality of their work is relayed back to them every day.

The nurse manager in this story also made it easier to change by training the team in the 3Ms and process improvement. The team of nurses and nurse manager all shared equally. The nurse manager could have forced the change by threatening disciplinary actions if the nurses did not spend more time with patients and specifically to chart in the room with the COWs. That change might have been met with an equal and opposing force. What would the effect have been on the patients? Well, there are many studies that correlate staff satisfaction with patient satisfaction.

Explain

Explaining the reasons for the issues that hinder the change is to validate the contributing factors. In the nurse example, simple observation can confirm that the COWs don't work, that there is a lot of printing required with the only printer being located at the nurse's station, and the other issues discovered exploring together. "Asking why five times" is a powerful tool in explaining and validating the contributing factors.

Explaining can take a more statistical approach. When data are available, it is useful to use data to explain correlations. Simple line charts showing the variable that one thinks is an issue and a line representing the measure to change can suggest correlation visually. People who are trained in testing for correlation can speed change by speeding and improving the quality of the Explain phase.

Measure, again, is the vehicle to explain the issues affecting the process and thus the reason for change. We measure the contributing factors' effects. An example would be to measure the time away from patients caused the nurses needing to leave the room for supplies. In one study in the ORs (operating rooms) at a major hospital, the OR staff left the OR an average of seven times for at least 10 minutes lost. Add this up for the 40 rooms, and an average of three or more cases per OR per day.

The organization's leader and I didn't get the chance to see if the supply issue was the same on the Med/Surg floors, but if they have issues in the OR with supplies, it is likely supply issues hinder the nurses on the floor from staying with the patient as well. Use measure to help explain the issues and make the change easier to spend more time with patients. Measure the correlation of the changes the team is making with the change desired: $Y = f(xs)$. The Y outcome of what you are leading the change to achieve is a function of the Xs, the inputs that the team needs to change to get the outcome desired.

Without measuring the baseline, how would we know if we have improved?

Experiment, Explore, Build Consensus

Once the team has identified contributing factors, the countermeasures, solutions, the changes to be made, are self-evident. A strong process improvement leader will validate the changes to the variables to affect the change desired by experimenting and exploring the effects of the changes. Again, Measure is what the Change Leader and team use in the experiments and explorations. PDSA (plan, do, study, act) is based on measuring what happens in the "do." Study is using the Measure to know if the "do" had an effect. The "act" is to implement the change. It is critical to Measure the Y and the key Xs to ensure sustained change is critical.

Choosing the Best Countermeasures

Note the word *countermeasure:* counter and measure. Counter is to change the variables in the process that are causing the issue. Measure is included in the term countermeasure to reinforce measuring the change is critical to knowing if the countermeasure works. Countermeasure is sometimes synonymous with the word *improvement*. However, sometimes we aren't absolutely sure we know the root causes, so countermeasure is a more conservative term. The team sees the question to be answered in this phase on our Roadmap.

Piloting and Choosing the Best Countermeasures

Before you pilot and after you pilot, a process to find the best set of countermeasures to achieve the goals on your charter will make it easier for you and your team. I include an easy-to-use decision matrix. Here is how to use it and it is available at www.rpmexec.com (see Figure 15.2).

Choosing the Best Countermeasures

	Rating of Importance to Customer	10	10	10	10	10	10	10	10	10	10	10	
		Criteria for Choosing the Best Solution											
	Countermeasure ideas	Contribution to the charter goals	Ability to implement	Cost to implement	Empowerment of the process members	Relia-bility	Risk	Scalability to other areas	Technology available	Learning opportunity	Safety	Builds on Core Competency	ImportanceTotal
1													
2													
3													
4													
5													
6													
7													
8													
9													
10													
11													
12													
13													
	Total												

Figure 15.2   Solution selection matrix.

Step 1. Brainstorm for all improvement ideas and list them in the matrix in the Countermeasure Ideas column.

Step 2. Choose the criteria that add value in your decision. Simply zero out the row labeled "Rating of Importance to Customer" to completely eliminate a criteria from your process.

Step 3. Rate the criteria. Often, some criteria are very important to you and the team. Weight these criteria with a high value, say 9 or 10. Rate the least important criteria as a 1, 2, or 3. Finally, rate the balance of the criteria using some number between 3 and 9.

Step 4. Have your team rate each improvement idea for each of the criteria. Use the following values with a 9 as high impact (1, 3, 9).

Step 5. Sort the ideas using the "Total Importance" column.

Step 6. Choose the best countermeasures from among the highest values in the "Importance Total" column.

Now, the team has a set of countermeasures that makes piloting much easier and more productive.

Piloting to See If the Measure Moves

Measure now comes back into play for the team. It is time to measure the impact that the countermeasures have on the measures on the charter. Piloting and building consensus is much easier when measure has proved the change has been achieved. We mentioned a fact-based and data-driven methodology not only validates the change has occurred, it validates the contributing factors and helps the Change Leader build consensus through facts. Debating without facts not only wastes time, it may increase resistance on this change and future changes that you may attempt.

Sampling practices again add value as well as ensuring our measurement system is able to accurately and precisely measure the impact the countermeasures have. Of course, SPC is the right tool to use during the pilot. Basically, circle back on the Roadmap to ensure that all the questions that needed to be answered are not forgotten (Figure 15.3).

The last phase of Change Leadership separates those who think they achieved change and those who actually did.

Train, Enable, Empower, and Hold Accountable

This phase is to ensure the Stakeholders are trained in the changes, enabled to enact the change, empowered to continuously improve, and that a control system exists that includes holding people accountable. One of the key accountabilities for people in the process is to continue the 3Ms. Only in those changes where the process is stable, capable, and mistake-proof can the 3Ms be relaxed. People are identified to maintain control and act or

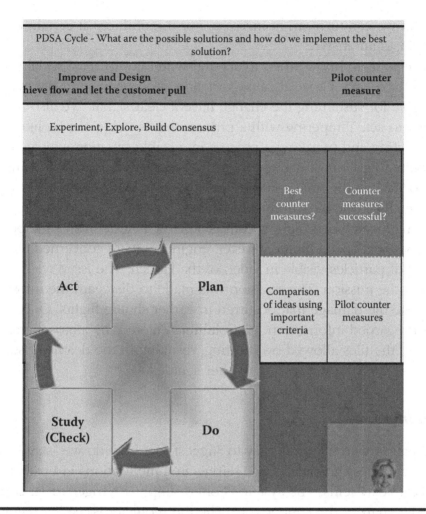

Figure 15.3   Roadmap improve and pilot.

report when special causes occur. We share stories later when managers have failed to utilize the 3Ms.

Mindfulness and Control[3]

Control comes from knowing if control is occurring. Statistical Process Control (SPC) gives the team in the process real-time knowledge if its process is in control. What better tool. Mindfulness is what High Reliability Organizations (HROs) practice, and SPC and mindfulness go together well. Did you wonder how HROs can be mindful all the time? Isn't that exhausting, if not impossible? To be ever mindful is a nice catch phrase, but is there a way that we can turn on, or increase, our mindfulness at certain times? SPC, again, is an answer.

SPC helps us to know when to act and when not to act. Special causes are identifiable when special cause variation is occurring and the persons accountable for sustaining the change have a clear signal. We also know when not to act. Tampering with a process that is stable can be like "crying wolf." Reacting and tweaking a process in a stable situation may also cause the stability to go out of control and achieve exactly what is not wanted. And, soon, when the time comes to act, the people in the process may disregard signals in the measurement system.

What happens when there is confusion to act? Accidents can happen. In the Columbia space shuttle disaster, engineers were concerned about the cloud of particles visible in video of the launch. The issue was brought up during the mission. The decision was made to disregard the information despite tile damage that occurred in earlier shuttle flights. Once again, NASA disregarded information. As Columbia entered the atmosphere, the damage to the tiles allowed overheating, resulting in the deaths of seven more astronauts and the loss of another shuttle.

Mindfulness

Preoccupation with failure is easy to suggest, but how do we "stay on our toes?" In countless hospitals, I see refrigerated medications in unstable and unpredictable systems. The system is often simply a refrigerator, thermometer, and a chart of the temperature. The thermometer is read at regular intervals and the temperature is plotted on the chart, such as in Figure 15.4.

I found a similar setup to this one and noticed there was a dot plotted in the upper red zone on a refrigerator for medicines in a hospital medical surgical floor. The pencil mark was crossed out, however, and there was another dot directly below this dot, but it was in the acceptable range. I was curious, having seen this all too often. I asked the nurse to tell me about this chart. She mentioned that it is important to make sure the refrigerator keeps the meds from getting too cold or hot, or they could change properties and either not provide the benefit, or worse, injure the patient. I thanked her and she was quick to walk away (yes, she was really busy and probably wondered who this "bloomin' idiot" was asking about the obvious need to control the temperatures of refrigerated meds). Note she did not mention the

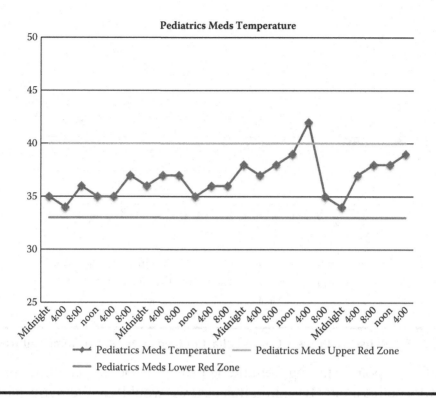

Figure 15.4 Refrigerated medicine temperatures.

two points. I asked her if she could answer one more question. I asked her about the point in the red zone. She remarked that she called maintenance as soon as she saw the temperature was too high. She went on to say that maintenance checked something on the refrigerator and told her that her plot was wrong. The maintenance engineer must have corrected her point, she said, and she returned to her duties.

What happened here? Have you switched on your state of mindfulness? Maintenance came, said all is well, and remarked the chart showing the refrigerator is in the safe zone. What would happen in an HRO? To start, maybe some would buy self-recording temperature devices in their med refrigerator systems and have alarms if the temperature exceeds boundaries. Many hospitals have these, but not all. There is nothing wrong with manu-ally recording data on the refrigerators, so how could we improve on what this hospital, and many others do?

First, let's take the same data and plot it on SPC (see Figure 15.5).

How can SPC help us heighten our mindfulness? Understand please that the control limits would have been set long ago on this refrigerator. The

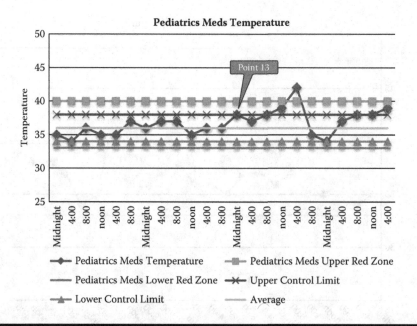

Figure 15.5 Statistical Process Control chart of meds refrigerator temperatures.

first 10 or 12 points starting from the left show no points out of the upper or lower control limits. Based on this test, we would say the refrigerator temperatures are stable. We also can see they are within the danger zones denoted by the uppermost line and lowermost line. There are a couple of points (points 8 and 9) that might be two standard deviations consecutively above the mean. Referring to our handy SPC interpretation diagram in Figure 15.6, we now have reason to be mindful.

Ah, so going out of control helps us to heighten our mindfulness. The nurses and maintenance person were not only *not* mindful, they also failed at another element in mindfulness, they oversimplified. The maintenance person dismissed completely why the nurse had plotted a point in the red zone. When he or she came to check the temperature, they found it to show a temperature below what the nurse had noted and evidently thought the nurse misread the thermometer. Heavens, who would think a nurse knows how to read a thermometer? Unfortunately, both the maintenance person and nurse oversimplified the root cause, dismissed the information gained, and went on about their business.

Look at point 13 in Figure 15.5. If this hospital was in Houston, we might say, "Houston, we have a problem." The refrigerator temperature has gone out of control. Deference to expertise, another element in mindfulness

SPC Interpretation

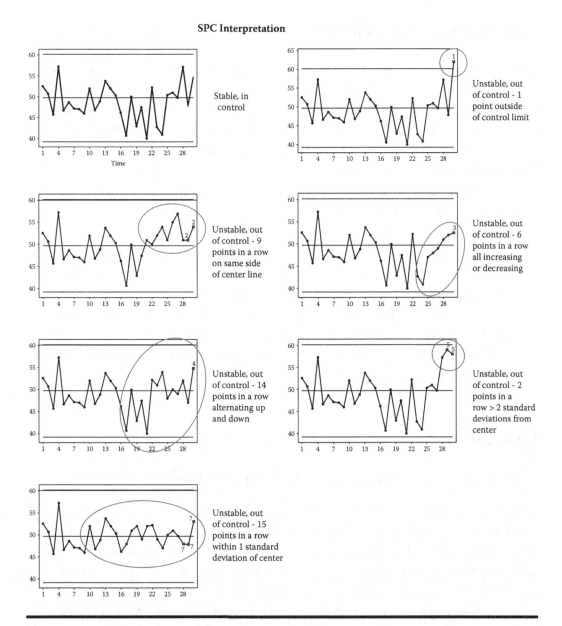

Figure 15.6   SPC Interpretation.

would have been to trust that the nurse knows how to read a thermometer, as we know nurses are well trained. Maybe the refrigerator had just finished cycling and the temperature was simply low by the time the maintenance person checked it. As we can see in SPC, the temperatures vary, and the control limits denote the normal operating variation in the temperatures.

Commitment to Resilience

Another element of mindfulness is commitment to resilience. The refrigerator and temperature measurement system are not very resilient to failure. There is not a fail-safe when the temperature gets too high in this piece of equipment. In your refrigerator at home, you might have resilience in your fresh food section. Refrigerators with a fresh and frozen food section may have a design that allows colder air in the freezer compartment to flow into the fresh food section if the temperature is not maintained low enough.

In summary, I fear the meds reached a temperature beyond their limit and should have been removed. The nurse and maintenance person should have become mindful back around the 9th point and had a higher sensitivity to operations in monitoring the temperature. At point 13, they definitely should not have oversimplified by merely plotting a new point and carrying on. If they had acted with a commitment to resilience back when the chart went out of control, they would have prevented the temperature from exceeding the allowed upper temperature by repairing the system.

Case Study

University of Pennsylvania, Penn Medicine Utilizing the 3Ms

At the University of Pennsylvania Health System, Dr. Dan Feinberg, chief medical officer (CMO) at Pennsylvania Hospital, said, "This chart (holding up his team's SPC chart of children who were getting immunizations) is what High Reliability Organizations use and healthcare needs to do more of it."[5] Penn Medicine's teams are utilizing the 3Ms and Statistical Process Control charts taught in their Performance Improvement in Action course. Every team is truly interdisciplinary with most teams comprised of physicians, nurses, and staff from services most relevant to the project that they are working on, such as pharmacy, radiology, finance, IT, quality, and other services and professions. They learn together as a team using a unique Lean, Six Sigma, and Change Leadership and PDSA. Healthcare Performance Partners developed the course with Kristi Pintar, corporate director of organizational development and leadership practice, and the Penn Medicine faculty. Judy Schueler, vice president of organizational development, and Pat Sullivan, vice president of patient safety and quality at UPHS, lead the initiative that has grown quickly and delivered results. What you may find most amazing is the productivity of learning and getting results. The latest class size is 120 people, in eleven projects, and all learning the entire roadmap. What's not so amazing is that all teams measure, manage to the measure, and make it easier for the people in the process to do the right thing.

One last point. The SPC also prevents tampering with temperatures. How many times have you seen people adjusting the thermostat in a conference room only to end up at the other extreme? Often, the discomfort is not from an out of control heating system. The system simply has a wide variation in temperatures as it cycles on and off. This is especially true in forced air systems compared to hot water radiant systems. If there was an SPC chart on the room temperature, it may show the variation is in control. When someone adjusts the thermostat, it doesn't reduce the variation that makes us uncomfortable, but the new extreme now has increased the variation and results in an even higher or lower temperature depending on the direction the person turned the thermostat.

SPC Making It Easier

Using SPC in making change easier is a wise move. It gives the team early notice that the change really does make a difference and how much of a difference. It gives the team an easier way to know if the change is starting to slip away, too. And, SPC provides them a tool to continuously improve—to continue to change.

The people who are targets of the change should be trained, enabled, empowered, and held accountable. Training them in SPC will be the start to leading change successfully. They must be enabled to make the change with a minimum of difficulty—making it easier. Empowerment allows the Stakeholders to continuously improve to sustain the change. Complex changes are seldom without issues. Empowering the people to problem solve in improving the change is a powerful way to reduce resistance to the change. Empowerment does not mean blind abdication of authority. Empowerment has been referred to as freedom to make decisions with boundaries to keep the system and Stakeholders safe.

The 3Ms Are the Most Important Tool for Leadership and Process Improvement Leaders Including Change Leaders to Sustain the Gains

In the hundreds of organizations where I have worked, many have asked how to sustain the gains. I have asked a number of consultants how the organization they left has sustained the changes they were a part of before leaving the company. Many report, embarrassingly, that their organization has reverted to its old ways. Why? In every case that I have observed, at least one of the 3Ms was missing. Most often all three were missing. It is surprisingly simple. We know to lead change; the 3Ms can make the difference between achieving the change, and wasting time. The 3Ms are also necessary in human controlled processes to sustain the changes.

Key Points

- This chapter walked us through the entire Roadmap.
- Process improvement utilizes the 3Ms from start to finish.
- Without all 3Ms, sustain is unlikely.
- The next chapter shares how to reduce the reliance on all 3Ms, but it isn't that easy.

Endnotes

1. Isaac Newton, *The Principia*, A new translation by I. B. Cohen and A. Whitman. (Berkeley, CA: University of California Press, 1999).
2. Fred Reichheld and Rob Markey, *The Ultimate Question*. (Cambridge, MA: Harvard Business School Publishing, 2006).
3. Karl Weick and Kathleen Sutcliffe, *Managing the Unexpected*. (John Wiley & Sons, 2007).
4. Used with permission, University of Pennsylvania, Penn Medicine, Dan Feinberg, M.D.

Chapter 16

High Reliability

Even when we think we have done the 3Ms well, there may still be difficulty. The third M is Make it *easier,* not easy. We can't always make doing
the right thing and change easy.

   This is a story of a change that seemed easy to me. However, it wasn't
so easy for a plant engineer despite being in a High Reliability Organization
(HRO). The plant was one of many in SKF.[1] SKF is based in Sweden with
locations around the world. SKF services healthcare, aerospace, aviation, automotive, industrial, mining, and countless other smaller companies specializing
in reliable products. SKF is referenced in textbooks on reliability engineering
because of its pioneering work in design and performance reliability.

Case Study: SKF

SKF is considered one of the highest quality manufacturers and service
companies in the world evolving from a bearing and seal manufacturer to
one that makes products found deep in space to the deepest depths of
the oceans. SKF makes products where safety is critical, such as in the rotor
connector for military aircraft that holds the entire rotor system to the heli-
copter. SKF also has made "brake-by-wire" systems that demand the highest
reliability to protect the vehicle and passengers. These systems have a higher
hurdle for reliability than conventional hydraulic braking systems, which
have failed in the past.

   Claes Rehmberg, quality leader for the corporation, was my superior
when I was vice president of Total Quality. Rehmberg was also my coach

and mentor who taught me much about high reliability. We later worked together in another role as we launched the 3Ms with SKF's Lean Six Sigma initiative globally. In my first meeting with Rehmberg, he began teaching me how an HRO operates. He shared with me two programs that I needed to learn. He also thought my business unit especially needed these programs because it was behind most of SKF's other units in quality and reliability. Here are several practices SKF pioneered that were instrumental in its success achieving high reliability.

High Reliability Program Number 1

The first program was named Zero Defects. Ah, you are thinking, another buzz word. That is why I did not put the words in the header for fear that you wouldn't even read the story coming up. You say that even Dr. Deming said that Zero Defect programs were ill-advised? Let me explain what SKF meant by Zero Defects. Zero Defects meant zero, period. Yes, no defects reaching the customer were allowed to be recognized as a zero defects product line. SKF even had a poster clarifying it really meant zero. And, they had products that had achieved zero defects for over five consecutive years. Okay, so maybe zero defects with a time attached to it is cheating? I was not a believer at first, either. I found out soon that SKF had quality management systems that exemplified what we are sharing in this book. SKF truly had achieved zero defects. But, how does an SKF product line get to truly zero defects quality to the customer?

High Reliability Program Number 2

SWOC. SWOC? This is an acronym for Scrap without Compromise. It took SKF years to get to zero defects in some product lines. SKF also is one of the oldest manufacturing companies and has had lots of opportunities to learn. One thing SKF learned is that even the best production processes occasionally have a defect escape to the customer. After applying process improvement similar to what we are sharing in this book, SKF found a recurring, although very infrequent, root cause to a defect escaping. They found that the defects came from a process that had stopped flowing or that some variation started occurring. The process often quit flowing because SKF had designed it to stop when a process measure showed the process was starting to get out of control.

The Products Surrounding the Variation

Sometimes the escaped defective product that reached the customer was traced back to one of the products that was taken out of the process for inspection when a process problem occurred. The product was one that came before, during, or after a process issue. Stopping the process is what all good companies do. Toyota even has a term for stopping the line when a quality abnormality occurs. It is called *jidoka*. In healthcare, we reinforce stopping a procedure if anyone senses something is wrong. This is jidoka. Not stopping the process or procedure has often been cited in accident investigations. The "time out" in surgical procedures is required in many countries and is a pause to reflect on whether the patient, the site of the incision, and the procedure are all correct. Too often, we hear people wish that they had stopped instead of going on.

What SKF discovered in analyzing these escaped defects is what many miss. These products could get inserted back into the wrong sequence, be damaged in the effort to ensure they are not damaged, or put back with a defect because human inspection is not reliable enough to catch all defects.

Scrapping versus Inspecting

Once a process becomes reliable, the defects and wastes may be miniscule. It may be far less risky to throw them out than to inspect and reinsert them into the process. SKF swallowed hard and pioneered doing what many do today. They scrap the products around a process failure without question—without compromise. The risk of a defect escaping to a customer is less than the cost of the product scrapped.

Utilizing the 3Ms in Zero Defects and SWOC

Zero defects and SWOC cannot occur without utilizing the 3Ms. SKF measures critical parameters in its processes to know there is an issue early enough to prevent an escaping defect. The frontline people manage to the measure, too. When the Statistical Process Control (SPC) chart or other measure suggests, SKF's people manage to the measure by stopping the process until all is well. Lastly, they learn from earlier failures and make it easier to do the right thing. There is nothing any easier than scrapping products after a process issue with no fear of punishment. It is easier to scrap products than inspect them, especially when many of the features can only be measured using advanced test equipment in a remote location.

High Reliability Program Number 3: Building a Safety Culture[2]

A safety culture is not discussed much at SKF. As one of its leaders, I didn't have to discuss it, because it is truly a way of life. I surely didn't create it, but I benefitted from it every day. To be fair, zero defects and SWOC compromise would not have been achieved without SKF's safety culture. For the sake of time, let me get on with the story, but please realize SKF's leadership created a culture that promotes reporting and learning, is just, and flexes across the organization to ensure safety.

A Story of a Seal and Its Grease

The 3Ms were found throughout SKF. One example was in its sealing group. A seal is found in virtually every high performance pump, whether it is for water, IVs, blood, or waste. In medical pumps, aircraft engines, faucets in your home, and countless other devices that make our life better and safer, seals protect the function of these vital products. Seals are a critical component of many systems, especially systems with bearings in them for parts that rotate or move linearly as in many high technology and safety products, such as medical pumps. Actually, a seal is often a system itself.

The sealing system consists of a seal, an installation tool to minimize damage to the seal in assembling it into the pump, jet engine, etc., and, lastly, grease. I learned that what seemed like a simple piece of rubber connected to a metal casing was engineered to do some amazing things, with specifications so incredibly tight that one could not see with the naked eye the quality level needed. A flaw that could only be seen with magnification could cause a failure.

In this story, the 3Ms paid off despite a change that seemed difficult for one plant engineer. This lesson is how this one plant engineer struggled with a change to measure and manage to the measure, but, in the end, did the right thing.

One purpose of a seal is to ensure that there is a barrier from contaminants, such as water. Water reaching the bearing may destroy it, resulting in catastrophic failure. Bearings that are damaged may allow high friction, which results in extreme heat and eventual failure of the device. In the case of surgical instruments, the failure can result in delayed surgeries and perhaps risk to the patient. In the transportation industry, "wheel offs" have occurred when the bearing failed and the wheels flew off the tractor. Sometimes worse, the heated assembly did not fly off, but created a fire and consumed the tractor and risked injury to the driver and the environment. Wheel offs occur for a variety of reasons including mishandling at the truck assembly plant and improper maintenance. SKF worked to ensure this didn't happen because of their products.

Measuring the seal greasing process, managing to the measure, and making it easier to get grease into the seal makes sense. What do we measure? We can measure if grease is in the seal by weighing the seal after grease is installed. This is a bit late, though, requiring rework to apply grease or scrapping the seal. We would prefer to measure the key input variables that tell us how well the grease process is working. But, some processes don't lend themselves to measuring what we want. But, there is always a way to measure. Let's start with the one type of process to manufacture the seal.

Grease is pushed into the seal using a pneumatic injection system. Pneumatic equipment is often unreliable for the precise control of dispensing grease. If the pneumatic pressure that pushes the grease into the seal varies, this variation could result in too little or too much grease. Insufficient grease may not provide enough of a barrier to water, especially from high pressure washers found in some wash stations. This water, if allowed to reach the bearings, may cause early failure of the bearing and the unit where the bearing is installed.

Unfortunately, one cannot see inside the seal to know if grease is present. Thus, measuring the linear distance of the rod that pushes grease into the seal is one way to measure the process to ensure grease is in the seal. However, there is another variable called air gaps that occur in the grease container. The same travel distance in the action of the rod, therefore, does not guarantee the correct amount of grease is applied if an air gap is pushed instead of grease. Therefore, until a system to apply a stable and capable amount of grease is in place, each seal needs to be weighed to see if the correct amount of grease was applied. SPC charts on the weight of the greased seal are a good way to know if the process is starting to vary and to check the quality of the grease process. Inspection is never completely reliable and we didn't know of a mistake-proof process. It was better to weigh and chart than not measuring at all.

This is exactly what we did in one seal-making process. We used an SPC chart to track the amount of grease installed in each seal and asked the worker to stop the process if the control chart showed the process was out of control. The Measurement System Analysis (MSA) proved the SPC would assess the amount of grease accurately and precisely enough. The chart was doing its job. We hadn't completely eliminated seals with insufficient grease, but we were catching them now before they "escaped." Measure was working. We were on our way to zero defects.

Some time later I was out in the shop and saw that the SPC chart was not being updated. I asked the worker why this wasn't happening and he said that his manager said it wasn't needed. Managing to the measure had failed. The chart was being ignored by the frontline and by management. Not managing to the SPC measure was one thing, but worse was the fact that management allowed Measure to stop. They told the people in the process they didn't need to measure the grease any more.

Concerned that we might have seals without grease, we sampled production and found seals without the required amount of grease. We were not surprised knowing that the process varied and the SPC was to be an early indication that the process was starting to fail. I immediately went to the plant engineer and asked him if he knew the SPC had stopped. He said he had and he allowed it to stop after hearing that it was time consuming to measure every seal and chart the results. After showing him the seals with insufficient grease and how easy it was to chart compared to the rework we now had, he agreed to reinstate the SPC.

Change Isn't Always Easy, Except...

I guess change for the wrong reason can be easier in the short run, such as in this story. Changing back to the old ways of not measuring and managing to the measure was easier in the short run for them, I guess. This is a story that has been told countless times because people don't utilize the 3Ms. I wish I knew how to prevent this story from reoccurring.

Stakeholder Analysis Revisited for Making It Easier

Those who ignore the stakeholders, make change very difficult. Sustaining the change is impossible long term if the stakeholders resist and the 3Ms are not achieved.

Another reason that change is difficult is we didn't reengage the stake-holders in the selection of changes. One proven way to make change easier is to engage the stakeholders in selecting the changes using the solution selection matrix covered in Chapter 15. Part of the selection process is the discussion of the countermeasures and the rating of each. We often find that stakeholders add much value in the process because they know things that the Change Leader and team may not be aware of.

Designing an Experiment Should Start with the People Doing the Work

I don't think I will ever forget a pilot of a countermeasure in Puerto Rico. We had worked long and hard to identify the variables that were causing the problems in safety products. Defects in the plastic casing of the circuit breaker could result in failure of the circuit breaker to cut the flow of electricity and, thus, not stop an electrical hazard. The team of managers designed a pilot to test the variables at levels that they thought would mini-mize the potential of defects. When the managers went out to the shop to ask the machine attendants to set the controls to the levels desired, the attendants said they couldn't.

At first, I wondered if there was some subordination or at least heavy resistance. Actually, the change was difficult not because the machine atten-dants were resisting. The reason that they refused to set the controls for the pilot the way that management wanted was because the levels extended beyond the capability of the machines. Management asked for levels that were not possible. We should have engaged the people who do the work to help us judge the best countermeasures. This would have made the change easier for all.

Key Points

■ HROs utilize the 3Ms for process improvement.
■ SKF has pioneered HRO practices, such as a true Zero Defects program and a culture where it is safe to scrap products rather than try to sal-vage them due to inherent risks.

■ A safety culture and mindfulness are key to becoming an HRO.
■ HROs measure their cultures and mindfulness.
■ HROs use Change Leadership principles.
■ Maintaining the 3Ms is critical.

Endnotes

1. Used with permission, SKF, Claes Rehmberg.
2. James Reason, *Managing the Risks of Organizational Accidents,* (London: Ashgate Publishing, 1997).

Chapter 17

Summary

Utilizing the 3Ms is the answer to process improvement that is real and sustains. We leave you with one technique that reduces the need for the 3Ms.

Mistake-Proofing?

Mistake-proofing is any method that can help workers avoid mistakes, and equipment and other resources from failing. This concept recognizes that the optimal location to prevent or correct mistakes is at the point of creation of the problem. Late recognition of a mistake or defect is never as efficient and typically has a cumulative effect. Is it better to mistake proof or fail safe? What are the differences?

Fail safe by definition involves a failure. An example is when an electrical circuit has a short, the circuit breaker "trips" and stops the flow. The fault still occurred, but it failed safely. Mistake-proofing would prevent the failure from occurring in the first place. Shigeo Shingo[1] believed that zero defects are possible, but it takes strong stability, capability, and techniques to stop a process if variation begins to occur at abnormal levels. Even Statistical Process Control (SPC) is often not robust enough to prevent some failures. Shingo researched methods for mistake-proofing and most industries are using some, if not most.

Mistake-Proofing Promotes Defect Prevention versus Detection

Mistake-proofing also should respect the intelligence of workers by taking the judgment out of repetitive tasks where errors are likely to occur. It utilizes people working in the process to mistake-proof the work because they *own* the process.

Shingo, expert in problem solving and creator of mistake-proofing methodologies, found:

■ SPC greatly improved quality, but sampling and SPC alone may not guarantee zero defects in unstable processes.
■ The need to focus on detecting errors before they escaped with defects and reached the customer.

Types and Levels of Mistake-Proofing Devices

■ A *prevention* device renders the process so that it is impossible to make a mistake at all.
■ A *detection* device signals the user when a mistake has been made, so that the user can quickly correct the problem. Detection devices typically warn the user of a problem, but they do not enforce the correction.
■ Levels to mistake-proofing:
  – 1. Basic visual. 5. Bypassing the risk
  – See Figure 17.1: Mistake-proofing levels

Start with failure modes and effects analysis. Then mistake-proof the high risks.

Errors cause defects:

■ Proactive tool to detect ways of failing and prevention.
■ Design the process so that errors are eliminated, or at least easily detected and corrected.
■ Suppliers should be required to do a failure mode and effect analysis (FMEA) before awarding business.

Mistake-Proofing Types and Levels

Level 1	Level 2	Level 3	Level 4	Level 5
Type: <u>Detection</u>	<u>Detection</u>	<u>Detection</u>	<u>Prevention</u>	<u>Prevention</u>
Minimal protection	Low-level	Mid-level	Mid-level	High-level
	Single sensory alert	Dual sensory	Dual + Barrier	Bypass fail-safe
100% Inspection required.	100% Inspection required.	Redundant inspection suggested.	Minimal inspection.	No inspection.
Real-time measurement required of fail-safe operation. (Knowledge of train approaching.)	Real-time measurement.	Real time measurement.	Minimal measurement required.	No measurement required.
		Calibration testing of alert required periodically.	Calibration testing of barrier periodically.	Inspection of structure infrequently.

Figure 17.1   Mistake-proofing levels.

Human Error Drives Need for Mistake-Proofing

Errors are slips, lapses, mistakes or purposeful mistakes, according to James Reason.[2] It is very difficult, if not impossible, to eliminate entirely these incidents. Therefore, utilizing the 3Ms continuously is critical until the system can ensure any slip, lapse, or mistake will not result in a failure.

Examples of mistake-proofing in healthcare are seen in Figure 17.2.

Mistake-Proof Approaches

- Facilitate: Make the task easier
- Detection/magnify the sensing
  - Install sensors to detect the problem or the preventive measure.
  - Redundancy: Failure requires two or more things to go wrong simultaneously.
- Fail safe device that the staff understands its operation. Fail safe devices have actually caused catastrophic failures, such as when a pilot overrode his stick bypassing the fail safe that would have probably saved the flight.

Mistake Proofing in Healthcare

Dialysis and IV pumps – Air detector – prevents air from entering the patient's bloodstream

Smart pumps: in an area where decimal-point medication errors can be fatal, smart infusion pumps are adding a line of defense

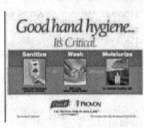

Hand hygiene

Childproof medicine bottles

Figure 17.2   Mistake-proofing in healthcare.

Train, Engage, Enable, and Empower the People Doing the Work

Dr. W. Edwards Deming and High Reliability Organizations (HROs) practice:

■ Process owners check themselves at the source, not final audit.
■ 100% fail-safing for nonrobust processes.
■ Immediate action versus inspect and sort out defects.

Physical mistake-proofing may include both parties pointing to the control. This is in addition to verbal attention to the control. Pointing and touching the surgical site is a mistake-proofing technique used by some organizations to reduce the risk of wrong-site surgery (WSS).

Mistake-proofing relies on plans to maintain control of the variation or make the system robust to variation.

Control plans include:

■ Anything and everything required to sustain the gains.
■ Often, the measurement system is critical to sustain the gains because the variation is not fail-safed completely.

- Make charting in real-time and posted in the area.
- The sampling may be reduced once stability is achieved and capability well within customer needs.

Reinforcing Continuous Process Improvement

If you read the first few lines in my book and these last few lines, you are vastly more knowledgeable than all those who have failed to improve processes and sustain the gains. These last paragraphs may be some of the most important lessons in sustaining your process improvement and, thus, your real desired outcome—performance excellence. We will utilize the 3Ms to share with you that this is the only proven way to reinforce people to improve their processes.

In some cultures, the desire to work for the good of the many is more pronounced than in other cultures. It is well known that Toyota measures its managers on the number of ideas implemented. Note that this is *implemented*. This is not a suggestion box where ideas sit and staff are not trained or empowered to implement.

In America, very few organizations have begun counting and Managing to that measure. I think it is a shame because it is an easy way to Measure, Manage to the measure, and Make it easier to reinforce process improvement. I implemented it while at Motorola and our Asian vice president, Lee King Tan, found strong results by simply counting the ideas implemented and sent to him monthly.

Maybe individual certification is one answer? We have had clients ask for programs that result in an opportunity to certify that the individual is trained *and* has improved processes and designs. I invite you to try one or both of these methods. It is Utilizing the 3Ms.

Thank you for reading and I look forward to hearing of your successes at www.rpmexec.com.

Key Points

Utilizing the 3Ms for process improvement:

- *Measure* accurately and frequently.
  - Keep score: The more real time the better.
  - Use statistical process control to validate changes.

- Ensure everyone can see the score; "the entire game."
- *Manage to the measure*; Just-In-Time.
- Don't pass up a chance to coach.
- Reinforce to the charts.
- Share the Control charts daily, and reference them.
- Be a role model.
- *Make it easier.*
- To Measure and to improve performance.
- Make it easy to do the right things:
  • Hand hygiene
  • Operate on the correct knee
  • Do standard work
- Reinforce process improvement continuously to achieve performance excellence.
- Practice the skills of the Change Leaders and remember:

The best fertilizer for a piece of land is the footprints of its owner.

Lyndon B. Johnson

Endnotes

1. Shigeo Shingo's works as cited in, Yasuhiro Monden, *Toyota Production System, An Integrated Approach to Just-In-Time*, 2nd ed. (Norcross, GA: Industrial Engineering and Management Press, 1993).
2. James Reason, *Managing the Risks of Organizational Accidents*. (London: Ashgate Publishing, 1997).

Appendix 1: Roadmap for Performance Excellence™

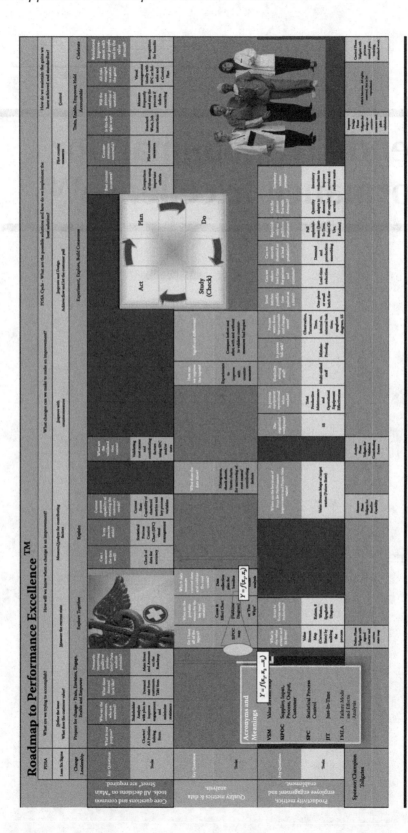

Figure A1.1   Roadmap to Performance Excellence

Appendix 2: Process Improvement Foundational Tools

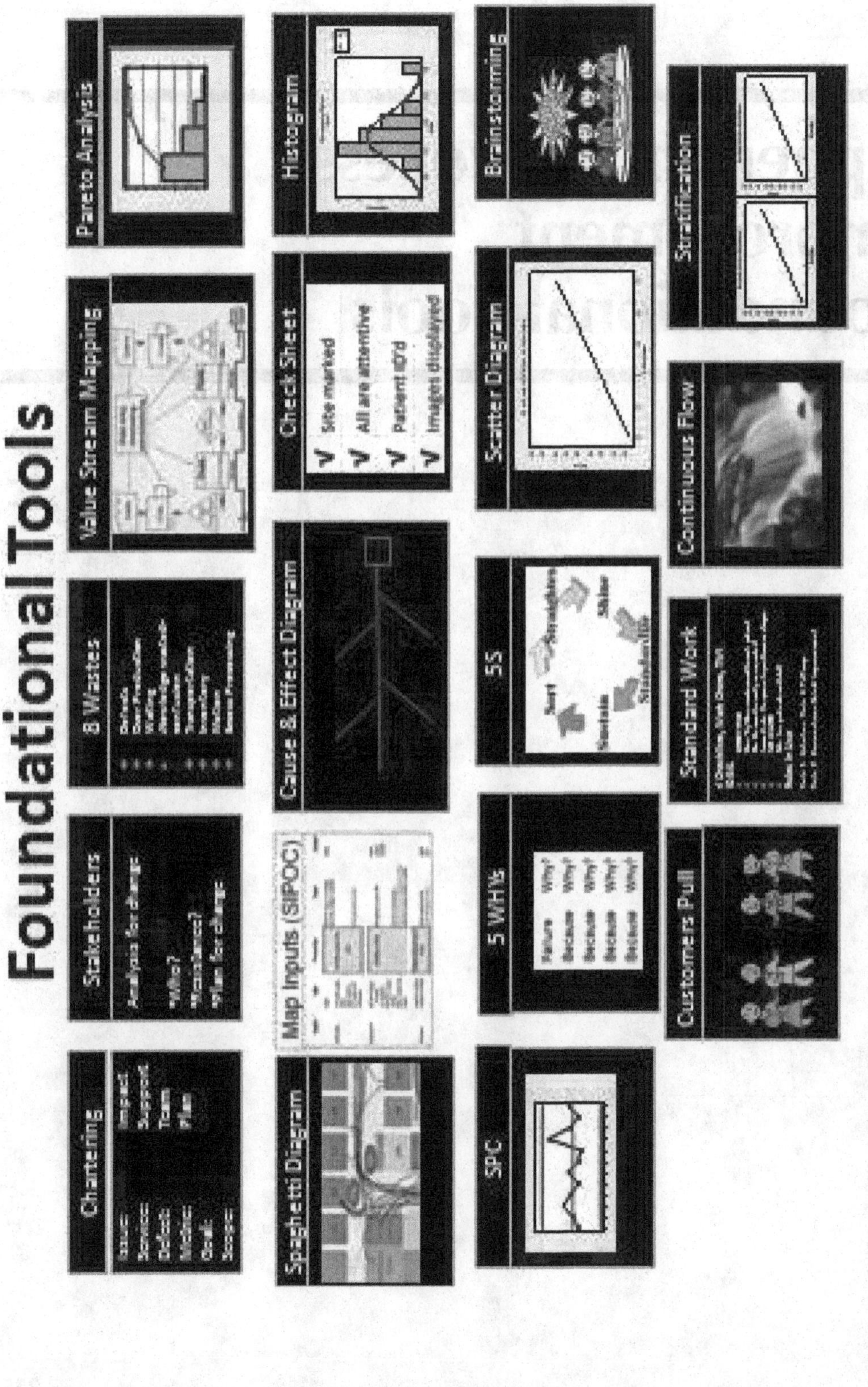
Foundational Tools
Chartering
Issues:
Scenarios:
Defects:
Metrics:
Goals:
Scope:
Impact
Support
Team
Plan
Stakeholders
Analysis for change
Who?
Resistance?
Plan for change
8 Wastes
Value Stream Mapping
Pareto Analysis
Spaghetti Diagram
Map Inputs (SIPOC)
Cause & Effect Diagram
Check Sheet
Site marked
All are attentive
Patient ID'd
Images displayed
Histogram
SPC
5 WHYs
Failure Why?
Because Why?
Because Why?
Because Why?
Because Why?
5S
Sort
Straighten
Shine
Standardize
Sustain
Scatter Diagram
Brainstorming
Customers Pull
Standard Work
Continuous Flow
Stratification

Figure A2.1

Appendix 3: The Emancipation Proclamation

January 1, 1863
A Transcription
By the President of the United States of America
A Proclamation.

Whereas, on the twenty-second day of September, in the year of our Lord one thousand eight hundred and sixty-two, a proclamation was issued by the President of the United States, containing, among other things, the following, to wit:

> That on the first day of January, in the year of our Lord one thousand eight hundred and sixty-three, all persons held as slaves within any State or designated part of a State, the people whereof shall then be in rebellion against the United States, shall be then, thenceforward, and forever free; and the Executive Government of the United States, including the military and naval authority thereof, will recognize and maintain the freedom of such persons, and will do no act or acts to repress such persons, or any of them, in any efforts they may make for their actual freedom.
>
> That the Executive will, on the first day of January aforesaid, by proclamation, designate the States and parts of States, if any, in which the people thereof, respectively, shall then be in rebellion against the United States; and the fact that any State, or the people thereof, shall on that day be, in good faith, represented in the Congress of the United States by members chosen thereto at elections wherein a majority of the qualified voters of such State shall have participated, shall, in the absence of strong countervailing

testimony, be deemed conclusive evidence that such State, and the people thereof, are not then in rebellion against the United States.

Now, therefore I, Abraham Lincoln, President of the United States, by virtue of the power in me vested as Commander-in-Chief, of the Army and Navy of the United States in time of actual armed rebellion against the authority and government of the United States, and as a fit and necessary war measure for suppressing said rebellion, do, on this first day of January, in the year of our Lord one thousand eight hundred and sixty-three, and in accordance with my purpose so to do publicly proclaimed for the full period of one hundred days, from the day first above mentioned, order and designate as the States and parts of States wherein the people thereof respectively, are this day in rebellion against the United States, the following, to wit:

Arkansas, Texas, Louisiana, (except the Parishes of St. Bernard, Plaquemines, Jefferson, St. John, St. Charles, St. James Ascension, Assumption, Terrebonne, Lafourche, St. Mary, St. Martin, and Orleans, including the City of New Orleans) Mississippi, Alabama, Florida, Georgia, South Carolina, North Carolina, and Virginia, (except the forty-eight counties designated as West Virginia, and also the counties of Berkley, Accomac, Northampton, Elizabeth City, York, Princess Ann, and Norfolk, including the cities of Norfolk and Portsmouth), and which excepted parts, are for the present, left precisely as if this proclamation were not issued.

And by virtue of the power, and for the purpose aforesaid, I do order and declare that all persons held as slaves within said designated States, and parts of States, are, and henceforward shall be free; and that the Executive government of the United States, including the military and naval authorities thereof, will recognize and maintain the freedom of said persons.

And I hereby enjoin upon the people so declared to be free to abstain from all violence, unless in necessary self-defense; and I recommend to them that, in all cases when allowed, they labor faithfully for reasonable wages.

And I further declare and make known, that such persons of suitable condition, will be received into the armed service of the United States to garrison forts, positions, stations, and other places, and to man vessels of all sorts in said service.

And upon this act, sincerely believed to be an act of justice, warranted by the Constitution, upon military necessity, I invoke the considerate judgment of mankind, and the gracious favor of Almighty God.

In witness whereof, I have hereunto set my hand and caused the seal of the United States to be affixed.

Done at the City of Washington, this first day of January, in the year of our Lord one thousand eight hundred and sixty three, and of the Independence of the United States of America the eighty-seventh.

By the President: Abraham Lincoln
William H. Seward, Secretary of State

Appendix 4: Charter Template

Charter Title:					Role	Responsibility
1. Issue Statement Elements a. Customer name:		Business Case:			**Executive Sponsor:**	Senior Level manager who selects work. Has authority to solve cross-functional issues.
b. Characteristic to improve:					*Signature*	
c. Process name(s):					**Champion:**	Leader who owns the process and manages staff. Prime responsibility with Project Leader for success.
2. Product/Unit: *Name of what is produced in the process*					*Signature*	
					Clinical Leader	Decision-maker for clinical issues.
					Signature	
3. Defect: *How we sense a failure in the product or service*					**Process Owner(s):**	Responsible for the design, continuous improvement, and sustaining the process.
4. Metric(s) to Improve		Current Baseline	Goal (S.M.A.R.T.)	Date to Achieve	*Signature(s)*	
					Project Leader:	Leads the team and execution of the methodology. Shares prime responsibility with Champion for success.
					Signature	
5. Financial Impact Metrics:		Type of Impact	Traceable	Non-Traceable	Mentor/Coach	Coaches and mentors sponsor, champion, and project leader in their roles.
		$ Annualized Amount			*Signature*	
6. Scope: Process Begins and Ends when....		**7. Scope: What must be included or excluded is...**			**Team Members**	Key contributor to work. Participates with Project Leader in methodology and responsible for success.
					Core Member	
					Core Member	
					Core Member	
					Core Member	
					Core Member	
					Core Member	
High Level Project Plan: Rick Morrow					Core Member	
Phase	Planned Start Date	Planned End Date	Actual Start Date	Actual End Date		
Define/Charter signed						
Measure/Baseline obtained					Subject Matter Expert	
Analyze/Root Cause validated					Subject Matter Expert	
Improve/Improvement piloted					Subject Matter Expert	
Control/Sustainability plan					Author name:	

Figure A4.1

Appendix 5: Stakeholder Analysis Template

Stakeholder Analysis											
Project			Stakeholder role						Contributor names:		
Date											
Organization/ Location/ Area	Name (or group name)	Role or Title	Customer of the process	Process owner	Decision-maker/ Appro-ver	Target of the change	Interested party	Supplier to the process	Current level of buy-in to change. Rate 0 - 10 with 0 being no buy-in - heavy resistance	Needed level of buy-in to change. Rate 0 - 10 with 0 no buy-in needed	Gap	Strategy to close the gap

Figure A5.1

Appendix 6: Hand Hygiene Data Collection Sheet

Hand Hygiene Observation and Contributing Factor Form

Collected by: Date of observations:

Possible Contributing Factors to Washing

Observable by asking person

Observable

																							Comments
	8	9	10	11	12	13	14	15	16	17	18	19	20	21	22	23	24						

Column 7 header: **Did person perform hand hygiene?**
- 3 After fluid risk
- 5 After patient contact with pt surroundings
- 2 Before aseptic task
- 4 After patient contact
- 1 Before patient contact

Column 6: Grade role of health professional observed
(RN=Nurse, T=Therapy, HSK=Housekeeping, Con=Consultant)
(others please identify in the comments section)
CATR=Caterer, Plb=Phlebotomist,
ThStf=Staff, ThPor=Porter, ODP=Con

Column 5: Circle time of observation (AM is 0801-1700, PM is 1701-0800)

Column 4: Unit name (2 South, ITU, etc.)

Observation Number	Unit name	AM/PM	Grade	Before/After	Yes/No
1		AM PM	RN T MD Diet Rx PHL HSK CATR ThStf ThPor ODP Con	1 2 3 4 5	Yes No
2		AM PM	RN T MD Diet Rx PHL HSK CATR ThStf ThPor ODP Con	1 2 3 4 5	Yes No
3		AM PM	RN T MD Diet Rx PHL HSK CATR ThStf ThPor ODP Con	1 2 3 4 5	Yes No
4		AM PM	RN T MD Diet Rx PHL HSK CATR ThStf ThPor ODP Con	1 2 3 4 5	Yes No
5		AM PM	RN T MD Diet Rx PHL HSK CATR ThStf ThPor ODP Con	1 2 3 4 5	Yes No
6		AM PM	RN T MD Diet Rx PHL HSK CATR ThStf ThPor ODP Con	1 2 3 4 5	Yes No
7		AM PM	RN T MD Diet Rx PHL HSK CATR ThStf ThPor ODP Con	1 2 3 4 5	Yes No
8		AM PM	RN T MD Diet Rx PHL HSK CATR ThStf ThPor ODP Con	1 2 3 4 5	Yes No
9		AM PM	RN T MD Diet Rx PHL HSK CATR ThStf ThPor ODP Con	1 2 3 4 5	Yes No
10		AM PM	RN T MD Diet Rx PHL HSK CATR ThStf ThPor ODP Con	1 2 3 4 5	Yes No

Contributing factor column headers (9–24):
- 9 Dispenser location not in path of person or obstructed/hidden
- 10 Dispenser empty
- 11 Leaves patient room
- 12 Dispenser broken
- 13 Hands full: supplied/equipment (e.g. food trays, lab supplies)
- 14 Hands full: Meds
- 15 Gloves – Did not wash before or after gloving
- 16 Urgency to act for patient safety concern
- 17 Person entering/exiting followed someone who did not wash
- 18 Frequent entry and exit
- 19 Admissions or discharge process
- 20 Isolation area
- 21 Lack of immediate feedback to person who did not wash
- 22 Distractions/forgot/lack of knowledge (gown + gloves)
- 23 Perception that hand hygiene is not required)
- 24 Perception that if resting in the patient area is needed/Chose not to wash/Chose pot to use hand hygiene compliance/dislike of skin irritation or dislike of alcohol based cleanser

Instructions:
1. Use a separate row for each entry or exit.
2. When known, check any contributing factor for each observation.
3. Emergency situations are EXCLUDED from the data collection process.

Calculate compliance for this sheet	Count of "yes"	=	Count of observations (rows used)	=

Figure A6.1

Appendix 7: Hand Hygiene Compliance Chart for Posting

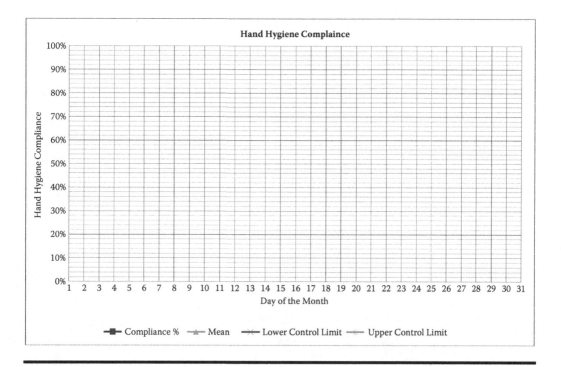

Figure A7.1

Appendix 7: Hand Hygiene Compliance Chart for Posting

Appendix 8: Measure: Data Collection Tool

Visitor (remember patient confidentiality rules, so use something like a number or destination)	Outcome metric — number of wrong turns in getting to the destination	Errors in giving (count the times you change your instructions, regardless of reason)	Signage — missing, wrong, confusing, too many signs, blocked	Visitor taking a wrong turn (turning differently than the directions that you gave or the signage directs)
1				
2				
3				
4				
5				
6				
7				
8				
9				
10				
11				
12				

Figure A8.1

Appendix 9: FMEA Severity, Occurrence, Detection Tables

The team defines the rating scale (1–10) for the Severity, Occurrence, and Detection ratings. You and your team choose the levels and numbers (as long as they are on a scale of 1 to 10).

How **s**evere is it?
    Not severe = 1
    Somewhat = 3
    Moderately = 5
    Very severe = 10 (VERY BAD)

How often does it **o**ccur?
    Never/Rarely = 1
    Sometimes = 3
    Half the time = 5
    Always = 10 (VERY BAD)

How well can you **d**etect it?
Always = 1
Sometimes = 3
Half the time = 5
Never = 10 (VERY BAD)

Rating	Severity of Effect	Likelihood of Occurrence	Ability to Detect
10	Hazardous without warning	Very high: Failure is almost inevitable	Cannot detect
9	Hazardous with warning		Very remote chance of detection
8	Loss of primary function	High: Repeated failures	Remote chance of detection
7	Reduced primary function performance		Very low chance of detection
6	Loss of secondary function	Moderate: Occasional failures	Low chance of detection
5	Reduced secondary function performance		Moderate chance of detection
4	Minor defect noticed by most customers		Moderately high chance of detection
3	Minor defect noticed by some customers	Low: Relatively few failure	High chance of detection
2	Minor defect noticed by discriminating customers		Very high chance of detection
1	No effect	Remote: Failure is unlikely	Almost certain detection

Figure A9.1

Appendix 10: The Soda Drink Challenge to Learn Attribute Agreement Analysis

Set-Up for the Challenge

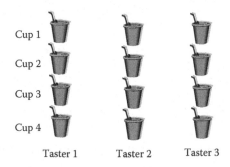

Cup 1

Cup 2

Cup 3

Cup 4

Taster 1   Taster 2   Taster 3

Data Collection Plan and Tests

Collect two samples from each cup from each Taster

Discrimination –
    Able to differentiate one product from another

Stability –
    Same decision through time

Accuracy –
    Correct decision

Repeatability –
    Same cup from same Taster should get the same decision

Reproducibility –
    Same cup (1,2,3,or 4) with same product by different Taster gets
    the same decision

Data Collection Template for The Soda Drink Challenge to Learn
Attribute Agreement Analysis

Taster	Cup	Decision. Brand A or Brand B.	Truth if Brand A or Brand B.
2	2		
2	4		
2	1		
3	1		
2	3		
1	2		
2	3		
3	1		
3	3		
3	3		
1	1		
1	1		
3	2		
3	2		
2	4		
1	4		
1	2		
2	1		
1	4		
2	2		
3	4		
3	4		
1	3		
1	3		

- Run the tasting in the order of the randomized worksheet.
- It is OK to have each taster drinking simultaneously as long as they drink in the order of the data collection worksheet.
- It helps to dedicate a "Runner" to each Taster.
- Someone directs the runners by saying which Taster and holding up fingers noting which of four cups.
- Record the decisions as the Tasters taste.

Appendix 11: Gage Repeatability and Reproducibility Measurement System Analysis

Purpose: Assess the quality of a measurement system used in measuring the pounds of force before two electrical plugs safely can be pulled apart.

Method: Stress gage showing the force at disconnect.

Analysis technique: Gage repeatability and reproducibility (R&R).

Software: Minitab®

We will demonstrate how to do a Gage R&R by showing the screen navigation from Minitab version 16 and utilizing its "Assistant" menu feature that guides us in setting up an experiment, worksheet, and the analysis. We will have the three operators who work in the process measure seven different parts.

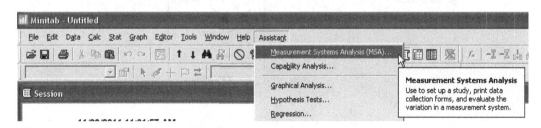

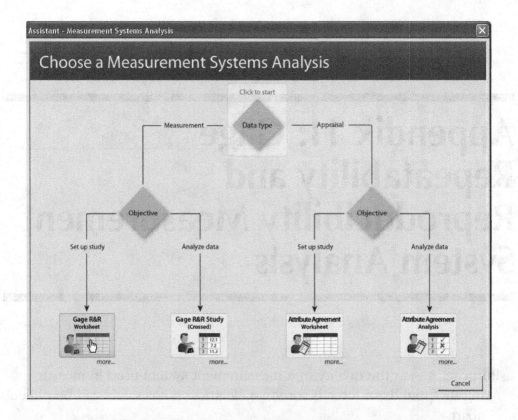

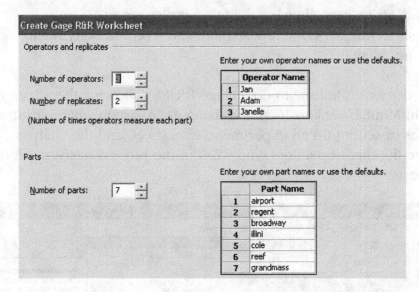

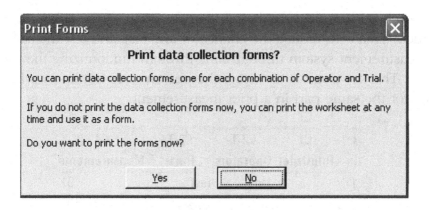

This is a convenient feature that prints a data collection sheet for each operator.

Have each person measure the parts in the order of the column named "RunOrder." This is to reduce the chance of any bias and test the stability of the measurement system through time through randomizing the parts measured. The key point is to ensure the person does not know what they recorded for the same part in a prior measurement.

↓	C1	C2-T	C3-T	C4
	RunOrder	Operators	Parts	Measurements
1	1	Jan	reef	91
2	2	Jan	cole	103
3	3	Jan	illini	94
4	4	Jan	regent	81
5	5	Jan	broadway	105
6	6	Jan	airport	90
7	7	Jan	grandmass	82
8	8	Adam	airport	90
9	9	Adam	reef	89
10	10	Adam	illini	95
11	11	Adam	broadway	104
12	12	Adam	grandmass	84
13	13	Adam	regent	84

Return to Minitab's Assistant

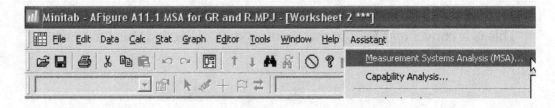

Select the option to analyze the data.

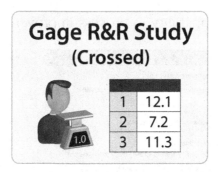

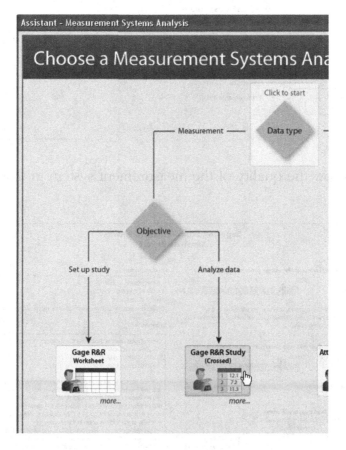

Let's analyze the measurement system this time in its ability of assessing if the force meets the requirements of the customer. Later, we will assess the measurement system's capability in process improvement.

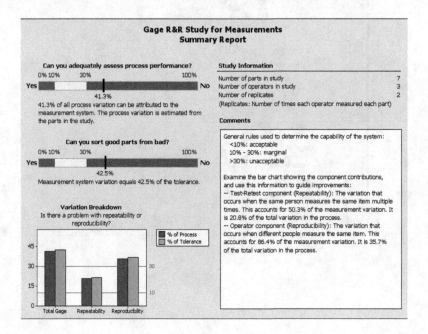

We now know the quality of the measurement system in the report in Figure A11.11.

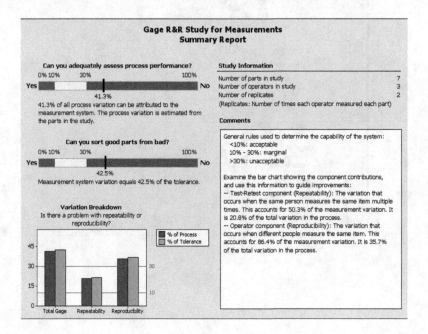

The measurement system is not capable of determining good parts from bad. See the vertical marks in the scale named, "Can you sort good parts from bad?"—42.5% of the variation is from the error in the measurement system. Thus, it is difficult to tell what the force actually was. The chart at the bottom left suggests we should improve the Reproducibility of the measurement system for the biggest improvement. The three operators are not in agreement on the forces. Look for a bias between operators, such as one operator consistently measuring a lower force at disconnect than the other two. Then, use your DMAIC (demand, measure, analyze, improve, control) training to determine the root cause of the variation, improve reproducibility, and perform a Measurement System Analysis (MSA) again to see if the system is now capable.

Next, we will use the Gage R&R to assess the measurement system's ability to measure process improvement regardless whether the parts meet the customer's requirement. Highly reliable organizations meet the customer requirements very easily and consistently and want to continuously improve to become even more reliable. They need measurement systems that can tell them if they are really improving.

Read the scale in the top left named, "Can you adequately assess process performance?" Again, the answer is "no" because 41.3% of the variation measured is *not* from the parts. It is from the measurement system itself. Reproducibility is the major error. We would like the percent to be 10 or less, especially if personal injury may occur if the force is not what we think it is.

To demonstrate improving a measurement system, let's take the suggestion to look at each of the three operators and see if there is one operator consistently recording a lower or higher value than the others. This is not to suggest the one operator is wrong. Perhaps the other two have more error and are not as well trained as the one operator. Figure A11.12 is a simple statistical analysis showing if there is a statistically significant difference (bias) between operators.

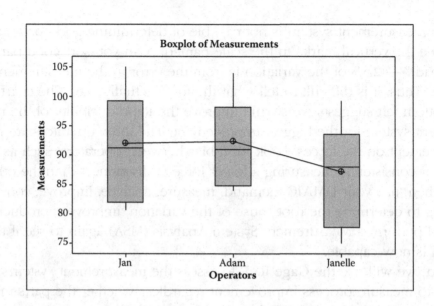

This is a boxplot chart. A boxplot chart shows the central tendency (median and mode) and the variation. The "box" represents the middle two quartiles of the data. The "whiskers" represent the remaining two quartiles of the data. The horizontal line in the box is the median and the circle within the box is the mean. Both the median and mean for Janelle is below the median and mean for Adam and Jan. This suggests a bias. Again, maybe Janelle is more correct than Adam and Jan. We need to apply our DMAIC and find out what the root causes are and improve.

After we think that we improved the system, we will run another MSA to see if we can get the percent of Process and percent of Tolerance closer to acceptable levels.

Index

Printed in the United States
by Baker & Taylor Publisher Services

Printed in the United States
by Baker & Taylor Publisher Services